W9-CIG-554

CrOSSWORDS WORD SEARCHES
LOGIC PUZZLES & SURPRiSES!

mind
STRETCHERS

BLUE EDITION

eDITED BY StANLEY NEWMAN

Reader's Digest

The Reader's Digest Association, Inc.
Pleasantville, NY / Montreal

Project Staff

EDITOR
Neil Wertheimer

PUZZLE EDITOR
Stanley Newman

PRINCIPAL PUZZLE AUTHORS
George Bredehorn, Stanley
Newman, Dave Phillips, Peter
Ritmeester

DESIGNERS
Rich Kershner, Erick Swindell

PUZZLE PROOFREADER
Sandy Fein

COPY EDITOR
Katharine O'Moore-Klopf

Reader's Digest Home & Health Books

**PRESIDENT, HOME & GARDEN
AND HEALTH & WELLNESS**
Alyce Alston

EDITOR IN CHIEF
Neil Wertheimer

CREATIVE DIRECTOR
Michele Laseau

EXECUTIVE MANAGING EDITOR
Donna Ruvituso

**ASSOCIATE DIRECTOR NORTH
AMERICAN PREPRESS**
Douglas A. Croll

MANUFACTURING MANAGER
John L. Cassidy

MARKETING
Dawn Nelson
Charlene Lancaster

The Reader's Digest Association, Inc.

**PRESIDENT AND
CHIEF EXECUTIVE OFFICER**
Mary Berner

**PRESIDENT,
CONSUMER MARKETING**
Dawn Zier

**VICE PRESIDENT,
CONSUMER MARKETING**
Kathryn Bennett

ISBN 978-0-7621-0782-7

Address any comments about *Mind Stretchers, Blue Edition* to:

The Reader's Digest Association, Inc.
Editor in Chief, Reader's Digest Books
Reader's Digest Road
Pleasantville, NY 10570-7000

To order copies of this or other editions of the *Mind Stretchers* book series, call
1-800-846-2100.

Visit our website at rd.com

For many more fun games and puzzles, visit www.rd.com/games.

Printed in the United States of America

3 5 7 9 10 8 6 4 2

US 4967/L-2

Contents

Dear Puzzler,

You already know that solving crosswords increases your vocabulary and knowledge, and you may be familiar with scientific studies that prove that crosswords can help protect against mental deterioration. But did you know that crosswords can have a more immediate benefit in your life?

By solving tricky clues and interpreting the multiple meanings of cross-word titles, you build exactly the sort of creative mind-set that helps you in real-life situations. Crosswords teach you to look deeper than the face value of words and to find hidden meanings. This skill can undoubtedly help you find solutions in nonpuzzling venues as well: at work, in the home, at the store, even dealing with bureaucracy.

How can I be so sure of this? Because I've seen these benefits time and time again in my own life. I've trained myself to "turn on the puzzle light" every time I find myself in a situation that doesn't lend itself to an easy answer. And while I don't always succeed, just the creative attempt, the "lateral thinking" process of trying to come up with a nonobvious answer, is fun.

For instance, a few years ago, I checked into a motel where the clock radio was glued to the night table, facing front. If you're like me, you want the clock radio facing toward the bed, where you can see it while lying down. I tried moving the clock radio, but it wouldn't budge.

Applying a puzzler's sensibility, I contemplated creative solutions. Place a mirror on the desk on the opposite wall? Sleep with my head at the foot of the bed? Then the simple solution came: Rotate the whole night table. Not so big a deal, perhaps, but I'll bet many people would just settle for things the way they were.

Are you good at abandoning preconceived notions and finding unconven-tional solutions? Here's an instant test:

A cowboy rides into town on Friday. He stays in town for three days, then he rides out on Friday. How?

If there are seven days in a week, how can this be? It all makes sense once you figure out that the cowboy's horse is named Friday. And you're well on the way to figuring it out once you carefully examine the sen-tence above for natural-but-erroneous assumptions you might be making.

Do you see how the answer to the crossword clue "The nation's capital" might well be DOLLARS as well as WASHINGTON, or the clue "Leaves home" might be TREE as well as GOES? If so, you're well on your way to an A in Real-Life Puzzle Solving 101.

Stanley Newman
Mind Stretchers Puzzle Editor

■ Foreword

Meet the Puzzles!

Mind Stretchers is filled with a delightful mix of classic and new puzzle types. To help you get started, here are instructions, tips and examples for each.

WORD GAMES

Crossword Puzzles

Edited by Stanley Newman

Crosswords are arguably America's most popular puzzles. As presented in this book, the one- and two-star puzzles test your ability to solve straightforward clues to everyday words. "More-star" puzzles have a somewhat broader vocabulary, but most of the added challenge in these comes from less obvious and trickier clues. These days, you'll be glad to know, uninteresting obscurities such as "Genus of fruit flies" and "Famed seventeenth-century soprano" don't appear in crosswords anymore.

Our 62 crosswords were authored by 17 different puzzle makers, many of them renowned for their creativity and cleverness.

Clueless Crosswords

by George Bredehorn

A unique Crossword variation invented by George, these 7×7 grids primarily test your

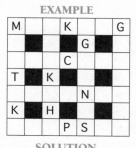

vocabulary and reasoning skills. There is one simple task: Complete the crossword with common uncapitalized seven-letter words, based entirely on the letters already filled in for you.

Hints: Focusing on the last letter of a word, when given, often helps. For example, a last letter of G often suggests that IN *are the previous two letters. When the solutions aren't coming quickly, focus on the shared spaces that are blank—you can often figure out whether it has to be a vowel or a consonant, helping you solve both words that cross it.*

Split Decisions

by George Bredehorn

Crossword puzzle lovers also enjoy this variation. Once again, no clues are provided except within the puzzle. Each answer consists of two words whose spellings are the same, except for two consecutive letters. For each pair of words, the two sets of different letters are already filled in for you. All answers are common words; no phrases or hyphenated or capitalized words are used. Certain missing words may have more than one possible solution, but there is only one solution for each word that will correctly link up with all the other words.

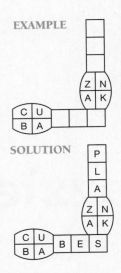

EXAMPLE

SOLUTION

Hints: Start with the shorter (three- and four-letter) words, because there will be fewer possibilities that spell words. In each puzzle, there will always be a few such word pairs that have only one solution. You may have to search a little to find them, since they may be anywhere in the grid, but it's always a good idea to fill in the answers to these first.

Triad Split Decisions

by George Bredehorn
This puzzle is solved the same way as Split Decisions, except you are given three letters for each word instead of two.

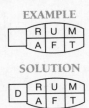

EXAMPLE

SOLUTION

Word Searches

Kids love 'em, and so do grownups, making word searches perhaps the most *widely* appealing puzzle type. In a word search, the challenge is to find hidden words within a grid of letters. In the typical puzzle, words can be found in vertical columns, horizontal rows, or along diagonals, with the letters of the words running either forward or backward. Usually, a list of words to search for is given to you. But to make word searches harder, puzzle writers

ANSWERS!

Answers to all the puzzles are found beginning on page 233, and are organized by the page number on which the puzzle appears.

sometimes just point you in the right direction, such as telling you to find 25 foods. Other twists include allowing words to take right turns, or leaving letters out of the grid.

Hints: One of the most reliable and efficient searching methods is to scan each row from top to bottom for the first letter of the word. So if you are looking for "violin" you would look for the letter "v." When you find one, look at all the letters that surround it for the second letter of the word (in this case, "i"). Each time you find a correct two-letter combination (in this case, "vi"), you then scan either for the correct three-letter combination ("vio") or the whole word.

Word Square Jigsaw

by George Bredehorn
Another logic and vocabulary game devised by George that can range from super easy to brutally hard. The task: Place the given pieces into the 4×4 blank diagram to form eight common words, four reading across and four reading down.

EXAMPLE

SOLUTION

Hints: Use pencil and have a good clean eraser! To start, identify letter combos provided that most likely end a word (such as NT and WS), and then look for letter combos that might go in front of them.

NUMBER GAMES

Sudoku

Sudoku puzzles have become massively popular in the past few years, thanks to their simplicity and test of pure reasoning. The basic Sudoku puzzle is a 9×9 square grid, split into 9 square regions, each containing 9 cells. Each puzzle starts off with roughly 20 to 35 of the squares filled in with the numbers *1* to *9*. There is just one rule: Fill in the rest of the squares with the numbers *1* to *9* so that no number appears twice in any row, column, or region.

EXAMPLE

SOLUTION

Hints: *Use the numbers provided to rule out where else the same number can appear. For example, if there is a 1 in a cell, a 1 cannot appear in the same row, column, or region. By scanning all the cells that the various 1 values rule out, you often can find where the remaining 1 values must go.*

Kakuro

First came Sudoku, then came Kakuro! This new puzzle form is actually more like a Crossword puzzle with numbers, though. Your task: Fill in the white boxes with the numbers *1* to *9*, so that each line of consecutive numbers adds up to the shaded number above it (for a column) or to the left of it (for a row). Each group of numbers must contain all different digits; that is, no digit may be repeated within a particular group of consecutive numbers.

EXAMPLE

SOLUTION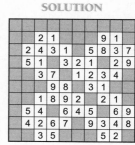

Hint: *Work on the two- and three-square lines first; they're the easiest. Remember: no line can have the same numeral twice, so if the clue is 7 for a three-square line, the answers have to be some arrangement of 4-2-1, because any other sequence requires two of the same number.*

Equation Construction
by George Bredehorn

These simple puzzles ask you to create a mathematical equation, using the digits provided and the standard operations of arithmetic (addition, subtraction, multiplication, division, parentheses, fractions), to generate the answer provided.

EXAMPLE: Use the digits 8, 2, 5, and 3 to create a mathematical expression that equals 13.
SOLUTION: $38 - 25 = 13$

Hints: *We've kept these relatively simple, so don't get too fancy! Most people try to use the numbers as is, but as in the example, the simplest answer often comes from combining numerals to create larger numbers.*

Three or More
by Peter Ritmeester

It seems simple: Enter the missing numbers from *1* to *9* in such a way that all pairs of numbers connected by a line have a difference of 3 or more. Remember: no number can repeat. But once you get started, you'll find that it is trickier than it seems!

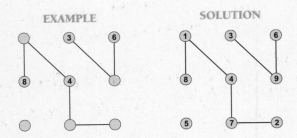

EXAMPLE   SOLUTION

Hints: *The easiest clues to solve are those that are linked to only two numbers, so you might wish to search those out first. A general approach is to pencil in all the possibilities for each circle and try to use elimination from there. For example, any circle linked to a 4 can only be a 1, 7, 8, or 9.*

LOGIC PUZZLES

Find the Ships

by Peter Ritmeester

If you love playing the board game Battleship, you'll enjoy this pencil-and-paper variation! In each puzzle, a group of ships of varying sizes is provided on the right. Your job: Properly place the ships in the grid. A handful of ship "parts" are put on the board to get you started. The placement rules:

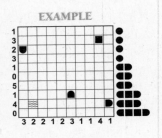

EXAMPLE

SOLUTION

1. Ships must be oriented horizontally or vertically. No diagonals!

2. A ship can't go in a square with wavy lines; that indicates hostile water.

3. The numbers on the left and bottom of the grid tell you how many squares in that row or column contain part of ships.

4. No two ships can touch each other, even diagonally.

Hint: *The solving process involves both finding those squares where a ship must go and eliminating those squares where a ship cannot go. The numbers provided should give you a head start with the latter, the number 0 clearly implying that every square in that row or column can be eliminated.*

ABC

by Peter Ritmeester

This innovative new puzzle challenges your logic much in the way a Sudoku puzzle does. Each row and column in an ABC puzzle contains exactly one *A*, one *B*, and one *C*, plus one blank. Your task is to figure out where the three letters go in each row. The clues outside the puzzle frame tell you the first letter encountered when moving in the direction of an arrow.

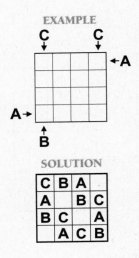

EXAMPLE

SOLUTION

Hint: *If a clue says a letter is first in a row or column, don't assume that it must go in the first square. It could go in either of the first two squares. A good way to start is to look for where column and row clues intersect (for example, when two clues look like they are pointing at the same square). These intersecting clues often give you the most information about where the first letter of a row or column must go.*

Circular Reasoning

by Peter Ritmeester

Lovers of mazes will enjoy these challenges. Your task: Connect all of the circles by drawing a single line through every square of the diagram. But there are a few rules:

1. All right-angle turns must alternate between boxes containing a circle and boxes without a circle.

2. You must make a right-angle turn out of every square that contains a circle.

3. The line can enter a square only once.

4. The line must end in the square that it began.

Hint: As with any logic puzzle, always look for those spaces that, because of the constraints in the instructions, allow for only one possibility. For example, according to the above rules, the path through any circle in one of the four corners must be a right angle around that corner.

EXAMPLE

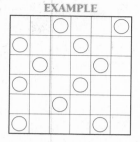

SOLUTION

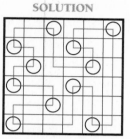

EXAMPLE

SOLUTION

Islands

by Peter Ritmeester
Here's a puzzle perfect for those who like to play Minesweeper on their computer (a free game that has come with Microsoft Windows for many years). Your task: Shade in some of the blank squares (as "water"), so that each remaining white box is part of an island. Here are rules:

1. Each island will contain exactly one numbered square, indicating how many squares that island contains.

2. Each island is separated from the other islands by water but may touch other islands diagonally.

3. All water is connected.

4. There are no 2×2 regions of water.

Hint: The most useful squares are those with 1 in them. Since an island with a "1" contains only that one square, you can black in every square adjacent to it.

Star Search

by Peter Ritmeester
Another fun game in the same style of Islands. Your task: find the stars that are hidden among the blank squares. The numbered squares indicate how many stars are hidden in squares adjacent to them (including diagonally). There is never more than one star in any square.

EXAMPLE

SOLUTION

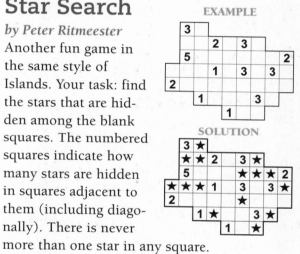

Hints: The number 8 in a square indicates that every other square adjacent to it has a star. And knowing that a particular square contains a star means that no square adjacent to it (even diagonally) can have one.

Throughout *Mind Stretchers* you will find unique mazes, visual conundrums, and other colorful challenges, each developed by maze master Dave Phillips. Each comes under a new name and has unique instructions. Our best advice? Patience and perseverance. Your eyes will need time to unravel the visual secrets.

In addition, you will also discover these visual puzzles:

Line Drawings

by George Bredehorn

George loves to create never-before-seen puzzle types, and here is another unique Bredehorn game. Each Line Drawing puzzle is different in its design, but the task is the same: Figure out where to place the prescribed number of lines to partition the space in the instructed way.

Hint: Use a pencil and a straightedge as you work. Some lines come very close to the items within the region, so being straight and accurate with your line-drawing is crucial.

One-Way Streets

by Peter Ritmeester

Another fun variation on the maze. The dia-

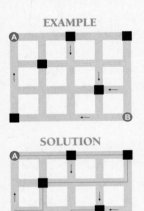

gram represents a pattern of streets. *A* and *B* are parking spaces, and the black squares are stores. Find a route that starts at *A*, passes through all the stores exactly once, and ends at *B*. Arrows indicate one-way traffic for that block only. No block or intersection may be entered more than once.

Hints: *The particular arrangement of stores and arrows will always limit the possibilities for the first store passed through from the starting point A and the last store passed through before reaching ending point B. So try to work both from the start and the end of the route. Also, the placement of an arrow on a block doesn't necessarily mean that your route will pass through that block. You will also use arrows to eliminate blocks where your path will not go.*

To round out the more involved puzzles are more than 100 short brain teasers. Stanley Newman is famous in the puzzle world for his inventive brain games. An example of how to solve each puzzle appears in the puzzle's first occurrence (the page number is noted below). The only exception is Word Wit, which is a mixed bag of one-of-a-kind word games. You'll find the following types scattered throughout the pages.

* Invented by and cowritten with George Bredehorn

But wait...there's more!

At the top of many of the pages in this book are additional brain teasers, organized into three categories:

• **QUICK!:** These tests challenge your ability to instantly calculate numbers or recall well-known facts.

• **DO YOU KNOW ...:** These more demanding questions probe the depth of your knowledge of facts and trivia.

• **HAVE YOU ...:** These reminders reveal the many things you can do each day to benefit your brain.

For the record, we have deliberately left out answers to the **QUICK!** and **DO YOU KNOW...** features. Our hope is that if you don't know an answer, you'll be intrigued enough to open a book or search the Internet for it!

■ Meet the Authors

STANLEY NEWMAN (puzzle editor and author) is crossword editor for *Newsday,* the major newspaper of Long Island, New York. He is the author/editor of over 100 books, including the autobiography and instructional manual *Cruciverbalism* and the best-selling *Million Word Crossword Dictionary.* Winner of the First U.S. Open Crossword Championship in 1982, he holds the world's record for the fastest completion of a *New York Times* crossword—2 minutes, 14 seconds. Stan operates the website www.StanXwords.com and also conducts an annual crossword-themed luxury-liner cruise.

GEORGE BREDEHORN is a retired elementary school teacher from Wantagh, New York. His variety word games have appeared in the *New York Times* and many puzzle magazines. Every week for the past 20 years, he and his wife, Dorothy, have hosted a group of Long Island puzzlers who play some of the 80-plus games that George has invented.

DAVE PHILLIPS has designed puzzles for books, magazines, newspapers, PC games, and advertising for more 30 years. In addition, Dave is a renowned creator of walk-through mazes. Each year his corn-maze designs challenge visitors with miles of paths woven into works of art. Dave is also codeveloper of eBrainyGames.com, a website that features puzzles and games for sale.

PETER RITMEESTER is chief executive officer of PZZL.com, which produces many varieties of puzzles for newspapers and websites worldwide. Peter is also general secretary of the World Puzzle Federation. The federation organizes the annual World Puzzle Championship, which includes difficult versions of many of the types of logic puzzles that Peter has created for *Mind Stretchers.*

■ Master Class: **Crosswords**

Simple Tips for Mastering America's Favorite Puzzle

Crossword puzzles are unique in the world of games in that they rarely come with a set of instructions. Publishers just assume that readers know what to do!

Having met thousands of puzzle fans over the past 20 years, I know that most crossworders have indeed figured things out for themselves, developing their own procedures and rituals for getting those little white boxes filled in.

But the first steps for new or infrequent puzzlers are not always obvious. So to help, we've put together this guide to the basic rules and tips that every crossword fan should know. If you're just getting started, keeping this "beginner's guide" handy while you're solving crosswords will undoubtedly make your puzzle experiences smoother, more pleasurable, and more mentally stimulating.

The First Step

Always look first at the puzzle title. It is there to give you a subtle hint about the theme of the puzzle—the subject matter or the common element among the longest answers. When you have filled in the first long answer, take another look at the title; you should be able to make a guess now as to what the theme is. Once you have correctly identified the theme,

the remaining theme answers should be much easier for you to puzzle out.

Here are some of my favorite puzzle titles that cleverly (and not too obviously) hint at the themes:

WHAT'S ON TODAY?

This might sound like a puzzle about TV shows, but the theme answers were all phrases that included an article of clothing, such as *coat of arms* and *brake shoes*.

FALLING LEAVES

This one had nothing to do with leaves on trees. The theme answers, all reading down (the *Falling* part of the title), were all different senses of the verb *leaves*, such as

- Leaves, as a hotel guest: *checks out*
- Leaves, as a rocket ship: *blasts off*

THE GREAT "S"-CAPE

This puzzle was all about Superman, with answers such as *X-ray vision* and *kryptonite*.

The First Clue

The first answer you should write in a crossword should always be one whose clue you are absolutely sure of. This may be the very first clue in a puzzle (1 Across), but crossword creators and editors don't automatically make the first clue the easiest one. Of course, people's vocabulary and knowledge differ anyway. So review the clue list carefully until you find one that you have no doubt is correct, and fill that in first.

Why is that so important? Because, if you're sure that first answer is correct, you know that every letter in that answer gives you one letter in each of the answers that cross it.

In an easier puzzle (one-star or two-star in this book), there should be quite a few clues whose answers you'll recognize right away. In more difficult (three- or four-star) crosswords, there will be fewer easy clues, but you'll find them if you look carefully.

What makes a clue easy? Both the clue and the answer play a part. An "easy" clue is one that points you clearly and unambiguously toward the answer. The clue "type of fruit" might sound easy, but if the answer is a 5-letter word, say, and you have no letters in the answer already filled in, the answer might be *lemon*, *apple*, *grape*, *mango*, or one of several others. A clue that's unambiguously easy has only one possibility. So, if the answer is *lemon*, the clue "sour citrus fruit" is clearly much easier than "type of fruit." Clues like these are hallmarks of well-edited easy crosswords.

Of course, it won't matter if a clue is clear if the answer is a word you don't know. That's why the best easy crosswords have all easy answers, common words that everyone knows. You might be surprised to learn that people who create crosswords find it more difficult to make easy crosswords than hard ones. That's because if the answer words are all to be genuinely easy, there is a far smaller base of words to pick from. One study showed that the average person uses only about 2,500 words during a week. With fewer words to pick from, the job of getting words to fit in a diagram is that much more difficult for a puzzle maker.

The Next Clues

The clues to look at after you get your first word are the ones that crisscross with the clue you just filled in. The reason: it's much easier to think of the answer once you have one or more of its letters written in.

Continue to focus on that area. Your solving will be smoother and faster if you concentrate on one area of the puzzle at a time, with each new answer you write connected to answers you've already filled in. If you're unable to fill in any answers in the area you're working in, look for another clue whose answer you're sure of elsewhere in the crossword and begin the process again.

If you've written in all the answers you can and some blank squares still remain, here are three of my favorite methods for getting unstuck:

• **Put the puzzle down,** and then come back to it later, tomorrow, or some other time. Many crossworders find if they take a break from a puzzle then take a fresh look at it later on, they're able to come up with answers that didn't occur to them before.

• **Try erasing one or more answers** that you may be less than sure of, and take another look at the area with the answers you've just erased. You may be stuck because you have one or more incorrect answers filled in.

• **It's completely okay to get help:** Look up a word in your dictionary, look up a fact in your encyclopedia or on the Internet, or even take a peek at the answer in the back of the book. No, it's *not* cheating! An important part of the educational benefits of crossword solving comes from learning new words and facts.

About Crossword Dictionaries

Many puzzlers own crossword dictionaries to have one handy volume with all the answers they're looking for. But crossword dictionaries vary widely in quality. The main shortcoming: not covering the vocabulary in *today's* crosswords.

Anyone who has been doing crosswords for a long time can tell you how much they've evolved. Much more than the crosswords of just a few years ago, contemporary puzzles are filled with a wide variety of vocabulary, including slang terms and brand names, current events, and facts that are just as likely to be from popular culture as from a history textbook. What today's puzzles are largely missing is "crosswordese": those strange, obscure words from the depths of the dictionary or from ancient mythology.

But most of the crossword dictionaries on booksellers' shelves are the same ones that were there 20 years ago. Just how useful do you think a 20-year-old crossword dictionary is going to be in solving a 21st-century crossword?

By all means, use a crossword dictionary. But be sure that you have one that's going to do the best job for you. Here are a few quick tests for you to make at your local bookstore:

Check the copyright date. If it's 10 or more years ago, drop it like a hot potato.

Do a name search. To make sure that a crossword dictionary covers nondictionary words, look up *Alda* (under which you should find *Alan*, and maybe *Robert*) and *Alan* (under which you should find *Alda*, *Shepard*, and other famous people named Alan).

Check for "fill-in-the-blank" clues. These are very common in today's crosswords. Any crossword dictionary you buy should have them. So look up a common crossword clue such as "from A __" (one answer: *to Z*). Or better yet, just skim through the pages to see if the book has any fill-in-the-blank clues at all.

You'll be surprised how few crossword dictionaries include them.

Look up a few "clues by example." This is my favorite way of testing whether a crossword dictionary was compiled from actual crosswords, or at least by someone who knows how crosswords work. Any crossword dictionary will have a long list of trees under *tree* (such as *spruce* or *sycamore*), but very few will have *tree* under *sycamore*. Because clues like "sycamore, for example" appear in crosswords all the time, it's important that the crossword dictionary you decide on organizes its information in both of these ways.

One crossword dictionary that I know will pass all of the above tests is *The Million Word Crossword Dictionary*, published very recently and cowritten by your humble puzzle editor. I invite you to check it out for yourself the next time you're in a bookstore or on a bookseller's website.

A Few Additional Tips

- Don't solve crosswords in pen unless it's an erasable pen or you never make mistakes.

- When you're done, always check your answers with the printed solution. If you've never done this before, you may be surprised how often you discover certain answers you've filled in aren't correct.

- The best crossword solvers have an insatiable curiosity. Always look up any new words you encounter in your crosswords and use unfamiliar facts as a springboard to learn more about new subjects. Your brain will thank you, and your increasing knowledge will undoubtedly improve your solving skill.

To get you started, the puzzles on the next three pages are all easy, "one-star" puzzles.
Good luck, and have fun!

—Stanley Newman

★ By the Book by Gail Grabowski

ACROSS

1 Stately home
6 Enlist again
10 *True __* (Wayne film)
14 Thunderstruck
15 What's more
16 Hasty
17 Cruise-drill wear
19 Norway's largest city
20 Superlative suffix
21 Curved molding
22 *The Prince and the __*
24 Tern, for one
26 Billboard
27 Dollar bill
28 Stops resisting
32 VI
34 Dutch cheese
36 Take place
37 Spring month
39 Pi follower
40 Suitor
41 Muffin alternative
42 Mrs. Chaplin
44 German cars, for short
45 Australian animal
47 Stinging bug
49 Ambush
50 Lodger
54 Small swimsuit
57 Promises to pay: Abbr.
58 *Norma __*
59 Word processing command
60 Legislative aide
63 Squeal, so to speak
64 Bothers
65 Cantered
66 Well-thought-out
67 House made of twigs
68 Psychics

DOWN

1 Colonist Standish
2 Licorice flavoring
3 1994 trade pact
4 Be indebted to
5 Come back to a group
6 Sped
7 Actress Sommer
8 Deplete, with "up"
9 Crusty entrée
10 Low-growing shrubbery
11 Grate
12 Capri, e.g.
13 God of thunder
18 Concur
23 Visibly happy
25 Pugilist's goal
26 Garfunkel's partner
28 Popular Web portal
29 Barge
30 Mon. follower
31 Bobby of hockey
32 Humane org.
33 Pump __ (lift weights)
35 Hang down
37 Inquire
38 Find out
43 Approximately
46 Dried grape
48 Studio stands
50 Blow one's own horn
51 Window curtain
52 Enthusiastic
53 Oboe features
54 Track transactions
55 Inventor's brainchild
56 Clay baker
57 Fills in, as a cartoon
61 Before, to Longfellow
62 "The Raven" writer

★ Scram by Sally R. Stein

ACROSS

1 Saloons
5 Book of maps
10 Frost
14 Class-reunion attendee
15 Pointy
16 __ Major (constellation)
17 Workday start for many
18 Aquarium fish
19 In the neighborhood
20 Bonnie and Clyde vehicle
22 __ *With the Wind*
23 Make noise while sleeping
24 Laughing African beast
26 Make illegal
29 Most achy
33 Clock part
37 Go first
40 Actor Sal
41 Memorable '50s-'60s sitcom
44 Trial and __
45 Peddle
46 Manhattan, on envelopes
47 Ten dimes
49 Airline stat: Abbr.
51 Take for oneself
54 Checkout-counter units
59 Big blow
62 Amish country dessert
65 Metered vehicle
66 Singer Lena
67 Warsaw resident
68 Norway's capital
69 Gardener's tool
70 Final or midterm
71 At what time
72 Six Day War general

73 Thesaurus entries: Abbr.

DOWN

1 Loud sounds
2 One with a green card
3 Total
4 Makeup stain
5 Whodunit canine
6 Those folks
7 Door closer
8 Well-ordered lineup
9 Bowling scores
10 Zsa Zsa Gabor, by birth
11 Black-and-white cookie

12 Wise __ owl
13 Very uncommon
21 Spider's creation
25 Alaska city
27 Muhammad __
28 Basketball targets
30 Jealousy
31 Taken a look at
32 British Conservative
33 Escaped
34 Aviation word starter
35 Poet Sandburg
36 Darwin's theory
38 Had a feast
39 North Carolina senator
42 Historical periods

43 Sandwich letters
48 Moved quickly
50 Feel poorly
52 *Mary Tyler Moore Show* spin-off
53 __ *and Bess*
55 Does word processing
56 Strong glue
57 City of Italy
58 Appears to be
59 Store away
60 Get ready for dinner
61 Wheel bar
63 Highest draft rating
64 Type of houseplant

★ Fill 'Er Up by Gail Grabowski

ACROSS

1 Fraction of a foot
5 Venomous vipers
9 Loathe
14 Lugosi of film
15 Immaculate
16 Playground equipment
17 Hawaiian island
18 High-school dance
19 Devastation
20 Baseball substitute
23 Sp. ladies
24 Partakes of
25 Airport car, e.g.
28 Onion coating
30 IRS employee
33 Hunter constellation
34 Wet weather
35 Loafer or moccasin
36 Hand-held lens
39 Tennis great Arthur
40 Chimed
41 Rustler's rope
42 Court divider
43 Summoned, with "for"
44 Shepherdess of rhyme
45 Pool stick
46 Bering and Caribbean
47 Rustic '50s film couple
53 Contented sounds
54 Leave out
55 Smidgen
57 Stage whisper
58 Vend
59 Gator kin
60 Slightest
61 Author ___ Stanley Gardner
62 Clark of the *Daily Planet*

DOWN

1 Apple Computer competitor
2 Close to
3 Hint
4 Icy pellet
5 Legal motion
6 Searches, as the Internet
7 Stage item
8 Highway hauler
9 Garbage container
10 Bored feelings
11 Honeybee home
12 Skunk's defense
13 Tape-deck button: Abbr.
21 Teheran resident
22 Person, place or ___
25 Julius Caesar, for one
26 Wipe away
27 Period after 43 Down
28 Canonized one
29 Chess piece
30 Pursue
31 Sheriff's group
32 Man of fables
34 Meg of *Sleepless in Seattle*
35 Keystone Kops comedy
37 Released
38 Crow (over)
43 Twilight time
44 Bailey of cartoons
45 Aces and jacks
46 Ability
47 Erato, for one
48 La Scala solo
49 Sit, as for a portrait
50 Part of U.S.A.: Abbr.
51 Like a folk tale
52 British prep school
53 Sidekick
56 Do something

★ Tea Time

Using each of the nine letters in the diagram exactly once, move through the gaps in the walls to spell out a type of tea.

EQUATION CONSTRUCTION

Use the digits 2, 4, 5, and 8 plus standard symbols and operations of arithmetic, to create a mathematical expression that equals the number 15. All the digits must be used.

$$= 15$$

★ A Puzzle

All the words and phrases on this list have at least two A's, and the diagram is appropriately shaped. Answers may be found across, down or diagonally.

ABERRATIONAL	ADAMANT	ALGEBRAICALLY	ANEMIA	APOCALYPTICAL
ABLATIVAL	ADAPTABLE	ALL-AMERICAN	ANESTHESIA	APPALOOSAS
ABLE SEAMAN	AEOLIAN HARP	ALPACA	ANTAGONISTICALLY	ARCANE
ABRACADABRA	AERONAUTICAL	ALPHABETICAL	ANTIAIRCRAFT	AREAWAYS
ACADIA	AFGHANISTAN	AMBILATERAL	ANTICAPITALIST	ARMADA
ACCLAMATION	AGORAPHOBIA	AMERICANA	ANTIQUARIAN	ARRAYAL
ACCUSATORIAL	AGRARIAN	ANABAPTIST	ANTIRATIONAL	AVAILABILITY
ACQUAINTANCE	ALAMEDA	ANAPHORA	APANAGE	AZALEA
ACROBATICALLY	ALASKA	ANAPLASMOSIS	APATHETICALLY	

```
        B A I S E H T S E N A C R A
      A N T I Q U A R I A N E M I A Z
    E G A N A P A T H E T I C A L L Y Q
  R A A E X A L P H A B E T I C A L Y J A
  A N A P L A S M O S I S N B R A T A M F
  N A I R A R G A C C U S A T O R I A L G
  T C J W C G A G O R A P H O B I A P A H
  I I I K I A A B W     O X P A B D O C A
  A R Y Y G C H D       P T T V E C I N
  I E T L O Q Z         F I K M A T I S
  R M I A L U             C I A L U S
  C A L N O A L G E B R A I C A L L Y A T
  R L I O E I C M L A V I T A L B A P N A
  A L B I A N T I C A P I T A L I S T O N
  F A A T Z T F E T Q R A P H Y L K I R O
  T R L A C A D I A S E B A G A M A C E I
  S E I R B N L A N O I T A R R E B A A T
  I T A I A C A P L A E N L D E M Z L D A
  T A V T N E P I S A S O O L A P P A A M
  P L A N A M A E S E L B A G W C G Y P A
  A I D A P N             A D A A T L
  B B A M H Y             Y T J R A C
  A M M A O Q             S R N R B C
  N A R D R U             N H R A L A
  A P A A A O             A Z A L E A
```

COMMON SENSE

What four-letter word can be found in the dictionary definitions of all of these words: BANG, FAIR, LOCK and PART?

— — — —

★ Sudoku

Fill in the blank boxes so that every row, column, and 3×3 box contains all of the numbers 1 to 9.

					6			2
4	6		9	2			8	1
	2	1	3	4	5			7
1				9	3			4
3				1	7	9		
6	5				8			
7		4		5		1		
	8		1		4			9
	1			3	9	4		8

MIXAGRAMS

Each line contains a five-letter word and a four-letter word that have been mixed together (the order of the letters in each word has not been changed). Unmix the two words on each line and write them in the spaces provided. When you're done, find a two-word answer to the clue by reading down the letter columns in the answers. Example: D A R I U N V E T = DRIVE + AUNT

CLUE: He had rafts of fun

S H L O R I F E T = _ _ _ _ _ + _ _ _ _

T H A U M I O L R = _ _ _ _ _ + _ _ _ _

R O C A T N E G T = _ _ _ _ _ + _ _ _ _

M O K E A N Y S U = _ _ _ _ _ + _ _ _ _

★ About Time by Sally R. Stein

ACROSS

1 Competed in the Indy 500
6 Family
10 Hair colorings
14 Sound of a sneeze
15 Oaf
16 Electrified swimmers
17 Antiques and relics
20 Fraction of a min.
21 Planet beyond Neptune
22 Al and Tipper
23 Mansion employee
24 Small fly
26 Costello's partner
29 Born and __
30 Sound booster
33 Untamed ranch horse
34 Lobster relative
35 Spiny houseplant
36 Something to open at a party
39 Singer Adams
40 Scratcher's target
41 Less than 90 degrees
42 "Absolutely!"
43 Medicine quantity
44 Thin soups
45 Author Morrison
46 Company div.
47 Fire-setting crime
50 After-bath need
52 Sound of a punch
55 Michael J. Fox film of '85
58 Donkey sound
59 Astronaut Armstrong
60 Uses a telescope
61 Casino city
62 Horse's gait
63 Nose, slangily

DOWN

1 *Peanuts* exclamation
2 Charley horse
3 Fashionable
4 Very long time
5 *Li'l Abner* locale
6 Cirrus or nimbus
7 Place for hay
8 Celebrity signature
9 To the __ degree
10 Bus station
11 Datebook capacity
12 Otherwise
13 Former JFK landers
18 Thin cut
19 Old-time exclamation
23 __ Carlo, Monaco
25 Neighbor of S. Dak.
26 Westminster, e.g.
27 Groom's mate
28 Actor Karloff
29 __ Canyon (Utah national park)
30 Alaska native
31 11 Down fraction
32 "For __ sake!"
34 Certain pet watcher
35 Wide tie
37 Singer Celine
38 Sound-blocking devices
43 Word of warning
44 Chicken alternative
45 Japan Airlines destination
46 Resided
47 20 Across or 25 Down
48 Very uncommon
49 Read quickly
51 Where Cincinnati is
52 *The Godfather* author
53 Popular cookie
54 Compass point
56 Toronto's prov.
57 Basker's shade

★ Circular Reasoning

Connect all of the circles by drawing a single continuous line through every square of the diagram. All right-angle turns of your line must alternate between boxes containing a circle and boxes not containing a circle. You must make a right-angle turn out of every square that contains a circle. Your line must end in the same square that it begins, and it cannot enter any square more than once.

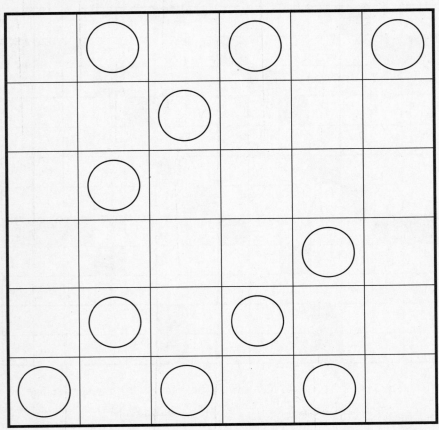

WORD SQUARE JIGSAW

Place the given pieces into the 4×4 blank diagram to form eight common words, four reading across and four reading down.

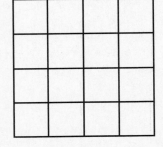

★ Line Drawings

Draw three straight lines, each from one edge of the square to another edge, so that the letters in each of the four regions spell rhyming words.

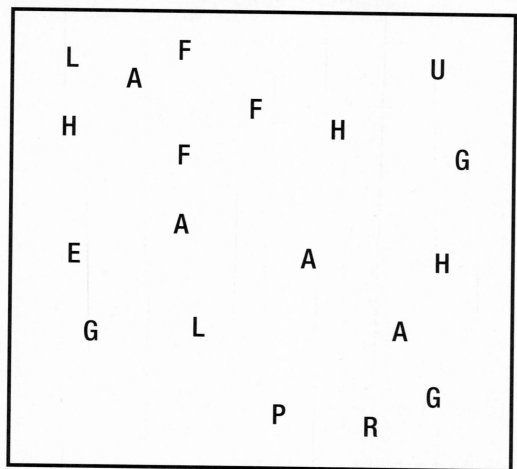

INITIAL REACTION

The "equation" below contains the initials of words that will make it correct, forming a numerical fact. Solve the equation by supplying the missing words. Examples:

60 = M. in an H. (Minutes in an Hour)

200 = D. for P. G. in M. (Dollars for Passing Go in Monopoly)

50 = S. on the A.F. _____

★ Z Puzzle

All the words and phrases on this list start with Z, and the diagram is appropriately shaped. Answers may be found across, down or diagonally.

ZABAIONE
ZACHARIAH
ZACHARY
ZAGGED
ZAGREB
ZAGS
ZAIRE
ZANIER
ZANY
ZANZIBAR
Z-AXIS
ZEALANDER

ZEALOT
ZEALOUS
ZEBRA CROSSING
ZEBRAS
ZEBU
ZED
ZEITGEIST
ZEMSTVOS
ZEPPELIN
ZEROES
ZESTY
ZETA

ZEUS
ZIGZAGGED
ZILLION
ZILLIONTH
ZIMMERMAN
ZINGS
ZIRCONIUM
ZOE
ZONATED
ZOO
ZOOGENOUS
ZOOGEOGRAPHICAL

ZOOLOGICAL
ZOOLOGIST
ZOOM LENS
ZOOMORPHISM
ZOOMS
ZOONS
ZOOPARASITIC
ZOOPATHOLOGY
ZOOPHILES
ZOOPHOBIA
ZOOPLANKTON
ZOOS

ZOROASTER
ZOROASTRIANISM
ZUCCHETTO
ZULU
ZYMOGENIC
ZYMOLYSIS
ZYMOPLASTIC
ZYMOSCOPE

```
N S I X A Z O O P H I L E S B E R G A Z
I D A I B O H P O O Z Y M O G E N I C J
L Z E A L O T T E H C C U Z A C H A R Y
E Z Y M O L Y S I S O V T S M E Z E B U
P Z I R C O N I U M S I H P R O M O O Z
P E E N D G B C I T S A L P O M Y Z I N
E T Z D G I             W G W M O Z
Z A I R E S             O G M T O D
Z E S T Y T       X L Y E K O E S
            Z X O Z R N G T F Y
          R A A H E F A E A R Z A
        X E N I T B R L N N A Z
      C I T I S A R A P O O Z
    I Z N S E A P A M O U Z
R R Z O A R R O C E O S
A Z E O S E O R E Z
B Z R L O Z O Z       V G E U N Z
I O T O G S         D Z L S A I
Z O Z G S E         O U U C M L
N M S I N A I R T S A O R O Z O H X R L
A S N C S G A Z N R E D N A L A E Z E I
Z G Z A B A I O N E M S S A R B E Z M O
S N E L M O O Z E I T G E I S T E E M N
E P O C S O M Y Z I G Z A G G E D U I T
J Z O O G E O G R A P H I C A L R S Z H
```

WORD WIT

The name of what well-known shoe company can be formed by adding one letter to the phrase SHOE FIRM, then rearranging all nine letters?

_____

★ In The Cards by Gail Grabowski

ACROSS

1 Ray of light
5 Iowa city
9 Former Russian rulers
14 __ Major (Big Dipper)
15 Novice
16 Devour
17 Mythological conflict
19 Following behind
20 Won __ soup
21 Rope loop
22 Licorice or lollipop
23 Mrs. Roosevelt
25 Kayak propeller
26 It's "falling down" in song
32 Garfield and Sylvester
35 Owl outcry
36 Physicians' org.
37 Black-and-white cookie
38 Fearless
40 "Woe is me!"
41 Tap beverage
42 Emulate an eagle
43 Mailed
44 Kind of newspaper column
49 Family member
50 *Wizard of Oz* song subject
54 Do a double take
57 Used up, as money
59 Starter for cycle or verse
60 God of Islam
61 Eli Whitney invention
63 Hill angle
64 Tennis champ Arthur
65 Succulent plant
66 Falk of *Columbo*
67 Perused
68 Pig homes

DOWN

1 Montana city
2 Flynn of film
3 United
4 Military officer: Abbr.
5 When many go to lunch
6 "Goodness!"
7 Historical chapters
8 Peeved
9 Server on wheels
10 African expedition
11 Memo abbr.
12 Regretted
13 Nimble
18 Part of A.D.
24 In addition
25 Orchestra member
27 Chicago airport
28 Thanksgiving mo.
29 Evans or Carnegie
30 Fed. agent
31 Toward the dawn
32 Fossil fuel
33 Folk singer Guthrie
34 High schooler, probably
38 Most Little Leaguers
39 Stadium sound
40 Part of 36 Across: Abbr.
42 Move like a snake
45 Get away
46 "Queen of Soul" Franklin
47 Fumed
48 Former leader of Yugoslavia
51 Reveille instrument
52 Burger topper
53 Napa Valley products
54 Hoarse sound
55 *Vogue* competitor
56 Considerably
57 Lasting mark
58 Sit, as for a portrait
62 Short snooze

★ Islands

Shade in some of the white squares in the diagram with "water," so that each remaining white box is part of an island. Each island will contain exactly one numbered square, indicating how many squares that island contains. Each island is separated from the other islands by water but may touch other islands diagonally. All water is connected, but there are no 2×2 regions of water in the diagram.

4				
2		3		3

AND SO ON

Unscramble the letters in the phrase FOOT SALES, to form two words that are part of a common phrase that has the word *and* between them. Example: The letters in LEATHER HAY can be rearranged to spell HALE and HEARTY.

_____ and _____

★ Loose Change

What is the only coin that appears only once in this picture?

EQUATION CONSTRUCTION

Use the digits 2, 4, 5, and 8 plus standard symbols and operations of arithmetic, to create a mathematical expression that equals the number 4. All the digits must be used.

| | = | 4 |

★ The i's Have It by Randall J. Hartman

ACROSS

1 Arizona neckties
6 The lion's share
10 Home of the Taj Mahal
14 Without company
15 Choir voice
16 Press, as laundry
17 Varnish ingredient
18 Eden resident
19 Trench around a castle
20 Business done over the Internet
23 Put into service
24 Before, to Burns
25 Singing and dancing
27 Actor Vigoda
30 Elemental building block
33 Related, as a story
34 Litter members
36 Precipitation
38 Kit contents
41 No-going-back moment
44 Keyboard user
45 Opera highlight
46 Director Kazan
47 Sterno product
49 Trip abroad
51 Fabergé ornament
52 Flew together, as bees
55 In mint condition
57 ___ Pan Alley
58 Moulin Rouge, for one
64 Landed
66 Skater Lipinski
67 Arm joint
68 Great joy
69 Give off
70 Idolize
71 Life of Riley

72 Too hasty
73 Gives temporarily

DOWN

1 Shakespeare, informally
2 Bread spread
3 ___ in Space
4 Out of service
5 Spanish lady
6 Polite address
7 Like a shoppe
8 Kickoff
9 Garfield, e.g.
10 Objective
11 Principle of conduct
12 Friars' fete
13 Chips in
21 Paris subway
22 Take the honey and run
26 Tickle pink
27 Datebook entry: Abbr.
28 Harbor marker
29 Sudden revelations
31 Dunderheads
32 North Dakota city
35 Curl one's lip
37 ___ contendere
39 Branch of math
40 Impediment
42 Chaplin persona
43 Ring-shaped
48 Move unsteadily
50 Cancel, as a law
52 54 Down venue
53 Author Cather
54 Serious work
56 Author Oscar
59 Part of the eye
60 Courtroom declaration
61 Black, to Byron
62 Telephone wire
63 Lea ladies
65 Golf peg

★ One-Way Streets

The diagram represents a pattern of streets. A and B are parking spaces, and the black squares are stores. Find the route that starts at A, passes through all stores exactly once, and ends at B. Arrows indicate one-way traffic for that block only. No block or intersection may be entered more than once.

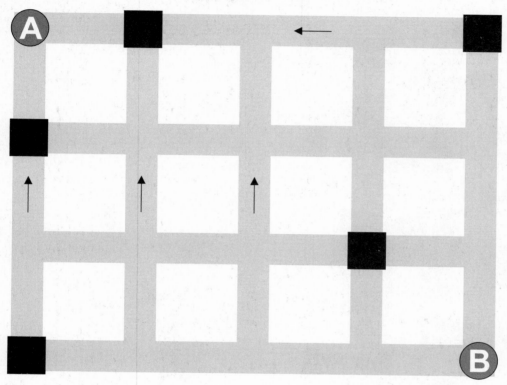

EQUATION CONSTRUCTION

Arrange these signs and numbers to form a correct number sentence. Numbers may be placed together to form a greater number (for example, a *1* and an *8* can be combined to form *18* or *81*). It is not necessary to use all the signs and numbers. No parentheses are needed.

$$1 , 2 , 3 , 7 , 12, \div , \div$$

	=	

★ Split Decisions

In this clueless crossword puzzle, each answer consists of two words whose spellings are the same, except for the consecutive letters given. All answers are common words; no phrases or hyphenated or capitalized words are used. Some of the clues may have more than one solution, but there is only one word pair that will correctly link up with all the other word pairs.

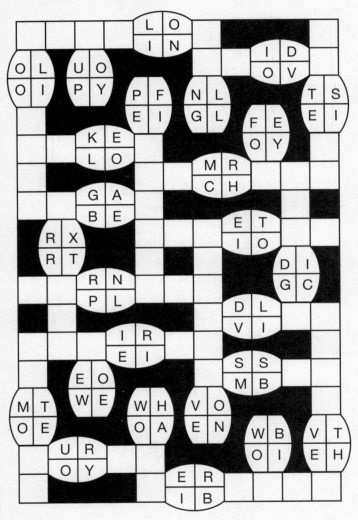

WORD WIT

The musical term "do" (a note of the scale) is a homophone of "dough," a slang term for money. What musical term for a type of singer is a homophone of a slang term for (a certain denomination of) money?

_____

★ Star Search

Find the stars that are hidden in some of the blank squares. The numbered squares indicate how many stars are hidden in the squares adjacent to them (including diagonally). There is never more than one star in any square.

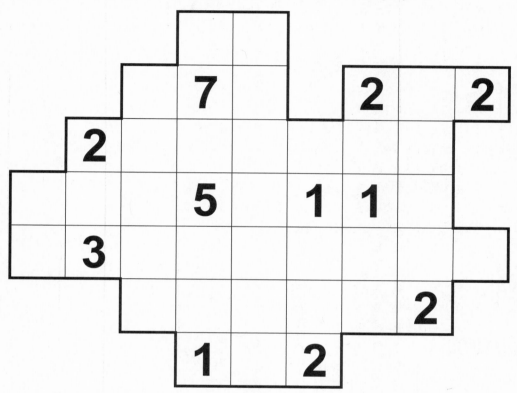

MIXAGRAMS

Each line contains a five-letter word and a four-letter word that have been mixed together (the order of the letters in each word has not been changed). Unmix the two words on each line and write them in the spaces provided. When you're done, find a two-word answer to the clue by reading down the letter columns in the answers.

CLUE: Where's the beef?

SLADUMITE   =   _ _ _ _ _   +   _ _ _ _

THIEOMNES   =   _ _ _ _ _   +   _ _ _ _

MAINUANEL   =   _ _ _ _ _   +   _ _ _ _

BAUTFATER   =   _ _ _ _ _   +   _ _ _ _

★ Smooth Sailing

Find the 14 types of sailing vessels that are hidden in the diagram. Answers may be found across, down or diagonally.

```
T R K K M U R C F L P C G Y S P R U F K
M H U J Z B O B L G O W Q D P K C R E C
O T S O R R Q H M S I Q A K L K E C D X
T E R F A Y R R E F T Y E R T N S R H P
J P I C Q G K Y A C V C E G I I F D D Q
P E L N W E Z O K F B P Y L R R X E E W
O E L S W R Z Y A E C N E I I A Q Y K Y
O I K Q E F T D P I H S L L A T B C R H
L H H A V A T Y P X I B C S E C L E A D
S M X B F Q J Z J U Z T R C R B N J Z T
Y Q P S X G J T R J S A A G M O C A O D
A K S D H F G C Y P Z F X O O J M M P N
A M T J F C A G G T Q P A H B R O U S S
T C C R J E L R H G G U C U C D C F B D
Z Z M K O F L Y V Z Q S G A C C E V A O
Y A C H T T E I A U Q B L B R U J E U I
Q H D T N L O P W C U H V I K I T B P L
S A H U Y F N C A T A M A R A N C I F S
I A P X W O J O Z P H O X Y Z I K O F B
F S F O A J S Q E B H I O C K I H R G S
```

TELEPHONE TRIOS

Using the numbers and letters on a standard telephone, what three seven-letter words from the same category can be formed from these telephone numbers?

486-3733   _ _ _ _ _ _ _

738-3689   _ _ _ _ _ _ _

645-5466   _ _ _ _ _ _ _

★ Cruising by Lee Weaver

ACROSS

1 Piece of bacon
6 Wall timepiece
11 Unhappy
14 Scarlett of fiction
15 Evita's surname
16 Put into service
17 "Say" farewell silently
19 Umbrella part
20 Group doctrines
21 Attend, as a film
22 Dieter's restriction
23 Consume
24 Small argument
26 Clumsy one
29 Basketball hoop attachment
31 Hidden away
34 Numero __
35 Confidence
37 Farm machine name
38 Wild guess
40 Nose, slangily
42 Unaccounted for, militarily
43 Oven adjunct
45 Spouse's mom, e.g.
47 Summer hrs. in St. Pete
48 Horror-movie sounds
50 Poet's "before"
51 Actress __ Arthur
52 Bring to naught
53 Tic-__-toe
55 Boxer's punch
57 Boise's state: Abbr.
59 Deli meat
62 Flow back
63 Prevailing price
66 Shoe width
67 Sci-fi bad guy, often
68 Actress Berry
69 According to
70 Starring roles
71 Alpine song

DOWN

1 Scatter seed
2 Not this
3 Great review
4 Goddess of peace
5 Beauty contest
6 Navy noncoms: Abbr.
7 Guided
8 Spheres
9 Most modest
10 Athlete's protective gear
11 Visit Internet sites
12 Largest continent
13 Something owed
18 Furry fish-eaters
25 On the briny
26 Throws out of office
27 Playful prank
28 Pillow material
30 North African capital city
31 Fur wrap
32 Deteriorate
33 River feature
36 Family member
39 Existed
41 Kilt pattern
44 Extreme
46 Well-to-do
49 Separable component
54 Chocolate source
55 All-terrain vehicle
56 Busy as __
58 Opera solo
59 State representatives: Abbr.
60 Gelatin shaper
61 Castaway's home
64 Blusher's color
65 __ Aviv

★ Hyper-Sudoku

Fill in the blank boxes so that every row, column, 3×3 box, *and* each of the four 3×3 gray regions contains all of the numbers 1 to 9.

1	4	5	9			7		
		7	5	8	4	1		
3				7	2		5	
5	9		4	2	7			
	6		8					7
	7	4				2	9	5
	1						8	
	5		2			6		
6			7			5		

TRANSDELETION

Delete one letter from the word ANNOTATIONS and rearrange the rest, to get the two-word name of a U.S. city.

_____

★ Loops

The diagram depicts a group of interconnected, unbroken loops. Carefully trace out all the paths, and determine how many different loops there are there.

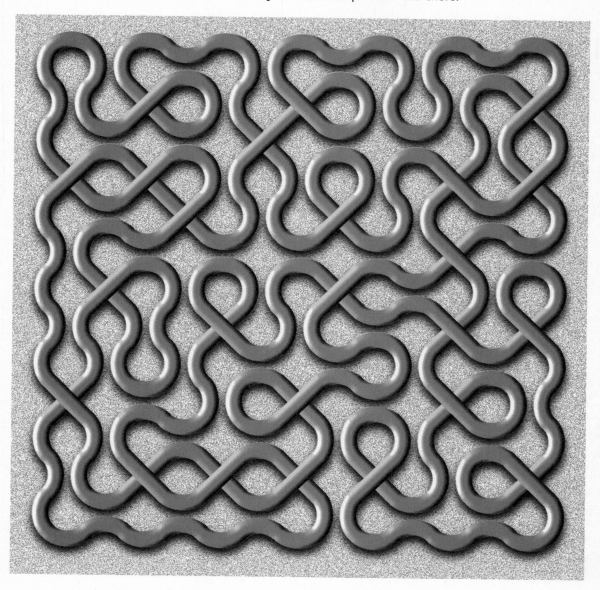

WORD WIT

The letters in the word ONE are in reverse alphabetical order. What is the only English name for a whole number whose letters are in alphabetical order?

_____

★ Kakuro

Fill in the blank white boxes of the diagram with digits from 1 to 9 so that each group of numbers adds up to the shaded number above it (for a column) or to the left of it (for a row). Each group of numbers must contain all different digits. That is, no digit may be repeated within a particular sum.

THREE OF A KIND

Find the three hidden words in the sentence that, read in order, go together in some way.
Example: I sold Norma new screwdrivers (answer: "old man river").

The tickets were at a concerto event.

★ Happy Day by Sally R. Stein

ACROSS

1 Grind, as one's teeth
6 __ and grill
9 Marsh bird
14 Juliet's love
15 Greek vowel
16 Make happy
17 Colorado resort
18 __ Baba
19 Bonnie of blues-rock
20 Happy
22 Does nothing
23 Biblical garden
24 Pie __ mode
25 Cherry's color
26 Deceives
28 Prince William alma mater
32 19 Across, e.g.
36 Early afternoon
37 World's longest river
38 Priests and ministers
40 Goes to
42 Where Siberia is
43 Hawaiian instrument
45 Sheriffs' IDs
46 Brewmaster's buy
47 At an angle
49 Smartness measures: Abbr.
51 Wide shoe
52 Zeus' wife
56 Messy situation
59 Happy
61 Nephew of Donald Duck
62 Modern music style
63 Writer Loos
64 Prefix for national
65 Ingested
66 Jeans fabric
67 Apt to sulk
68 Golfer Trevino
69 Rims

DOWN

1 A- or B+
2 Acted snoopy
3 More than enough
4 Escort to the door
5 __ Kong (Chinese region)
6 Paul or Ringo
7 Minimally
8 Police action
9 Spooky
10 Happy
11 Escalator part
12 Diminutive suffix
13 Vietnamese New Years
21 Barbershop offerings
25 Cola alternative
26 Floral necklace
27 Bygone airline
29 Dinner bell sound
30 Ye __ Shoppe
31 Monster's loch
32 Con game
33 Ingrid, in *Casablanca*
34 Sedaka or Diamond
35 Happy
39 Enjoy 17 Across
41 Little bit
44 Hoist
48 Comanche dwelling
50 "Who?" or "Where?"
52 Sharpened
53 Looking at
54 Adjust a knot
55 George Washington successor
56 Skinny
57 Forbidden thing
58 Coupe or convertible
59 Vocal
60 Green gem

★ ABC

Enter the letters *A*, *B*, and *C* into the diagram so that each row and column has exactly one *A*, one *B*, and one *C*. The letters outside the diagram indicate the first letter encountered, moving in the direction of the arrow. Keep in mind that after all the letters have been filled in, there will be one blank box in each row and column.

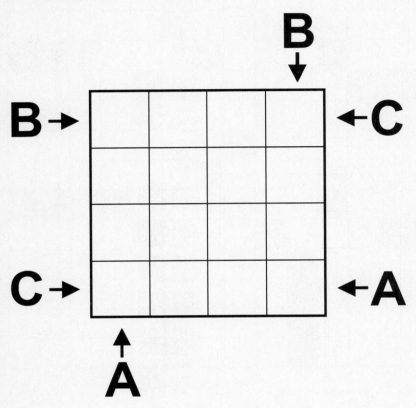

CLUELESS CROSSWORD

Complete the crossword with common uncapitalized seven-letter words, based entirely on the letters already filled in for you.

★ Find the Ships

Determine the position of the 10 ships listed to the right of the diagram. The ships may be oriented either horizontally or vertically. A square with wavy lines indicates water and will not contain a ship. The numbers at the edge of the diagram indicate how many squares in that row or column contain parts of ships. When all 10 ships are correctly placed in the diagram, no two of them will touch each other, not even diagonally.

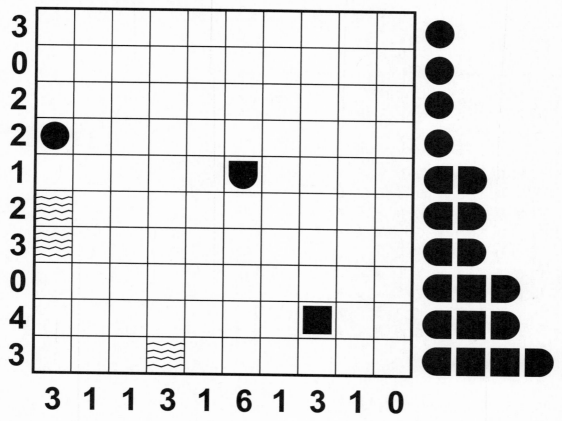

WORD WIT

The phrase DIAL TONE consists of two words that are both brand names of soap. What world nation's name consists of two words that are both brand names of soap?

_____   _____

★ Buried Treasure

Find the 16 precious stones that are hidden in the diagram. Answers may be found across, down or diagonally.

```
X R C H J H G I L U Z A L S I P A L T O
E I A W O O X R P Z C W L M Y K V L U G
L G M Q A H T O P A Z B K I D K S O R Y
F Y E Q B K W V F X H T J A J M A V Q B
U Y T A X V O V G F I Y S Q Z B P M U U
U T H A W A G I Z H O X P H S Z P G O R
V X Y A U G G Z C D L A R E M E H E I E
W Y S Z X K F C P G Z A L G N L I E S E
P P T U I Z O E E N X T P R Z Q R Y E Q
S O P X C M M I A R Q I S J U Y E W B A
S D O Y T F F R R M Y V L Y R E B P H J
H I B E V N L P L W O J M Z E U F X R I
S A U N G B F J J D E C D U P K U L Q P
Z M L O N D F G A R N E T W S G W M M Q
P O G T K X S U V G V Y A S A D U T E H
F N F S Y U M N D A C V L I J Z S F E O
E D I N Q F Z X H Y L N A M B E R O B K
Q A O O K E U J U V X T G R C S P D M A
C D F O Y T K T K K A E T R G A V N B I
J K W M L O Y X G C O N C A L E Z X X F
```

IN OTHER WORDS

HBO is a popular cable TV network. Words that contain the consecutive letters HBO include the compound words DASHBOARD and MATCHBOOK. What common eight-letter non-compound word contains the consecutive letters HBO?

— — — — — — — —

★ Anthem Phrases by Sally R. Stein

ACROSS

1 Is unable to
5 Highly sloped
10 Wild canine
14 Margarine
15 Traveler's stop
16 Jai __
17 "Star Spangled Banner" phrase
20 Donkey
21 Detective's job
22 Types of teeth
23 Move swiftly
24 Audiences' disapprovals
25 Cast members
28 Not at all loose
29 DVD player ancestor
32 Call up
33 Price-tag info
34 Dress of India
35 "Star Spangled Banner" phrase
38 Fabric fuzz
39 High cards
40 Occupied, as a seat
41 Tee preceder
42 Having no available seats
43 Says hello to
44 Canary's home
45 Chicago baseballers
46 Laundry bottle
49 Diva's performance
50 Skillet
53 "Star Spangled Banner" phrase
56 Muscle soreness
57 Gladden
58 Emcee Trebek
59 Boxing results: Abbr.
60 After-bath cover-ups
61 Pulsate

DOWN

1 Musical postscript
2 Regretful word
3 6 p.m. broadcast
4 Freight unit
5 Tailor's scissors
6 "Cheers!" is one
7 Raison d'__
8 Snakelike fish
9 Where the Pilgrims landed
10 Cries loudly
11 Gymnast Korbut
12 Cowardly Lion portrayer
13 Looks good on
18 Fearful
19 Crook's haul
23 Cruller alternative
24 Foundations
25 Pie fruit
26 Evert of tennis
27 Animated characters
28 Terry cloth product
29 Prize highly
30 Wave top
31 Takes a bus
33 Repetitive pattern
34 Trig functions
36 Music to a comedian's ears
37 Auto safety device
42 Portrait part
43 Museum employees
44 Dessert listings
45 Greek island
46 Unruly kid
47 Canal device
48 Reverberate
49 Lebanese, e.g.
50 Lacking color
51 Vicinity
52 On deck
54 Highway warning
55 Chemist's room

★ Cash Drops

The picture shows some euro currency that was dropped on the floor, one bill at a time. Which bill was dropped first?

WORD WIT

Boats are often referred to as "she." The letters of what five-letter word for a type of boat can be rearranged to form a girl's nickname, which is the name of the title character of a popular comic strip?

— — — — —

★★ Circular Reasoning

Connect all of the circles by drawing a single continuous line through every square of the diagram. All right-angle turns of your line must alternate between boxes containing a circle and boxes not containing a circle. You must make a right-angle turn out of every square that contains a circle. Your line must end in the same square that it begins, and it cannot enter any square more than once.

EQUATION CONSTRUCTION

Use the digits 2, 4, 5, and 8 plus standard symbols and operations of arithmetic, to create a mathematical expression that equals the number 16. All the digits must be used.

$$\boxed{} = \boxed{16}$$

★ Three or More

Enter the missing numbers from 1 to 9 into the diagram in such a way that all pairs of numbers connected by a line have a difference of three or more.

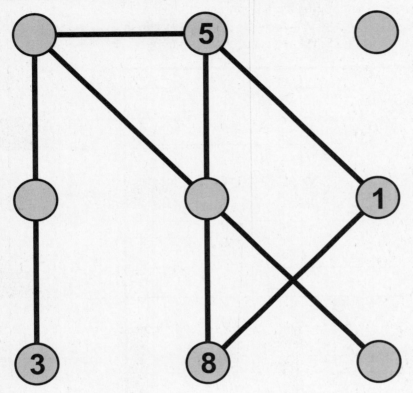

CITY SEARCH

Use the letters in SAN FRANCISCO to form common uncapitalized six-letter words. Plurals ending in S or verbs ending in S aren't allowed. We found eight words. How many can you find?

_____   _____

_____   _____

_____   _____

_____   _____

★ Cupfuls by Lee Weaver

ACROSS

1 Big fuss
5 __ one's time (wait)
9 Summary
14 Got off the horse
15 China's continent
16 Eat away at
17 Shopper's memo
18 Functions
19 Thin cookie
20 Tanning-lotion ingredient
23 Not masc. or neut.
24 Burros' relatives
25 Ballot casters
27 Segmented, as a flower
30 Double a knot
31 Turns topsy-turvy
32 Touched lovingly
35 Mermaid's habitat
36 Blond shade
37 Horse food
38 Disinclined
42 Take a stand against
45 Chris of tennis
46 Lost vitality
47 Breakfast bowlful
49 Israeli native
50 XIII x V
51 Charitable food source
56 Share one's thoughts
58 Flue fallout
59 Hawaiian seaport
60 Room style
61 Tiny thing
62 Author __ Stanley Gardner
63 Winter vehicles
64 Dressed
65 Business transaction

DOWN

1 Bath powder
2 Hodgepodge
3 Part of CD
4 Chair accessory
5 Doodads
6 Handed out
7 Tries to lose weight
8 Compass point
9 Overhauled the manuscript
10 Time period
11 Place for a quick bite
12 "Doe __ ..."
13 Salon hairstyles
21 "__ Lang Syne"
22 Always
26 Poetic contraction
27 Nudge
28 Fencing blade
29 Chinaware set
30 Pep-rally yell
32 St. Louis clock setting
33 Smooth the way
34 __-in-the-wool
36 Social insect
39 _Got a Secret_
40 Taunting ones
41 Singer Guthrie
42 Went around the earth
43 Red wine
44 Like some cooked eggs
46 Bismarck, North __
47 Dolts
48 Throw out, as of school
49 Go bad
52 Leathernecks' org.
53 Add staff
54 Singer Fitzgerald
55 Playwright Coward
57 Show approval

★ Split Decisions

In this clueless crossword puzzle, each answer consists of two words whose spellings are the same, except for the consecutive letters given. All answers are common words; no phrases or hyphenated or capitalized words are used. Some of the clues may have more than one solution, but there is only one word pair that will correctly link up with all the other word pairs.

EQUATION CONSTRUCTION

Use the digits 2, 4, 5, and 8 plus standard symbols and operations of arithmetic, to create a mathematical expression that equals the number 127. All the digits must be used.

| | = | **127** |

★ Kakuro

Fill in the blank white boxes of the diagram with digits from 1 to 9 so that
each group of numbers adds up to the shaded number above it (for a column)
or to the left of it (for a row). Each group of numbers must contain all different
digits. That is, no digit may be repeated within a particular sum.

AND SO ON

Unscramble the letters in the phrase SEND CONGA, to form two words that are part of a common
phrase that has the word *and* between them.

_____ and _____

★ Oops! by Gail Grabowski

ACROSS

1 Even exchange
5 Small spot
10 Was indebted to
14 Foot feature
15 Agile
16 Cleopatra's river
17 Salty snack
19 Organization: Abbr.
20 Night noise
21 Scottish skirt
22 Below-average grades
23 Lawn material
25 Medical facility
27 *Beetle Bailey* dog
29 Show scorn towards
32 Luxurious
35 Hubbub
37 Like old bread
38 Alias letters
39 Closely-cropped hair
42 Metal container
43 Court case
45 Forget-me-__
46 Revue unit
47 Airport structures
50 Hourly pay
52 Neatened, with "up"
54 Devastation
57 Style of type
59 Greenish blue
61 Plant in a new container
63 Diva's solo
64 Midday time-out
66 Diplomacy
67 Sections of seats
68 Singer Guthrie
69 Actress Sommer
70 Beginning
71 Highland girl

DOWN

1 Exhausts, as strength
2 Not correct
3 Film performer
4 Ancient Egyptian ruler
5 __-mo (replay speed)
6 Select
7 Moral principle
8 Puts in the fridge
9 Didn't let out
10 Trying to lose weight
11 Impertinent remark
12 "You're something __!"
13 Cozy places
18 Dry run
24 Sky sight
26 Hawk's home
28 Dedicated verse
30 Jai __
31 Canvas shelter
32 Hiker's trail
33 Gumbo ingredient
34 12/25 figure
36 Have
39 Dressed
40 Dairy animal
41 Colorado neighbor
44 Stir
46 A few
48 Theater district
49 Dress spangle
51 Attire
53 Desert features
55 Musical drama
56 Raked over the __ (reprimanded)
57 Destiny
58 Spoken
60 43,560 square feet
62 Boxing stats.
65 FDR successor

★ One-Way Streets

The diagram represents a pattern of streets. A and B are parking spaces, and the black squares are stores. Find the route that starts at A, passes through all stores exactly once, and ends at B. Arrows indicate one-way traffic for that block only. No block or intersection may be entered more than once.

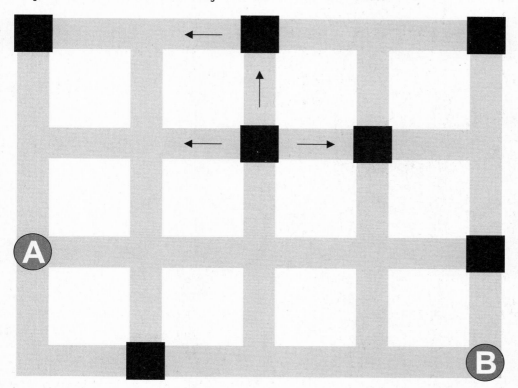

MIXAGRAMS

Each line contains a five-letter word and a four-letter word that have been mixed together (the order of the letters in each word has not been changed). Unmix the two words on each line and write them in the spaces provided. When you're done, find a two-word answer to the clue by reading down the letter columns in the answers.

CLUE: Camp kid

MABUNIRAN = _ _ _ _ _ + _ _ _ _

ROTHUSERT = _ _ _ _ _ + _ _ _ _

PRAINSTEM = _ _ _ _ _ + _ _ _ _

TOREILADY = _ _ _ _ _ + _ _ _ _

★ Mixed Nuts

Find the six varieties of nuts hidden in the honeycomb diagram. Form your words by moving from one letter tile to another as long as they have a side in common. All tiles must be used exactly once.

COMMON SENSE

What three-letter word can be found in the dictionary definitions of all of these words: WASHER, SHELL, THREAD and WRENCH?

— — —

★ Star Search

Find the stars that are hidden in some of the blank squares. The numbered squares indicate how many stars are hidden in the squares adjacent to them (including diagonally). There is never more than one star in any square.

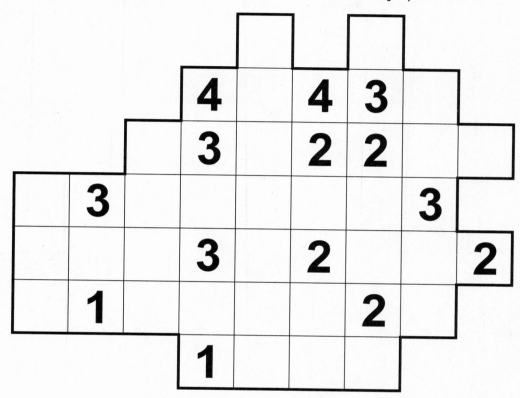

TELEPHONE TRIOS

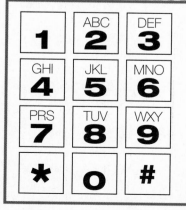

Using the numbers and letters on a standard telephone, what three seven-letter words from the same category can be formed from these telephone numbers?

242-9253 _ _ _ _ _ _ _

726-6837 _ _ _ _ _ _ _

876-5539 _ _ _ _ _ _ _

★ Summer Is Here by Sally R. Stein

ACROSS

1 Economist Greenspan
5 Bookcase part
10 Increased
14 "The Eternal City"
15 Backyard feature
16 Significant times
17 Hair grooming device
18 Church platform
19 Auction condition
20 Emporium summer
22 Disappeared
23 Becomes more mature
24 Clothes with belts
25 Cowboy ropes
28 Stayed home for dinner
31 Run ___ (go wild)
32 Commit larceny
33 Taste of soup
36 Summer without batteries
40 Mao ___-tung
41 Almighty of Islam
42 Top of the head
43 Puts back together
44 Siesta
46 Eagle claw
49 Singer Tennille
50 Actor Sharif
51 Ledger summer
57 Short letter
58 Dolt
59 Nevada neighbor
60 Part of the eye
61 Defiant one
62 Capitol topper
63 Dollar fraction
64 Wipe clean
65 Fencing blade

DOWN

1 Curved lines
2 Pillage
3 Rifle filler
4 Where Omaha is
5 Gaps
6 Building walkways
7 Suffix for leather
8 Dishonest sort
9 Place-setting piece
10 Jimmy Carter successor
11 Welles of Hollywood
12 Canonized person
13 Curved letters
21 Self-image
24 Aspirin unit
25 Endure
26 Wally "Famous" ___
27 Filet fish
28 Map book
29 Engineering school, for short
30 ___ de Cologne
32 Register ring-up
33 Comedian Laurel
34 Tiny amount
35 Get ready, for short
37 Wet forecast
38 160, to Caesar
39 Knack
43 Wooded area
44 Twosome
45 Actress Sothern
46 Pick-me-up
47 Dean Martin song subject
48 Nero's language
49 Heavy books
51 Real-estate unit
52 Sonny and ___
53 Island south of Florida
54 On the summit
55 Specify
56 You, to Quakers

★ Grin and Wear It

Find the 16 articles of apparel that are hidden in the appropriately shaped diagram. One word appears twice in the diagram. Which one is it?

```
    C A T                 O B O
  M A T H                 V E S G
O S L I N K           S H C C F G
J E K L A T R I H S T O R S A
B A T C R O I F S T N A P A N
A R R A O L D E H J C T A N K
    P O S E O H S H O
    M V E G I A S R T
    J K V L O V E S T
    A B L O N T R Y S
    F O Y V A S D O E
    L O N E L Y C A T
    A T W S G L O V V
    H S G R I H A T O
    S N A E J A T P I
```

WORD WIT

What U.S. state's current license-plate slogan consists of three words, where the first letter of each word spells a very common chat-room abbreviation?

_____

bRain BREATHER BELLY LAUGHS

Losing weight is serious business, which means it takes a lot of laughter to get you through it. Here are true-life jokes about weight loss submitted to *Reader's Digest*.

A friend had been working out hard, guided by her *Buns of Steel* exercise video. When she asked her husband if he thought she was showing any results from all her effort, he wrapped his arms around her, gave a squeeze, and replied, "Sure, honey. You're up to aluminum."

—Judy Couto

My friend Kimberly announced that she had started a diet to lose some pounds she had put on recently. "Good!" I exclaimed. "I'm ready to start a diet too. We can be dieting buddies and help each other out. When I feel the urge to drive out and get a burger and fries, I'll call you first."

"Great!" she replied. "I'll ride with you."

—Katina Fisher

Although I knew I had put on a few pounds, I didn't consider myself overweight until the day I decided to clean my refrigerator. I sat on a chair in front of the appliance and reached in to wipe the back wall.

While I was in this position my teenage son came into the kitchen. "Hi, Mom," he said. "Whatcha doin', having lunch?"

I started my diet that day.

—Betty Strohm

Although I was only a few pounds overweight, my wife was harping on me to diet. One evening we took a brisk walk downtown, and I surprised her by jumping over a parking meter, leapfrog style.

Pleased with myself, I said, "How many fat men do you know who can do that?"

"One," she retorted.

—R. T. McLaury

Early one Saturday I checked out a local yard sale and came across some exercise equipment I had been looking for. As I paid the owner for her ThighMaster and aerobic step, I inquired if she also had a ButtMaster. "No," she replied quickly, "but I should have it in time for my next yard sale."

—Melody Lear

After noticing how trim my husband had become, a friend asked me how I had persuaded him to diet. It was then I shared my dark secret: "I put our teenage son's shorts in his underwear drawer."

—Ruth J. Luhrs

My daughter couldn't muster the willpower to lose unwanted pounds. One day, watching a svelte friend walking up our driveway, she lamented, "Linda's so skinny, it makes me sick."

"If it bothers you," I suggested gently, "why don't you do something about it?"

"Good idea, Mom," she replied. Turning to her friend, she called out, "Hey, Linda, have a piece of chocolate cake."

—Doris E. Fletcher

Needing to shed a few pounds, my husband and I went on a diet that had specific recipes for each meal of the day. I followed the instructions closely, dividing the finished recipe in half for our individual plates. We felt terrific and thought the diet was wonderful— we never felt hungry!

But when we realized we were gaining weight, not losing it, I checked the recipes again. There, in fine print, was "Serves 6."

—Barbara Currie

★ Line Drawings

Draw three straight lines, each from one edge of the square to another edge, so that the letters in each of the six regions spell a three-letter word.

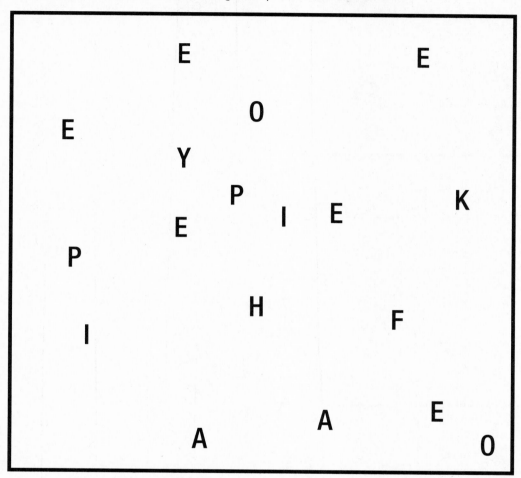

EQUATION CONSTRUCTION

Arrange these signs and numbers to form a correct number sentence. Numbers may be placed together to form a greater number (for example, a *1* and an *8* can be combined to form *18* or *81*). It is not necessary to use all the signs and numbers. No parentheses are needed.

5 , 7 , 1 , 10 , 4, × , ×

$$\boxed{} = \boxed{}$$

★ ABC

Enter the letters A, B, and C into the diagram so that each row and column has exactly one A, one B, and one C. The letters outside the diagram indicate the first letter encountered, moving in the direction of the arrow. Keep in mind that after all the letters have been filled in, there will be one blank box in each row and column.

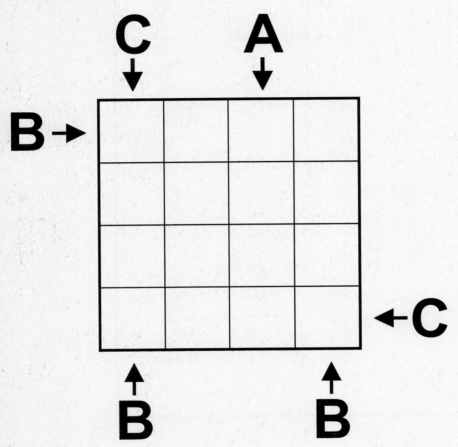

WORD WIT

What is the shortest common English word in which the letter F is pronounced like a V?

_____

★ Keeping Afloat by Norma Steinberg

ACROSS

1 Action-figure soldier
6 Babies' neckwear
10 "What time __?"
14 Curaçao neighbor
15 And others: Abbr.
16 Horse hair
17 Short skirts
18 Neutral color
19 Bandstand boxes
20 Invite
21 Where a baseball team sits
24 Tibia and fibula
26 Unforgettable performers
27 Dish washer's need
29 Dessert items
31 Stuff trapped in dryers
32 Sweetheart
34 Pale with fear
39 Cancel
40 Heroic tales
42 Sampras of tennis
43 Inhales suddenly
45 Actress Russo
46 Sculling poles
47 Poisonous snakes
49 Eats away at
51 Stress
55 Moonshine maker
56 Printer's copy
59 "Life __ cabaret ..."
62 Blind as __
63 Harness strap
64 Hermit
66 Poi ingredient
67 Killer whale
68 Upright
69 Panache
70 Close by
71 Classifies

DOWN

1 Vasco da __
2 Spring flower
3 Risky investments
4 Kimono sash
5 Slackening off
6 Borscht needs
7 Yearning
8 Unclothed
9 Engine gunk
10 Mental picture
11 South Pacific island group
12 Vocal contribution
13 Student's ordeals

22 Lacks
23 __ Major
25 Heading the list
27 Fake coin
28 __ colada
29 Senate aides
30 Modern Persia
33 Marshal Wyatt
35 Bobbin
36 Biggest name on the marquee
37 French 101 verb
38 Loch __ monster
41 Take care of
44 Of sound mind

48 *Sophie's Choice* author
50 Long-barreled weapons
51 Form of quartz
52 Conspiracy
53 Bow of the silents
54 Mr. John of rock
55 Underwater location device
57 Pierre's pop
58 Costa __
60 Religious subdivision
61 Linkletter et al.
65 Venezuelan gold

★ Sets of Three

Group all the symbols into sets of three, with each set having either all the same shape or all the same color. The symbols in each set must all be connected to each other by a common horizontal or vertical side.

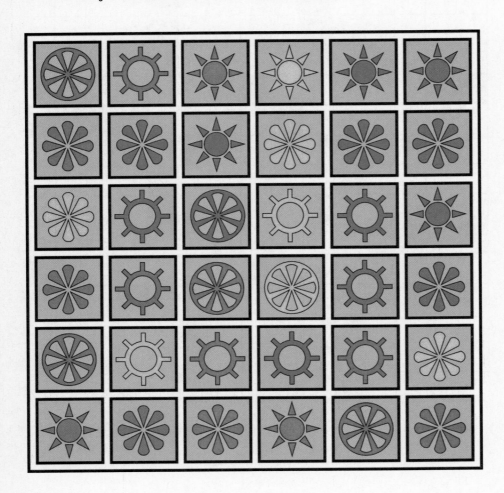

WORD WIT

What common six-letter word, that might be found in a real-estate contract, uses only two different letters, each repeated three times?

— — — — — —

★★ Mystery Guest

All of the 26 words to be found in the diagram come from the mini-biography of a famous person below. When you've found all the words, the unused letters in the diagram will spell out the name of the mystery guest.

This diminutive artist was born in Albi, France, in 1864. He started painting in child-hood and proved good enough to study for several years under some of the most respected French academic painters, but he was no dusty scholar. He preferred to spend his time in the company of actors, dancers, and ladies of the night in the shady districts of Paris. His portraits of the Moulin Rouge and other cabarets of Montmartre are some of the most vivacious ever committed to canvas. Despite standing a little under five feet tall and always being frail of health, this celebrated and talented soul lived his short life to the full, and produced a body of work that few others have equaled.

```
L T D A N C E R S T O U
A L B I A S O U L E L P
D O U N R R O U G E E A
I E V O S I E Y R F V I
E A T L C A E T H G I N
S C C A B A R E T S T T
A N V F R A N C E S U E
E I U S M B T F I F N R
V L I T T L E R R I S
I U N D E R R L E A M L
F O D E L A U Q E X I C
M M A C A D E M I C D L
```

TRANSDELETION

Delete one letter from the word DEVOURING and rearrange the rest, to get a phrase that you might find on the menu of a fine restaurant.

_____

★★ Find the Ships

Determine the position of the 10 ships listed to the right of the diagram. The ships may be oriented either horizontally or vertically. A square with wavy lines indicates water and will not contain a ship. The numbers at the edge of the diagram indicate how many squares in that row or column contain parts of ships. When all 10 ships are correctly placed in the diagram, no two of them will touch each other, not even diagonally.

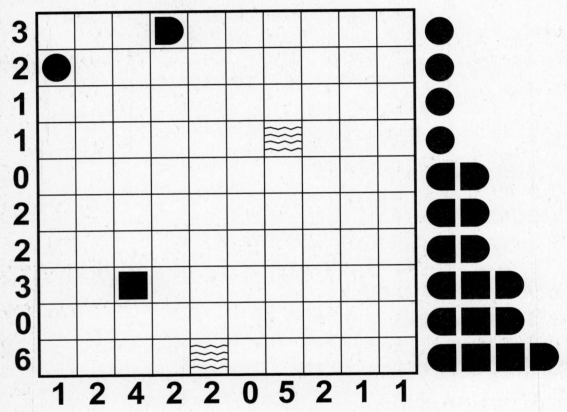

TRANSDELETION

Delete one letter from the word TREACHEROUS and rearrange the rest, to get a color.

— — — — — — — — — —

★ Sudoku

Fill in the blank boxes so that every row, column, and 3×3 box contains all of the numbers 1 to 9.

	4					7		5
7			6	3	9			
	2				5		6	9
3		4	2		6	5	1	8
		8			3		7	4
			1		4	2		
1		5			8	9		
	8		5	6			2	1
			4			8		

MIXAGRAMS

Each line contains a five-letter word and a four-letter word that have been mixed together (the order of the letters in each word has not been changed). Unmix the two words on each line and write them in the spaces provided. When you're done, find a two-word answer to the clue by reading down the letter columns in the answers.

CLUE: Stumblebum's pair

S C A H L A D E F = _ _ _ _ _ + _ _ _ _

C L U H E R E S T = _ _ _ _ _ + _ _ _ _

T A R F U F E I X = _ _ _ _ _ + _ _ _ _

D R O A T E U S T = _ _ _ _ _ + _ _ _ _

★ Hit for the Cycle by Randall J. Hartman

ACROSS

1 Flower areas
5 Chain piece
9 Went out with
14 Mishmash
15 Fairy-tale beginning
16 Draw forth
17 Arkin or Alda
18 Look over
19 Penalties for illegal parking
20 By oneself
23 Harasses
24 Long, long time
25 It follows Fri.
28 Jump-rope game
32 __ d'oeuvres
36 WWII entertainment provider
37 39 Across, e.g.
38 ``Yipes!''
39 Home of the Alamo
42 "Thanks __!"
43 Gymnast Comaneci
45 Ecology agcy.
46 Wife of Zeus
47 Horseracing coup
51 __ Jose, CA
52 __-mo replay
53 Making cow sounds
58 Bart's dad
61 Summoning device
64 Genuine
65 Where most people live
66 La Scala offering
67 Honeycomb section
68 A deadly sin
69 Iced-tea flavoring
70 Lodge members
71 Comprehends

DOWN

1 Talk oneself up
2 *Dallas* matriarch
3 Ross of the Supremes
4 Gershwin creations
5 Misses the boat
6 2.54 centimeters
7 March Madness org.
8 Sheepdog shelter
9 Supports, as a theory
10 Gung-ho
11 2,000 pounds
12 Barely manage, with "out"
13 __ Moines, IA
21 Was in front
22 Female deer
25 Tired, as an expression
26 Role player
27 Iota preceder
29 Take advantage of
30 One in the ring
31 2002 Winter Olympics site
32 Searches for prey
33 Mitchell mansion surname
34 *The Thinker* sculptor
35 Cruise vessel
40 Military mail drop: Abbr.
41 Logs' destinations
44 Election loser
48 Shade tree
49 Twist one's arm
50 __ de plume
54 October birthstones
55 *Vogue* copy
56 Reason for earplugs
57 Annoying insects
58 Medal of Honor recipient
59 Angler's gear
60 Polio vaccine developer
61 Legislator, for short
62 Monkey kin
63 Topaz or amethyst

★★ Circular Reasoning

Connect all of the circles by drawing a single continuous line through every square of the diagram. All right-angle turns of your line must alternate between boxes containing a circle and boxes not containing a circle. You must make a right-angle turn out of every square that contains a circle. Your line must end in the same square that it begins, and it cannot enter any square more than once.

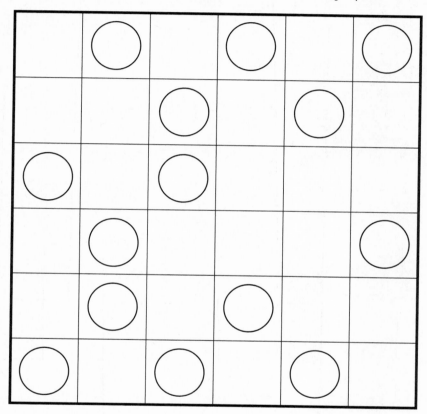

WORD SQUARE JIGSAW

Place the given pieces into the 4×4 blank diagram to form eight common words, four reading across and four reading down.

★★ Triad Split Decisions

In this clueless crossword puzzle, each answer consists of two words whose spellings are the same, except for the consecutive letters given. All answers are common words; no phrases or hyphenated or capitalized words are used. Some of the clues may have more than one solution, but there is only one word pair that will correctly link up with all the other word pairs.

EQUATION CONSTRUCTION

Use the digits 5, 2, and 7 plus standard symbols and operations of arithmetic, to create a mathematical expression that equals the number 18. All the digits must be used.

$$\boxed{} = \boxed{18}$$

★★ Kakuro

Fill in the blank white boxes of the diagram with digits from 1 to 9 so that each group of numbers adds up to the shaded number above it (for a column) or to the left of it (for a row). Each group of numbers must contain all different digits. That is, no digit may be repeated within a particular sum.

WORD WIT

Think of the name of a major consumer electronics company. If you add the letter A, and rearrange the letters, you'll get the name of another major consumer electronics company. What are the two companies?

_____   _____

★ The Green Stuff by Sally R. Stein

ACROSS

1 "The final frontier"
6 Actress __ Pinkett Smith
10 Kimono sashes
14 Book of photos
15 From __ (completely)
16 Final
17 Scales of the zodiac
18 Satirist Sahl
19 Londoner's exclamation
20 South Florida dessert
22 Perfume bottle
23 __ Misérables
24 Physics or optics
26 Obstacle
30 Flow back
32 Piece of turf
33 Singer Vikki
34 Legal wrong
36 Pressed for
40 Cambodia's continent
41 Displeased expression
43 Female voice
44 Civil rights org.
46 Copenhagen native
47 German city
48 Geologic time unit
50 Double-helix molecule
51 Home-run blow
52 Western mountain range
56 Frosty
58 Land unit
59 Breath-powered weapon
65 Dinner or brunch
66 Assistance
67 WWII sub
68 Weep loudly
69 One watching
70 Yankee manager
71 Merely
72 Texas city
73 Head-over-__

DOWN

1 Polio vaccine developer
2 Ballet bend
3 Dear __ (advice column)
4 Ringlet
5 AOL service
6 Agent 007
7 On the summit of
8 Actress Day
9 Ancient Mexicans
10 Army uniforms
11 Washbowl
12 Sir __ Newton
13 Fashion
21 Runs into
25 Promissory note
26 Read electronically
27 Cape Canaveral org.
28 Opera solo
29 Actress who married a prince
31 Diner freebie
35 Graf or Sampras
37 Shine softly
38 Sicilian volcano
39 Word of warning
42 Attain
45 Luau side dish
49 Family member
52 Stallone role
53 Vast body of water
54 Move on all fours
55 "Bye-bye!"
57 Child
60 Actor Baldwin
61 Woodwind instrument
62 Ripped
63 British noble
64 Hwys.

★ Islands

Shade in some of the white squares in the diagram with "water," so that each remaining white box is part of an island. Each island will contain exactly one numbered square, indicating how many squares that island contains. Each island is separated from the other islands by water but may touch other islands diagonally. All water is connected, but there are no 2×2 regions of water in the diagram.

1		4		
		4		
1				

WORD WIT

PANAMA is spelled with alternating vowels and consonants. What member of the United Nations has the longest full name that is spelled with alternating vowels and consonants?

_____

★★ Tire Maze

All of the people shown in the diagram, except one, are following the same path to the center. Find the one person who is not on the same path.

INITIAL REACTION

The "equation" below contains the initials of words that will make it correct, forming a numerical fact. Solve the equation by supplying the missing words.

39 = B. of the O.T. _____

★ Three or More

Enter the missing numbers from 1 to 9 into the diagram in such a way that all pairs of numbers connected by a line have a difference of three or more.

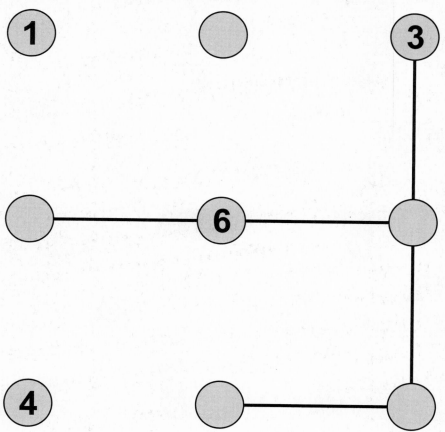

COMMON SENSE

What five-letter plural noun can be found in the dictionary definitions of all of these words: SOLAR BATTERY, VITAMIN E, HONEYCOMB and PROTOPLASM?

__ __ __ __ __

★ Easy Going by Gail Grabowski

ACROSS

1 Luggage attachment
6 "Safe!" sayers
10 Paradise
14 Audacity
15 Make a ringing sound
16 Gasoline name
17 Amphibious aircraft
19 Car wheel
20 DDE's command
21 Mottled horse
22 Complete view
24 Eminem and Ice-T
26 Used up, as money
27 Acorn bearers
29 1914-18 conflict, for short
32 Extremely bad
35 Damage
36 Feedbag tidbit
37 Disney of Disneyland
38 Bards
40 Style of type
41 Hubbub
42 Clumsy one
43 Comedian Hackett
44 Evergreen tree
45 Fiery-tempered one
48 Graduating group
50 Keep separate
54 South Pacific island
56 Restaurant handout
57 Finished first
58 Shah's land, once
59 Maritime patroller
62 Unhip type
63 56 Across, basically
64 Writer Bret
65 London farewell
66 Born Free lioness
67 Suit material

DOWN

1 Deduce
2 River mouth
3 Boy Scout unit
4 Actress Gardner
5 "That's ridiculous!"
6 Like a final batter
7 Have in mind
8 Skillet
9 Pullman cars
10 Worn away
11 Timber that washes up on beaches
12 Hosiery hue
13 Playwright Coward
18 Chinese entree
23 Polite reply, briefly
25 Sulk
26 County hub
28 Scarlett's spouse
30 Magician's stick
31 ___-bitty
32 Not at home
33 Walk in water
34 Computer programmer's graph
38 Frozen treat
39 French affirmatives
40 Coal or gas
42 Aspiring atty.'s exam
43 Took along
46 Spanish celebration
47 "Say it ___ so!"
49 Vocalist Ronstadt
51 In the know
52 Rich dessert
53 Stopped
54 Color gradation
55 Vicinity
56 Religious service
60 Salad-dressing ingredient
61 Detroit labor org.

★ One-Way Streets

The diagram represents a pattern of streets. A and B are parking spaces, and the black squares are stores. Find the route that starts at A, passes through all stores exactly once, and ends at B. Arrows indicate one-way traffic for that block only. No block or intersection may be entered more than once.

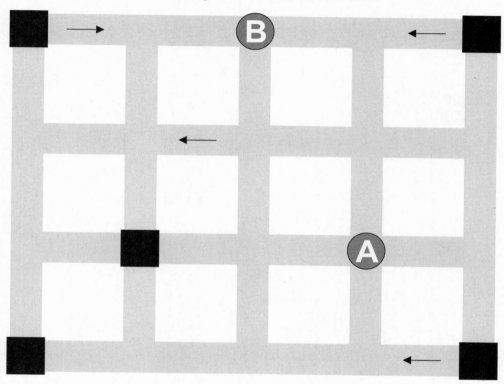

WORD WIT

What six-letter word that starts with the letter B (and has the same meaning as one of the words in this sentence) has all its letters in alphabetical order?

— — — — — —

★★ Hyper-Sudoku

Fill in the blank boxes so that every row, column, 3×3 box, *and* each of the four
3×3 gray regions contains all of the numbers 1 to 9.

7	4	8		1			9	
5	2							
1		6	5	8				4
		1		3	4	5		2
		5	9					8
			6		1			
6	5	9	1	4	3			
	3		7	9				1
		7	2					

TELEPHONE TRIOS

Using the numbers and letters on a standard telephone, what
three seven-letter words from the same category can be formed
from these telephone numbers?

297-7377   _ _ _ _ _ _ _

364-9663   _ _ _ _ _ _ _

436-5625   _ _ _ _ _ _ _

★★ Star Search

Find the stars that are hidden in some of the blank squares. The numbered squares indicate how many stars are hidden in the squares adjacent to them (including diagonally). There is never more than one star in any square.

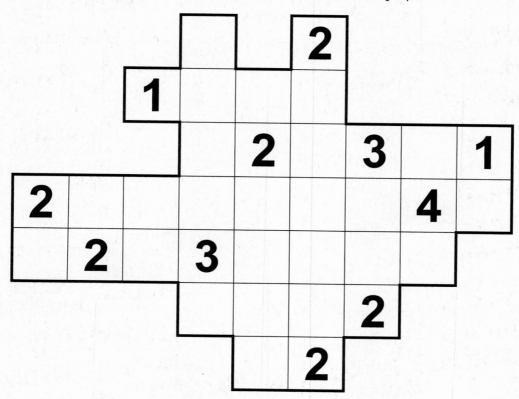

EQUATION CONSTRUCTION

Use the digits 5, 2, and 7 plus standard symbols and operations of arithmetic, to create a mathematical expression that equals the number 33. All the digits must be used.

| | = | 33 |

★ Comparatively Speaking by Gail Grabowski

ACROSS

1 Striped safari sight
6 Frog relatives
11 Corn core
14 Shoelace tip
15 Chef's protector
16 "__ we there yet?"
17 Fun-loving guy
20 Talk together
21 Aviator
22 Pose a question
24 Teheran native
27 Door ringer
28 Oyster product
31 Summer cooler
33 Below-average grade
34 Invest, as a minister
36 Sidestep
38 Not as unruly
42 Bushy plant
43 Brunch entrée
45 T-shirt size: Abbr.
48 Asner and Ames
49 Scornful smile
50 Southwest art center
52 Puppeteer Lewis
56 Use a lever
57 Bewildered
59 Salad vegetable
62 "First impression" advice
67 Soap ingredient
68 Financial review
69 Stately home
70 Curvy letter
71 Takes the bus
72 Pays for poker

DOWN

1 Zig partner
2 Self-image
3 Military embargo
4 Make over
5 Envelope abbreviation
6 Circus star
7 La Scala offering
8 Rainbow shape
9 Play-__ (kid clay)
10 Break sharply
11 Telephoned
12 Baltimore baseballer
13 Bailey of the comics
18 "See __ care!"
19 Barbecued piece
22 Letters on military mail
23 Belgrade resident
25 Church section
26 Boise's locale
29 "Darn it!"
30 Agile
32 Dutch cheeses
35 Those in the out crowd
36 Wane
37 Not odd
39 Hustle
40 GOP emblem
41 Bambi, e.g.
44 Give it a go
45 Seabiscuit's abode
46 Sailor's pals
47 Figures in red
51 Harden, as cement
53 Jazzman Shaw
54 Floating platforms
55 Familiar vow
58 Miles away
60 __ la Douce
61 Long-necked bird
63 Yes, to Yvette
64 Off-the-wall
65 Canapé topping
66 AMA members

★★ ABC

Enter the letters A, B, and C into the diagram so that each row and column
has exactly one A, one B, and one C. The letters outside the diagram indicate
the first letter encountered, moving in the direction of the arrow. Keep in mind
that after all the letters have been filled in, there will be one blank box in each
row and column.

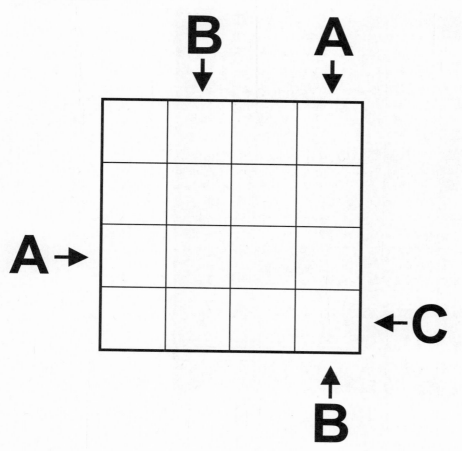

AND SO ON

Unscramble the letters in the phrase LIKED CRAFT, to form two words that are part of a common
phrase that has the word *and* between them.

_____ and _____

★★ Bookworm

A bookworm starts at the first page of Volume 1 and ends at the last page of Volume 3, as shown in the picture. If the front cover and back cover of the volumes are a quarter of an inch thick each, and the paper within each volume is four inches thick, how far does the bookworm travel?

WORD WIT

If the first three letters and last three letters of the word "German" are interchanged, the uncapitalized word "manger" is formed. What six-letter woman's name becomes an uncapitalized word when the first three letters and last three letters are interchanged?

— — — — — —

★★ Sudoku

Fill in the blank boxes so that every row, column, and 3×3 box contains all of the numbers 1 to 9.

1				6		3		
	6	2		1				
4	3	7	9		8			
3		8		7			2	4
2	4						7	
6	7		2				1	
			4		3	1		7
	5							
8	1		7				9	

MIXAGRAMS

Each line contains a five-letter word and a four-letter word that have been mixed together (the order of the letters in each word has not been changed). Unmix the two words on each line and write them in the spaces provided. When you're done, find a two-word answer to the clue by reading down the letter columns in the answers.

CLUE: It's waste-full

RISCADENT = _ _ _ _ _ + _ _ _ _

TIBLUDALE = _ _ _ _ _ + _ _ _ _

LOTITEMOR = _ _ _ _ _ + _ _ _ _

LYDRUPIEC = _ _ _ _ _ + _ _ _ _

★ Thoroughfares by Lee Weaver

ACROSS

1 Rustle, as taffeta
6 Govt. commerce agency
9 Leeway
13 Pointy beard
14 Formal speeches
16 Overdue payment
17 Carom
18 Tempting but hazardous course
20 Sushi servings
21 Hawaiian port
22 "*Now* I understand!"
25 Like a fox
26 Likeness
28 Parceled (out)
30 Eventually
32 Jewels from the sea
36 Downy ducks
37 Where rumors may be heard
41 VIPs' wheels
42 Singer Helen
43 Fire residue
46 Mag. honchos
47 Building location
48 Eastern continent
49 Strike-and-spare place
53 Of lesser quality
56 Electrical interruption
57 Emulate hyenas
58 Boulders
59 Full of promise
60 Cyclone center
61 Masters of ceremonies

DOWN

1 Reddish brown horse
2 In a cautious manner
3 EXPRESS: 10 __ OR LESS
4 Char on the grill
5 Man of the hour
6 From another country
7 One of a matching three
8 Chocolate source
9 In the money
10 Sound of awe
11 Early afternoon
12 Denver hrs.
13 Shows astonishment
15 Preschool attendee
19 George Bernard __
22 Spiny houseplant
23 Learn of
24 Throws in
26 Is a lazybones
27 Forest growth
28 God or goddess
29 Former California fort
31 Pay attention to
32 Gdansk resident
33 City in Oklahoma
34 $$$ dispensers
35 Sigma preceder
38 *The Lord of the Rings*, e.g.
39 Leisure Village resident
40 Genesis garden
43 Obliquely
44 Prolonged attacks
45 Helen or Gabby
47 Pigs, collectively
48 Choir section
49 __ of beauties
50 Comstock load
51 "Gee whiz!"
52 Racing vehicle
53 Syr. neighbor
54 Sgt., for one
55 Musical notes

★★ Line Drawings

Draw three straight lines, each from one edge of the square to another edge, so there is a different amount of money in each of six regions.

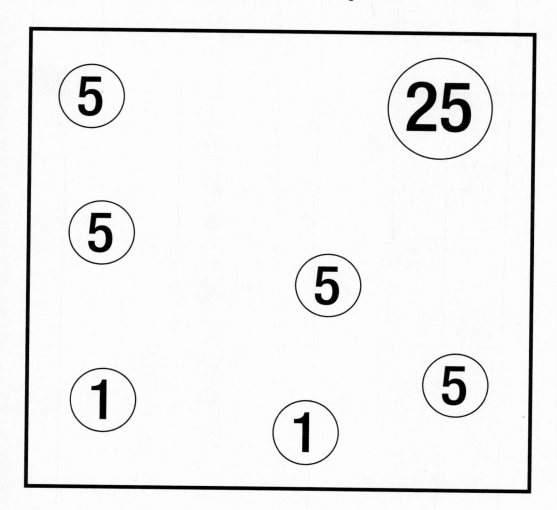

EQUATION CONSTRUCTION

Arrange these signs and numbers to form a correct number sentence. Numbers may be placed together to form a greater number (for example, a *1* and an *8* can be combined to form *18* or *81*). It is not necessary to use all the signs and numbers. No parentheses are needed.

1 , 2 , 5 , 8 , 15 , × , −

	=	

★★ Find the Ships

Determine the position of the 10 ships listed to the right of the diagram. The ships may be oriented either horizontally or vertically. A square with wavy lines indicates water and will not contain a ship. The numbers at the edge of the diagram indicate how many squares in that row or column contain parts of ships. When all 10 ships are correctly placed in the diagram, no two of them will touch each other, not even diagonally.

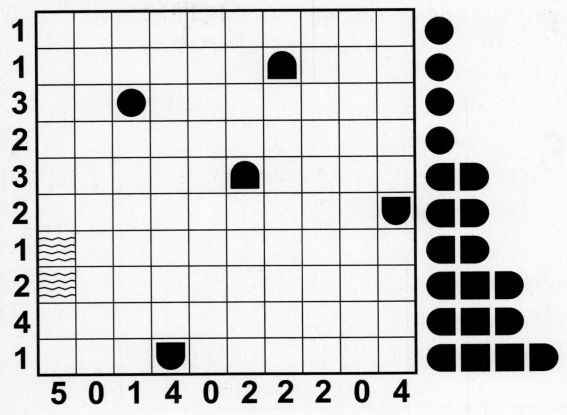

CLUELESS CROSSWORD

Complete the crossword with common uncapitalized seven-letter words, based entirely on the letters already filled in for you.

★★★ Circular Reasoning

Connect all of the circles by drawing a single continuous line through every square of the diagram. All right-angle turns of your line must alternate between boxes containing a circle and boxes not containing a circle. You must make a right-angle turn out of every square that contains a circle. Your line must end in the same square that it begins, and it cannot enter any square more than once.

WORD WIT

BEN BRADLEE is a former managing editor of the *Washington Post*. Delete one letter in his name and rearrange the remaining letters, to get the full name of an American singer.

_____

★ Continental Breakfast by Sally R. Stein

ACROSS

1 Tousle, as hair
5 Stage phone, e.g.
9 Infants
14 PDQ
15 Highly rated
16 Application, as of language
17 Acting part
18 Agitate
19 Toss
20 Breakfast order
23 Cattle groups
24 Pleasant
25 Allow
28 "__ port in a storm"
29 Have an evening meal
32 Submarine's weapon
34 Knickknack
36 Director Preminger
37 Breakfast order
41 "Get away!"
43 Mary Tyler __
44 Spotted wildcat
48 Not me
49 Gallery display
52 Make a selection
53 Surf and __
55 Hay machine
57 Breakfast order
61 Barton of the Red Cross
63 Final Four org.
64 Do a laundry chore
65 Sandwich shops
66 Held onto
67 Peruse
68 Arm of the sea
69 Numerical datum
70 Whirlpool

DOWN

1 Actress Mason
2 Major golf tournament
3 Worker's pay
4 Pay out
5 Avoid an F
6 Author Philip
7 Bagel flavor
8 Allow
9 Mansion employee
10 Arthur of tennis
11 Kind of pear
12 Swelled head
13 Assemble a shirt
21 Publish
22 Author Umberto
26 Summer clock setting in Ft. Myers
27 Also
30 Large coffee brewer
31 Photo
33 Sit for a photo
34 Wheat or soybeans
35 Electrical unit
37 Super Bowl sport
38 Plaything
39 Tic-tac-toe win
40 Caribbean resort island
41 Road warning sign
42 In the know
45 Finally
46 Floor covering
47 Bartender's offerings
49 __, Lord Tennyson
50 Put more film in a camera
51 Stylish
54 Gem surface
56 In flames
58 Great Lake
59 California wine center
60 Electrical unit
61 401, in old Rome
62 Author Deighton

★★ Four-Letter Word Routes

Using each of the 24 letters exactly once, find the six routes that form the six different four-letter words hidden in the diagram. For each route, start with the first letter in each word and spell the remaining letters in the word in order, by moving through the gaps in the walls.

CITY SEARCH

Use the letters in PITTSBURGH to form common uncapitalized six-letter words. Plurals or verbs ending in S aren't allowed. We found five words. How many can you find?

_____ _____ _____ _____

_____

★★ Kakuro

Fill in the blank white boxes of the diagram with digits from 1 to 9 so that each group of numbers adds up to the shaded number above it (for a column) or to the left of it (for a row). Each group of numbers must contain all different digits. That is, no digit may be repeated within a particular sum.

TRANSDELETION

Delete one letter from the word MINERALOGIST and rearrange the rest, to get the two-word name of a type of animal.

★★ Islands

Shade in some of the white squares in the diagram with "water," so that each remaining white box is part of an island. Each island will contain exactly one numbered square, indicating how many squares that island contains. Each island is separated from the other islands by water but may touch other islands diagonally. All water is connected, but there are no 2×2 regions of water in the diagram.

3					1
		1			
3				3	
	3				1

WORD WIT

CHAD is a man's name that is also the name of a world nation. The name of what world nation spells out two men's names consecutively if the order of the letters is reversed?

_____

★ Social Settings by Gail Grabowski

ACROSS

1 Mature fillies
6 Kayak kin
11 __ and outs
14 Toes the line
15 Sports complex
16 Command to a canine
17 Construction-site machine
19 Marvin or Majors
20 Beef dish
21 Takes a break
22 Place for makeup
23 Prestige
25 Pop singer __ Richie
27 "__ pin, pick it up ..."
28 Worn out
29 Coffeehouse selection
32 "Well done!"
33 Lunch meat
36 Water, to Pierre
37 Watercourse
40 Be in hock to
41 Fido's warning
42 Office staffer
43 Colorado ski spot
45 Brink
47 __ fide
49 Holmes or Poirot
51 Changing slowly
54 S. Dak. neighbor
55 Summer ermine
57 Takes to court
59 Actress Gardner
60 Posse, for example
62 Hodges of baseball
63 Kitchen appliance
64 "Here we go __!"
65 NBC weekend revue
66 Questioned
67 Birds' abodes

DOWN

1 Soft shoes, for short
2 Contributes to a crime
3 Held another session
4 Ocular solution
5 Nine-digit ID
6 Device with a lens
7 Crop up
8 Immediately following
9 Pizza portion
10 It's often pierced
11 Go from Kauai to Oahu to Maui
12 Dorothy, to Em
13 Iron alloy
18 __ Grit
22 Enemy
24 Food server on wheels
26 Home of the Blarney Stone
28 Metal container
29 Actress Ryan
30 Kayak propeller
31 Pitcher's delivery
32 Mobile-to-Montgomery dir.
34 Bowl over
35 Tom, Dick and Harry
38 Oceans
39 Fruity drink
44 Pizza topping
46 Where Ger. and It. are
47 Supported, as framework
48 Courtroom ritual
49 Hosiery problems
50 Novelist Ira
51 Chasm
52 Mystical glows
53 "__ Be" (Beatles song)
56 Armored vehicle
58 Dict. entries
60 Madrid Mrs.
61 Skillet

★★ Apple Tree Maze

Enter the maze at one of the two openings at the bottom, find a path that passes through all the apples, then exit through the other opening. You may not retrace your path.

EQUATION CONSTRUCTION

Use the digits 5, 2, and 7 plus standard symbols and operations of arithmetic, to create a mathematical expression that equals the number 45. All the digits must be used.

	=	45

★★ Split Decisions

In this clueless crossword puzzle, each answer consists of two words whose spellings are the same, except for the consecutive letters given. All answers are common words; no phrases or hyphenated or capitalized words are used. Some of the clues may have more than one solution, but there is only one word pair that will correctly link up with all the other word pairs.

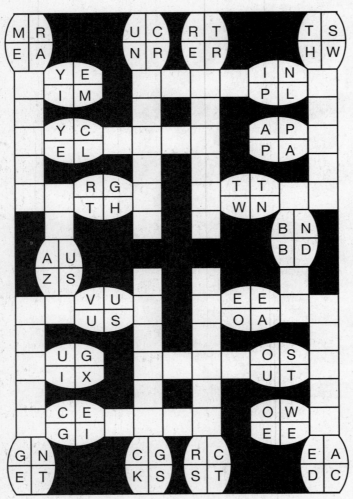

COMMON SENSE

What four-letter word can be found in the dictionary definitions of all of these words: SCIENCE FICTION, GARDEN, ACTION and GRAPH?

— — — —

★★ Hyper-Sudoku

Fill in the blank boxes so that every row, column, 3×3 box, *and* each of the four 3×3 gray regions contains all of the numbers 1 to 9.

			5	4	9	6		
					6			3
4		9	3				5	7
								6
		6	2		1			
2	7						9	
					2		6	
	5							4
	9	1				3	2	8

MIXAGRAMS

Each line contains a five-letter word and a four-letter word that have been mixed together (the order of the letters in each word has not been changed). Unmix the two words on each line and write them in the spaces provided. When you're done, find a two-word answer to the clue by reading down the letter columns in the answers.

CLUE: Igloo

WACHORINP = _ _ _ _ _ + _ _ _ _

CHOARMEON = _ _ _ _ _ + _ _ _ _

ASMOLARGM = _ _ _ _ _ + _ _ _ _

NECROANZE = _ _ _ _ _ + _ _ _ _

★ Going Solo by Gail Grabowski

ACROSS

1 Canyon sound
5 Spanish miss: Abbr.
9 Balance-sheet plus
14 Persuade
15 Lettuce purchase
16 Nut tree
17 Person with no siblings
19 Long look
20 "Take your paws off me!"
21 Robin's retreat
23 Reunion attendee
24 City in Oklahoma
26 Coffee containers
28 Office-memo specification
33 Hosp. workers
34 Pastoral place
35 Like a lot
37 Solemn statements
40 Piña colada ingredient
42 Equip anew
43 Boy Scout unit
44 Short sleep
46 King Kong, e.g.
47 Nickname for Texas
52 Whirlpool
53 News clipping
54 Depend (on)
57 Quick look
59 Synagogue leader
63 Suspect's story
65 Brief jokes
67 Safe spot
68 Gumbo ingredient
69 Pass out cards
70 Glossy
71 Poet Ogden
72 Johnson of *Laugh-In*

DOWN

1 Environmental sci.
2 Ice-cream holder
3 Sentry's order
4 Gas in the air
5 "No talking!"
6 Blitzen or Dasher
7 Folk story
8 Totals
9 Stomach muscles
10 Place in reserve
11 Marine mammal
12 Hosiery hue
13 Those people
18 Capitol Hill grp.
22 Singing syllable
25 Not feeling well
27 Tenn. neighbor
28 Traffic tie-up
29 Playground retort
30 Steam bath
31 Diet-food label phrase
32 Complain
33 Go bad
36 Summer, in France
38 Hive inhabitant
39 Went fast
41 Sailors
45 Seattle clock setting: Abbr.
48 Radical '60s org.
49 Powerful businessperson
50 Actress Garr
51 Blake of *Gunsmoke*
54 Stadium sounds
55 Airline to Israel
56 Not taped
58 "Puppy Love" singer
60 Bar brew
61 Pesky kid
62 Capri, e.g.
64 Pen filler
66 __-di-dah

★★ Three or More

Enter the missing numbers from 1 to 9 into the diagram in such a way that all pairs of numbers connected by a line have a difference of three or more.

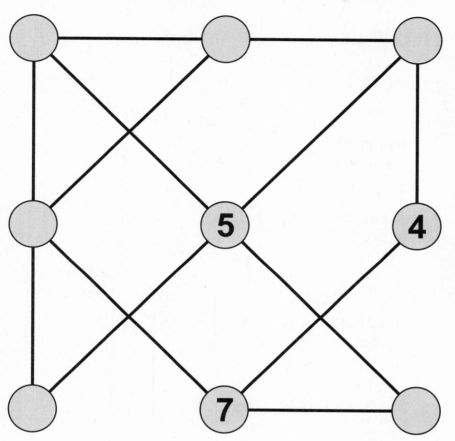

WORD WIT

Actors have to learn their LINES in their job. The full name (13 letters in total) of what film actor contains only the letters in the word LINES?

_____

bRain BReather MEETING MANIA

If you've ever sat in a meeting, bored to tears at the endless droning and debate, then these quotes and quips about meetings, committees, and bureaucracy will ring oh so true.

A conference is a gathering of important people who singly can do nothing, but together can decide that nothing can be done. —FRED ALLEN

You will never understand bureaucracies until you understand that for bureaucrats procedure is everything and outcomes are nothing.

—THOMAS SOWELL

A committee is a group that keeps minutes and loses hours. —MILTON BERLE

There is no monument dedicated to the memory of a committee.

—LESTER J. POURCIAU

The perfect bureaucrat everywhere is the man who manages to make no decisions and escape all responsibility.

—BROOKS ATKINSON

To get something done, a committee should consist of no more than three men, two of whom are absent.

—ROBERT COPELAND

A COMMITTEE IS A CUL-DE-SAC DOWN WHICH IDEAS ARE LURED AND THEN QUIETLY STRANGLED.

—BARNETT COCKS

If you see a snake, just kill it— don't appoint a committee on snakes.

—H. ROSS PEROT

A committee can make a decision that is dumber than any of its members.

—DAVID COBLITZ

Meetings are indispensable when you don't want to do anything.

—JOHN KENNETH GALBRAITH

★★ One-Way Streets

The diagram represents a pattern of streets. P's are parking spaces, and the black squares are stores. Find the route that starts at a parking space, passes through all stores exactly once, and ends at the other parking space. Arrows indicate one-way traffic for that block only. No block or intersection may be entered more than once.

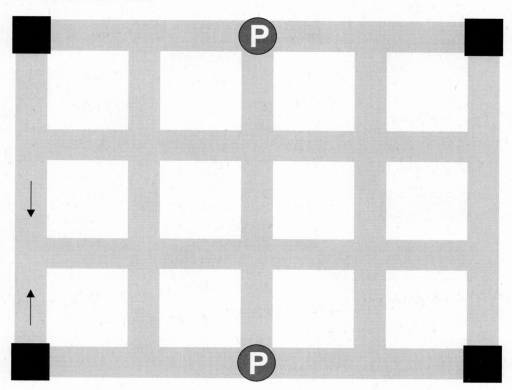

TRANSDELETION

Delete one letter from the word VACATIONING and rearrange the rest, to get a useful skill for some vacationers.

_____

★ Be Calm by Bob Frank

ACROSS

1 Model-kit item
5 Pennsylvania sect
10 Sweet potatoes
14 Morales of *NYPD Blue*
15 Roping and riding show
16 Coup d'__
17 "Be calm!"
19 Infrequent
20 Diminish gradually
21 Alternatively
22 Shipshape
23 Cry away
25 Rap-sheet info
26 *The Thin Man* dog
29 Ilie of tennis
33 Ships' rears
35 Li'l Abner creator
36 Annoy
39 "Be calm!"
42 June grads: Abbr.
43 Movie lioness
44 Winter eave hanging
45 Immersed
47 "That was close!"
48 Superb grade
51 Contemporary of 29 Across
53 Chow __
54 Tons
57 Cancel
61 Rural stopovers
62 "Be calm!"
64 Wise person
65 What majorettes do
66 Practice boxing
67 Piggy-bank feature
68 In the blink of __
69 Bank vault

DOWN

1 Annoyer
2 Largest continent
3 Inclined pathway
4 Sci-fi travel medium
5 Part of ETA
6 Vintage Ford
7 Worshiped one
8 Plies a needle
9 Sharpen
10 Seuss turtle
11 Video-game pioneer
12 *West Side Story* heroine
13 Apple holders
18 Historic period
24 Shoe part
25 Savory jelly
26 Makes an inquiry
27 Young or hip ending
28 Shirt types
30 Cloth remnant
31 Prof.'s aides
32 Plant pests
34 Russian refusals
36 Hankering
37 Actor's part
38 Was aware (of)
40 Take advantage of
41 Banana buyer's concern
45 Day's end
46 Diner, e.g.
48 Not quite right
49 Word before code or colony
50 Jargon
52 Skimmer or derby
54 "__ boy!"
55 Sodded surface
56 *The Grapes of Wrath* figure
58 Western wine valley
59 Military fliers' org.
60 Ancient stringed instrument
63 __ de France

★★ Labyrinth Walk

If one person starts at the beginning of the labyrinth (at the yellow star), walking toward the center, and another person starts at the center of the labyrinth (at the blue star), walking toward the entrance, how many times will they pass each other on adjacent concentric circles? Assume that the two people walk at the same pace, advancing one red dot at a time. The point where the two people meet on the same path does not count.

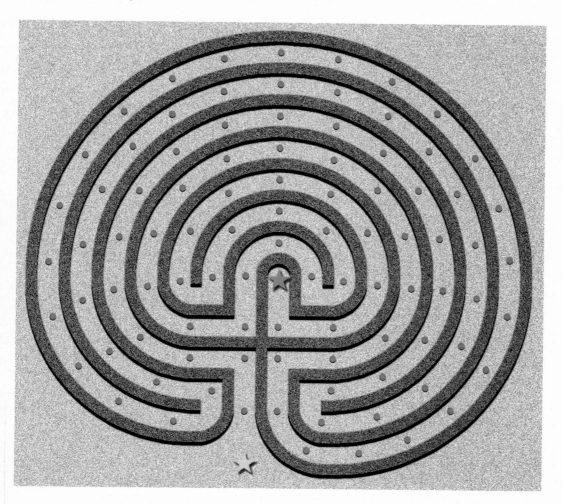

THREE OF A KIND

Find the three hidden words in the sentence that, read in order, go together in some way.

The food was bland, unseasoned, and barely fair.

★★ Star Search

Find the stars that are hidden in some of the blank squares. The numbered squares indicate how many stars are hidden in the squares adjacent to them (including diagonally). There is never more than one star in any square.

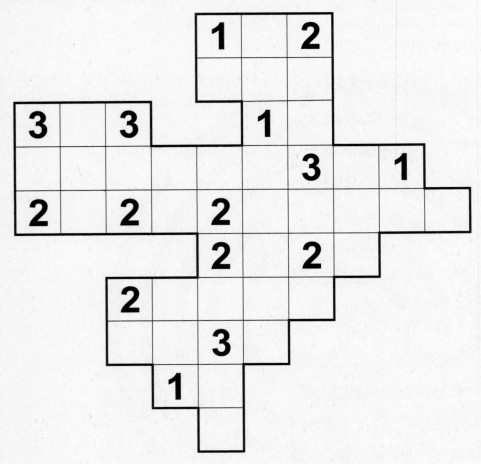

TELEPHONE TRIOS

1	ABC **2**	DEF **3**
GHI **4**	JKL **5**	MNO **6**
PRS **7**	TUV **8**	WXY **9**
✱	**0**	**#**

Using the numbers and letters on a standard telephone, what three seven-letter words from the same category can be formed from these telephone numbers?

227-8246 _ _ _ _ _ _ _

265-6635 _ _ _ _ _ _ _

774-8283 _ _ _ _ _ _ _

★★ Triad Split Decisions

In this clueless crossword puzzle, each answer consists of two words whose spellings are the same, except for the consecutive letters given. All answers are common words; no phrases or hyphenated or capitalized words are used. Some of the clues may have more than one solution, but there is only one word pair that will correctly link up with all the other word pairs.

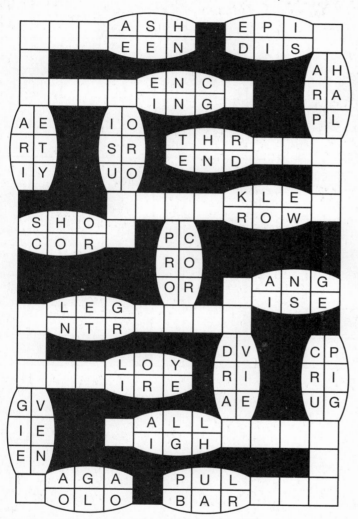

EQUATION CONSTRUCTION

Use the digits 5, 2, and 7 plus standard symbols and operations of arithmetic, to create a mathematical expression that equals the number 25. All the digits must be used.

[   ] = 25

★★ Burning Issues by Robert H. Wolfe

ACROSS

1 Right-angled shapes
5 Support, with "up"
9 Circus employee
14 Purely academic
15 Car takeback, for short
16 Writer Calvino
17 Building girder
18 Fifty-fifty
19 Seamstress Ross
20 Colorful firework
23 Intelligence grp.
24 Substandard
25 Small case
27 Prefix for hazard
30 Color variation
32 Buddies
33 Sweeping tale
35 B.B. of blues
37 Of birth
40 "Cool it!"
42 Place for a sow
43 Cathedral topper
44 Tempest
45 Cooking additive
47 Highlander
48 Oxen, often
50 Ratso, for Dustin
52 Marciano stats
53 Was blue
56 Cries audibly
58 Jackie's second
59 Item for MacArthur
64 __ cum laude
66 Unpleasant destiny
67 Like some cars
68 Erstwhile anesthetic
69 Rodeo throw
70 "Dern it!"
71 Was overaffectionate
72 Supplemented, with "out"
73 "Auld Lang __"

DOWN

1 Moslem ruler
2 Gray wolf
3 Rich soil
4 Handbag holder
5 Recipe instruction
6 Treat parquet again
7 Tourney for all
8 Little lakes
9 Certain Asians
10 Wolfed down
11 Fire starter
12 Bovine trademark
13 Like some flushes

21 "I should say __!"
22 Drink like a cat
26 Shows approval
27 Not his
28 In __ (ticked off)
29 Gas stove device
31 Make a record of
34 Insertion mark
36 Device with a rotating wheel
38 Buck ender
39 "Shall we?" response
41 Dec. 25th greeting

46 Yielded flowers
49 Big name in China
51 Flow back
53 Widely known
54 Muse for poets
55 Noted rapper
57 Taters
60 Secluded corner
61 "Do as __, not as ..."
62 Where Mt. Pocono is
63 Sharp side
65 Society page word

★★★ ABC

Enter the letters *A*, *B*, and *C* into the diagram so that each row and column has exactly one *A*, one *B*, and one *C*. The letters outside the diagram indicate the first letter encountered, moving in the direction of the arrow. Keep in mind that after all the letters have been filled in, there will be two blank boxes in each row and column.

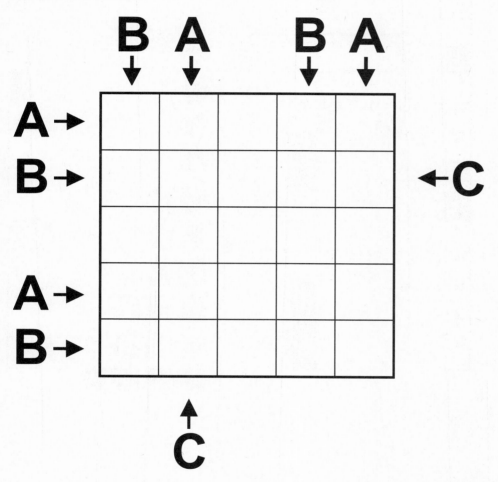

IN OTHER WORDS

The abbreviation FHA is short for "Federal Housing Administration." The shortest common word that contains the consecutive letters FHA has seven letters in all. What is the word?

_____

★★★ Find the Ships

Determine the position of the 10 ships listed to the right of the diagram. The ships may be oriented either horizontally or vertically. A square with wavy lines indicates water and will not contain a ship. The numbers at the edge of the diagram indicate how many squares in that row or column contain parts of ships. When all 10 ships are correctly placed in the diagram, no two of them will touch each other, not even diagonally.

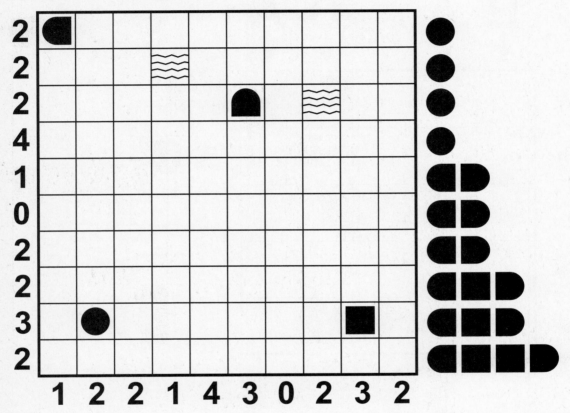

AND SO ON

Unscramble the letters in the phrase HE LOBS FOLD, to form two words that are part of a common phrase that has the word *and* between them.

_____ and _____

★★ Quiet on the Set by Fred Piscop

ACROSS

1 "__ is more"
5 Phobia
9 Cool in manner
14 "__ boy!"
15 McEntire of music
16 Prickly plants
17 Chaim Potok novel
20 Hospital staffer
21 G-man or T-man
22 W.C. Fields persona
23 Turndowns
24 Modest cigar
27 Ballerina Shearer
28 Tossed dishes
34 Field of expertise
37 Lighten up
39 Lawful, for short
40 Clown with a photog
43 No-frills
44 Cork's land
45 Too stylish, perhaps
46 Emotionally cool
48 Willy-__
50 Actress Lansbury
52 Instrument for Bird or Trane
55 William Tell's canton
58 TGIF day
59 Treat badly
61 Unheard from, slangily
65 Turns white
66 Cut and paste
67 "__ cost to you!"
68 Built for speed
69 Fishing spot
70 "It's __ real!"

DOWN

1 Livy's language
2 Starter for centric
3 Dele reversers
4 Kemo __
5 Crockett's milieu
6 Comics shriek
7 Blood-typing system
8 Children's singer
9 Etcher's fluid
10 Fall behind
11 Protest singer Phil
12 Snorkel's pooch
13 Ring weapon
18 Guesser's phrase
19 Wine sediment
25 Speechify
26 Cutting deeply
27 Word not heard in *The Godfather*
29 __ carte
30 Curtis of the Air Force
31 Ripening agent
32 Tabloid gossip
33 Collar stiffener
34 Concert lineup
35 Hold sway
36 "Holy smokes!"
38 Unworldly
41 Ottawa's prov.
42 Pen pal, perhaps
47 Bring home
49 Not of the clergy
51 Actor __ Bruce
52 Hospitality spot
53 In sync
54 Inert gas
55 Baseball crew
56 Iranian money
57 Tropical spot
58 Carlton in Cooperstown
60 Wild guess
62 "Told ya so!"
63 Actress Lupino
64 Beat or peace ender

★★ Knife, Fork, Spoon

Enter the maze at one of the four openings, pass through all the silverware in this order: knife, fork, spoon, knife, fork, etc., and exit the maze without retracing your path.

WORD WIT

Think of the name of a well-known company in the transportation business. If you delete one of its letters, then reverse the order of the letters, you'll get a word for a type of festive meal. What are the company and meal?

_____   _____

★★ Sudoku

Fill in the blank boxes so that every row, column, and 3×3 box contains all of the numbers 1 to 9.

2					9	7	1	
	8			5	6			4
		8		6	9	5		
5				8				9
9		2		1				6
						4	2	
	9		1	4				7
	3		5					
4			8	2				

MIXAGRAMS

Each line contains a five-letter word and a four-letter word that have been mixed together (the order of the letters in each word has not been changed). Unmix the two words on each line and write them in the spaces provided. When you're done, find a two-word answer to the clue by reading down the letter columns in the answers.

CLUE: Cranium

GRAHROSET = _ _ _ _ _ + _ _ _ _

ROARMUSYE = _ _ _ _ _ + _ _ _ _

FANENEUXD = _ _ _ _ _ + _ _ _ _

DYOAUTISH = _ _ _ _ _ + _ _ _ _

★★★ Circular Reasoning

Connect all of the circles by drawing a single continuous line through every square of the diagram. All right-angle turns of your line must alternate between boxes containing a circle and boxes not containing a circle. You must make a right-angle turn out of every square that contains a circle. Your line must end in the same square that it begins, and it cannot enter any square more than once.

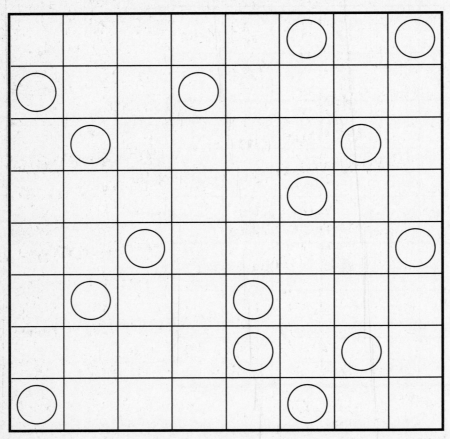

EQUATION CONSTRUCTION

Arrange these signs and numbers to form a correct number sentence. Numbers may be placed together to form a greater number (for example, a *1* and an *8* can be combined to form *18* or *81*). It is not necessary to use all the signs and numbers. No parentheses are needed.

$$4 , 6 , 7 , 7 , 9 , 12 , \div , -$$

	=	

★★ Hookups by Fred Piscop

ACROSS

1 Tooth tips
6 Jiggly dessert
11 Belfry resident
14 Mete out
15 Celestial hunter
16 *Tres - dos*
17 "Wake up!"
19 Indy 500 entrant
20 Alehouse
21 Actors' workplace
22 Comedy sketch
23 Writer Earl __ Biggers
25 Drive back
27 Deteriorate
31 Seldom found
32 Sudden fancy
33 Battery fluid
35 Climber's rest stop
38 Suffix with ethyl
39 Apple pie order
41 Assn.
42 Coveted prize
44 Soccer immortal
45 Gulp from a flask
46 Fridge foray
48 Flight finishes
50 *Gunsmoke* deputy
53 Calamitous
54 Furnace output
55 Routing word
57 " ... __ your ears"
61 Well liquid
62 Nine-digit code
64 Break an oath
65 Sharp as a tack
66 Touch of color
67 "__ Bingle" (Crosby)
68 Coke rival
69 Tent securer

DOWN

1 Start fishing
2 Forearm bone
3 Serb or Croat
4 John Paul II's reign
5 Mall units
6 Write hastily
7 Love god
8 Military careerist
9 Hang out
10 Toronto's prov.
11 Work determinedly
12 Diarist Nin
13 Rich cake
18 Imaginary
22 "You betcha!"
24 Postgame summary
26 Far from tanned
27 Broadway star Verdon
28 "This can't be!"
29 Overtime period
30 Nickel-and-__ (acted pettily)
34 Meted (out)
36 Sandy stuff
37 Morning fare
39 Touched down
40 Arnaz/Ball company
43 Toward sunup
45 Deemed appropriate
47 Contrivance
49 High points
50 Car-seat user
51 Skater Sonja
52 Tear to shreds
56 Rental units: Abbr.
58 Lady of Portugal
59 Gooey stuff
60 Art Deco master
62 Use a microwave
63 Luau garland

★★★ Islands

Shade in some of the white squares in the diagram with "water," so that each remaining white box is part of an island. Each island will contain exactly one numbered square, indicating how many squares that island contains. Each island is separated from the other islands by water but may touch other islands diagonally. All water is connected, but there are no 2×2 regions of water in the diagram.

1				1	
			2		
	2		3		
2			2		

COMMON SENSE

What three-letter word can be found in the dictionary definitions of all of these words: WHARF, TUXEDO, OBLIGATE and HITCH?

— — —

★★ Split Decisions

In this clueless crossword puzzle, each answer consists of two words whose spellings are the same, except for the consecutive letters given. All answers are common words; no phrases or hyphenated or capitalized words are used. Some of the clues may have more than one solution, but there is only one word pair that will correctly link up with all the other word pairs.

TRANSDELETION

Delete one letter from the word CHECKERS and rearrange the rest, to get a type of sound.

— — — — — — —

★★ Hold It by Daniel R. Stark

ACROSS

1 Fitness centers
5 In force
10 Australian mineral
14 Trumpet or bugle
15 Degrade
16 Nada
17 Jai __
18 Desert flora
19 Heavy burden
20 Canine predatory group
22 Apartment occupant
24 Army vehicle
25 Computer image bit
26 Thing
29 "Gotcha!"
30 Slot insert
33 Presides at tea
34 Copper alloy
35 Singer Sumac
36 Pitch
37 Feel off
38 Ski lift
39 *Addams Family* cousin
40 Chandelier pendant
42 Stood petrified
43 T'ai __ ch'uan
44 Slat
45 Persuaded
46 Lunch times
48 Skirt length
49 Tie types
51 Dress warmly
55 Bryce Canyon state
56 Speak publicly
58 To be, to Henri
59 Sly tactic
60 Web surfer's need
61 Increased
62 In dreamland
63 March composer
64 Break sharply

DOWN

1 *Major Barbara* author
2 Game with mallets
3 Inland sea of Asia
4 Brandy glasses
5 Empty
6 Take __ (disconcert)
7 Surplus opposite
8 Occupational suffix
9 Goddesses and gods
10 Atmospheric layer
11 Hockey area
12 Give __ for one's money
13 Going around in circles
21 Felt boots
23 Former mates
25 Choir selection
26 Of the eye
27 Kiosk
28 To be safe
29 From Donegal
31 Stun
32 Revealed
34 Prepares a hook
38 Tractor attachments
40 Story line
41 Kings' __ (large amounts)
42 Affectionate
45 Movie theater
47 Sounded impressed
48 Tones down
49 Mystique
50 Pencil end
51 Singer Erykah
52 Collar style
53 Bear constellation
54 Chirp
57 Aussie jumper

★★ Three or More

Enter the missing numbers from 1 to 9 into the diagram in such a way that all pairs of numbers connected by a line have a difference of three or more.

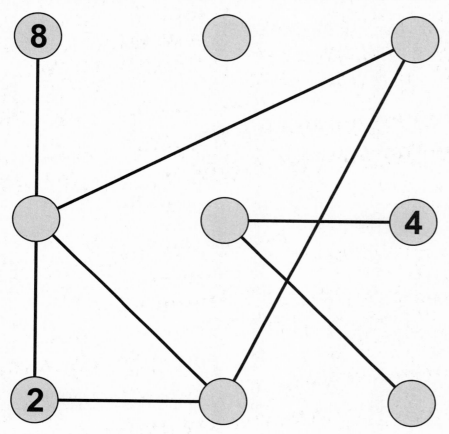

INITIAL REACTION

The "equation" below contains the initials of words that will make it correct, forming a numerical fact. Solve the equation by supplying the missing words.

10 = A. in the B. of R. _____

★★ Weather Maze

Find a path that enters the maze, passes alternately through suns and rain clouds (a sun first), then exits the maze, all without retracing your path.

AND SO ON

Unscramble the letters in the phrase START SCARF, to form two words that are part of a common phrase that has the word *and* between them.

_____ and _____

★★ Governmental by Fred Piscop

ACROSS

1 Unwashed
6 In a frenzy
10 Missing, militarily
14 Heavenly ram
15 *M*A*S*H* drink
16 Toy dog, for short
17 Novocain, e.g.
20 Son of Seth
21 Brightened up
22 Turkey moistener
23 Hamburg's river
25 Profs.' helpers
26 Fruity cocktail
29 __ it (leave quickly)
34 Duke U.'s sports org.
35 Nose, slangily
37 Visitor to Siam
38 Yearly address
42 Ponderosa trio
43 Pests on pets
44 Muscle spasm
45 Carriage-return equivalent
48 Wine and dine
50 Sculler's need
51 Out of kilter
52 Weather map line
56 Work wk. ender
57 Gone by
61 Daily DC bulletin
64 Arctic floater
65 New driver, often
66 *I Remember Mama* star
67 Knitting need
68 Editor's "keep it"
69 Struck down, Bible-style

DOWN

1 Over hill and __
2 Golf club
3 Puerto __
4 Afternoon service
5 Designer monogram
6 Sure-shot Oakley
7 Intersect
8 Cries of surprise
9 Knapsack
10 King Kong and kin
11 Sunset direction
12 Steinbeck migrant
13 King of tragedy
18 White rat, perhaps
19 "Slung" fare
24 Emit coherent light
25 Church donation
26 En __ (together)
27 Follow, as a tip
28 Quitter's words
29 With fervor
30 Basker's goal
31 Author Loos
32 How sardines may be packed
33 Knight's weapon
36 Put up for sale
39 Literary monogram
40 Insect with pincers
41 __-friendly
46 Crowd sound
47 Gold units
49 Plaster of Paris ingredient
51 Do not exist
52 Not certain
53 Actress Ward
54 Limburger quality
55 "It's __ real!"
56 On the house
58 Periodic table fig.
59 E-mailed
60 Sloth's hangout
62 Permit
63 Psyche segments

★★ One-Way Streets

The diagram represents a pattern of streets. P's are parking spaces, and the black squares are stores. Find the route that starts at a parking space, passes through all stores exactly once, and ends at the other parking space. Arrows indicate one-way traffic for that block only. No block or intersection may be entered more than once.

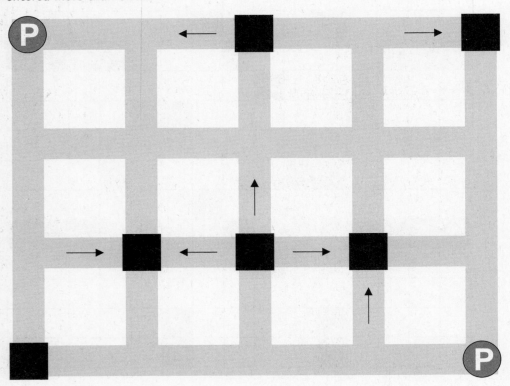

EQUATION CONSTRUCTION

Use the digits 9, 9, 8, and 4 plus standard symbols and operations of arithmetic, to create a mathematical expression that equals the number 3. All the digits must be used.

= 3

★★★ Kakuro

Fill in the blank white boxes of the diagram with digits from 1 to 9 so that each group of numbers adds up to the shaded number above it (for a column) or to the left of it (for a row). Each group of numbers must contain all different digits. That is, no digit may be repeated within a particular sum.

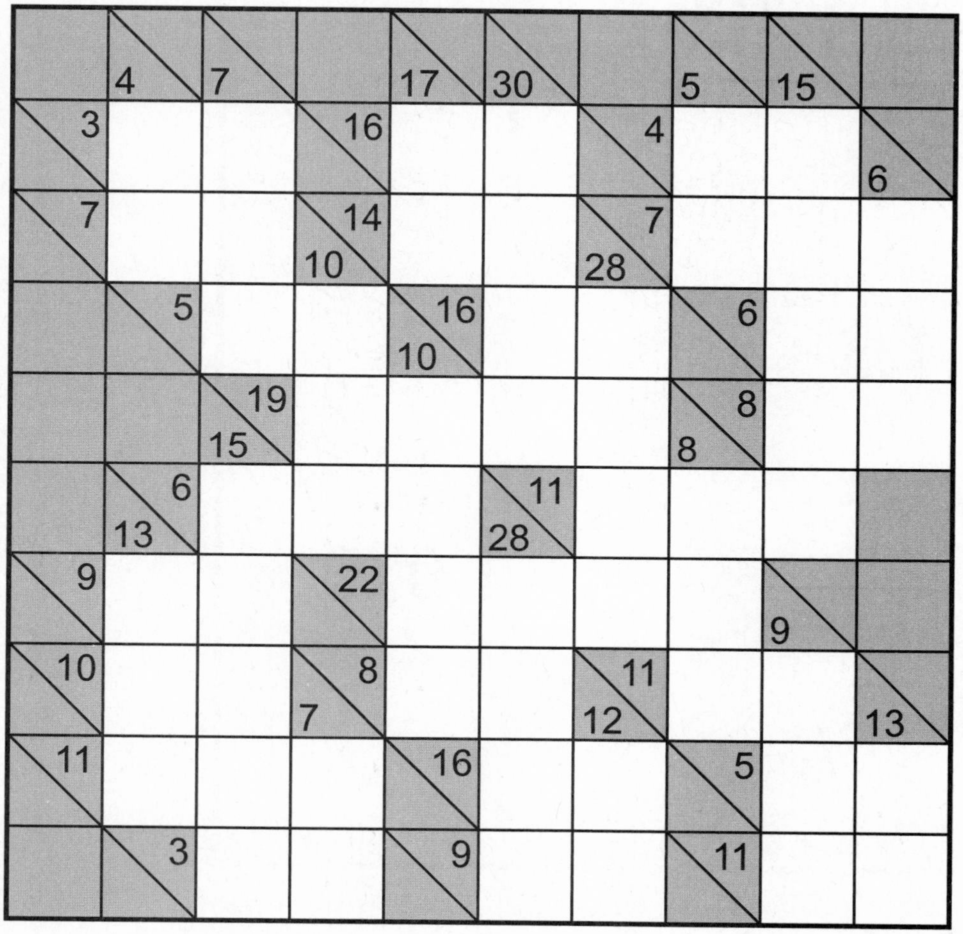

TELEPHONE TRIOS

1	ABC **2**	DEF **3**
GHI **4**	JKL **5**	MNO **6**
PRS **7**	TUV **8**	WXY **9**
*	**0**	**#**

Using the numbers and letters on a standard telephone, what three seven-letter words from the same category can be formed from these telephone numbers?

277-3642　　_ _ _ _ _ _ _

637-2879　　_ _ _ _ _ _ _

872-6486　　_ _ _ _ _ _ _

★★ Line Drawings

Draw two straight lines, each from one edge of the square to another edge, so that the numerical expressions within each region have the same value.

$$1.125$$

$$1\frac{1}{8}$$

$$1\frac{4}{5}$$

$$\frac{9}{8}$$

$$1.8$$

$$1\frac{3}{4}$$

$$1.075$$

$$\frac{7}{4}$$

WORD WIT

The letters in the plural word TACOS can be rearranged to form the name of an article of apparel: ASCOT. The letters in what four-letter singular word for a type of food can be rearranged to form the name of an article of apparel?

___ ___ ___ ___

★★ Sticking Points by Fred Piscop

ACROSS

1 Takes hold of
7 Is the right size
11 Regular: Abbr.
14 Like a modem connection
15 Job conditions agcy.
16 Luau staple
17 Collegian's jewelry
19 Rm. coolers
20 Truth
21 Snacks in shells
23 Room prettifier
26 "Help!"
27 Ms. Brockovich
28 Airline to Israel
31 Monopoly stack
32 Kitchen gadgets
35 *Seinfeld* character
37 Golfer Se Ri __
38 Genetic throwback
40 Mini-albums: Abbr.
43 Pea or peanut
45 "Not so fast!"
47 Get ready, for short
49 Putin's refusal
51 Actress Chase
52 Dieting successfully
54 Over-the-hill player
57 Pet protection org.
58 Be boiling mad
60 Deadlock
61 Indian peace symbol
66 Brewed beverage
67 Double reed
68 Maryland state bird
69 Bobble the ball
70 Coal holders
71 In a chair

DOWN

1 Mdse.
2 Carnival city
3 Berne's river
4 Ljubljana native
5 More moral
6 Church topper
7 A.J. of racing
8 Culp/Cosby series
9 Summer-weather stat.
10 Year-end temp
11 Seattle landmark
12 Still ahead
13 Insults, slangily
18 Poop out
22 Stratford's river
23 Cop's catch
24 Diva's delivery
25 Sandwich extra
26 Cut drastically
29 Flood control
30 Three-time heavyweight champ
33 Joplin tune
34 Attacked by a bee
36 "Who am __ say?"
39 Writer Tan
41 He reached his peak in 1806
42 Kenton of jazz
44 Grand in scale
46 Monrovia's land
47 River of Omaha
48 More optimistic
50 You, to the Amish
53 Fat cat
55 Periodic table figs.
56 Brokerage unit
58 Any minute
59 __ out a living
62 Stat for a slugger
63 Go bad
64 Bullring cry
65 Tie the knot

★★ Star Search

Find the stars that are hidden in some of the blank squares. The numbered squares indicate how many stars are hidden in the squares adjacent to them (including diagonally). There is never more than one star in any square.

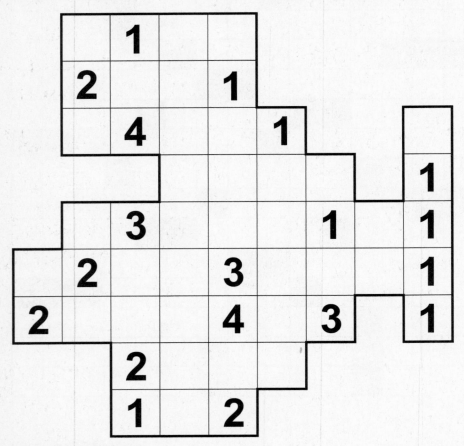

MIXAGRAMS

Each line contains a five-letter word and a four-letter word that have been mixed together (the order of the letters in each word has not been changed). Unmix the two words on each line and write them in the spaces provided. When you're done, find a two-word answer to the clue by reading down the letter columns in the answers.

CLUE: Sailor's drink?

GHAROWPEK   =   _ _ _ _ _   +   _ _ _ _

RIGELOINO   =   _ _ _ _ _   +   _ _ _ _

PENAIRNEL   =   _ _ _ _ _   +   _ _ _ _

MIDONETAH   =   _ _ _ _ _   +   _ _ _ _

★★ Twelve-Letter Word

Using each letter in the diagram exactly once, form a 12-letter word by starting with the first letter, and spelling the remaining letters in the word in order, by moving through the gaps in the walls.

EQUATION CONSTRUCTION

Use the digits 9, 9, 8, and 4 plus standard symbols and operations of arithmetic, to create a mathematical expression that equals the number 1/2. All the digits must be used.

| | = | 1/2 |

★★ Arctic Natives by Patrick Jordan

ACROSS

1 And others: Abbr.
5 Beethoven honoree
10 Pearl Mosque site
14 Rogers of *Austin Powers*
15 Anwar of Egypt
16 Seeks redress from
17 Love letter recipient's request
20 Everglades bird
21 Tried for office
22 Maiden name signaler
23 Mouse sound
24 Astrologer Dixon
26 "Dig in!"
27 Evil computer of film
28 Rogue
30 Smokehouse array
32 "Here on Gilligan's __"
34 AL arbiter
35 Simple Simon's weakness
36 Winter swim group
41 High-rise unit: Abbr.
42 City "by the sea-o"
43 Cozy
45 Word on a clapboard
48 Lyrics
50 Here: Fr.
51 It's cut and dried
52 Laughs loudly
54 Opts for
56 Consolidated
57 Lowly canine
58 Drama awards
59 Feature of Monopoly's mascot
64 *Paradise Lost* setting
65 Oklahoma oil center
66 Deere device
67 Bank deposit?
68 Pickle slice
69 Head, in Haiti

DOWN

1 Printers' squares
2 Haberdashery buy
3 Texas panhandle town
4 Purple shade
5 Italian dynasty surname
6 Mason's field
7 Dictator Amin
8 Despotic ruler
9 Hawke of Hollywood
10 "Try me!"
11 Papua New __
12 Usher elsewhere
13 Loan application list
18 Finishes a comic strip
19 Hardly hardy
23 Athenian's X
24 Door frame part
25 Napoleon title
29 Short-spoken
31 Sea wigglers
33 Impetuous ardor
35 Nudge
37 Instant insight
38 Plays on TV
39 Circus vehicle
40 12-gauge shells
44 USO visitors
45 Demonstrated
46 Alex Trebek's homeland
47 Hole in a sneaker
48 Prepare for aerobics
49 Dalmatian mark
53 Forces to abdicate
55 Not suitable
58 Alexis I or Nicholas II
60 "Messenger" molecule
61 Matador adorer's shout
62 '02 Winter Olympics host
63 Wool source

★★ Hyper-Sudoku

Fill in the blank boxes so that every row, column, 3×3 box *and* each of the four 3×3 gray regions contains all of the numbers 1 to 9.

		1	4					
					8			9
8					6	2	4	
2				1	7			6
			3		9			
		9		8	4			
	7			6			9	
				7	5		6	
			9	4		1		5

WORD SQUARE JIGSAW

Place the given pieces into the 4×4 blank diagram to form eight common words, four reading across and four reading down.

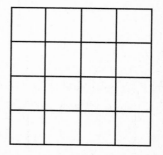

★★★ ABC

Enter the letters *A*, *B*, and *C* into the diagram so that each row and column
has exactly one *A*, one *B*, and one *C*. The letters outside the diagram indicate
the first letter encountered, moving in the direction of the arrow. Keep in mind
that after all the letters have been filled in, there will be two blank boxes in
each row and column.

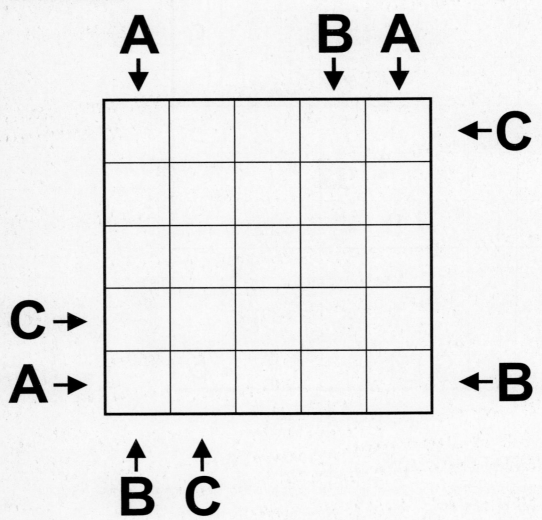

IN OTHER WORDS

The abbreviation KWH is short for "kilowatt-hour." What is the only common word that contains
the consecutive letters KWH?

_____

★★ Hat Shop by Fred Piscop

ACROSS

1 Software glitches
5 Furtive "Hey!"
9 Rustic dwelling
14 Canton's state
15 Need liniment
16 Tara family name
17 *Star Trek* helmsman
18 In shape
19 Carried on, as war
20 Music hit
23 Suffix for serpent
24 It means "resembling"
25 Nun's title
27 Recently
31 Under siege
33 Andes animal
34 Angry
35 Abba of Israel
39 Racetrack event
42 Kemo __
43 Top Untouchable
44 Sci-fi visitor
45 Point a finger at
47 At will
48 Lash out at
51 __ Lanka
52 Routing word
53 Demolitionist's device
60 Twine starter
62 Patchy in color
63 Seven Hills city
64 Tummy trouble
65 Pound of poetry
66 *QB VII* author
67 Has to have
68 Declare false
69 Most desirable

DOWN

1 Pear variety
2 Informal refusal
3 __ monster (large lizard)
4 Like a wrong note
5 Hamburger shape
6 New England catch
7 Cutter or clipper
8 Office fill-in
9 Brightly colored shell
10 "Gotcha!"
11 Brown __ (bring lunch)
12 Singer Cara
13 Common Cause founder
21 Completely wreck
22 Ruhr city
26 Pierce Brosnan TV role
27 Ransom Eli __
28 Boxer biter
29 Souvlaki meat
30 One-celled animal
31 Northwest capital
32 Bow-toting god
34 Goblet part
36 Mold-ripened cheese
37 Genesis victim
38 Big Apple inits.
40 Counting everything
41 "Splish Splash" singer
46 Many October babies
47 Crusoe's companion
48 Bird-related
49 Burn slightly
50 Composer Erik
51 Aft section
54 Mimicked
55 10 EEE, e.g.
56 Vittles
57 Central part
58 Writer Kingsley
59 28 Down, for one
61 LAX monitor info

★★ This Way

Enter the maze at the top right, pass through all arrows, and then exit the maze without retracing any part of your route. You must enter a chamber with an arrow in the middle of the arrow, and exit the chamber in one of the two directions the arrow is pointing.

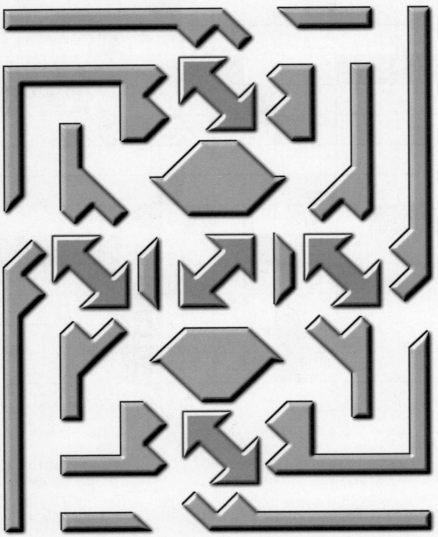

CITY SEARCH

Using the letters in BIRMINGHAM, we were able to form only one common uncapitalized six-letter word not ending in ING. Can you find the word?

★★★ Find the Ships

Determine the position of the 10 ships listed to the right of the diagram. The ships may be oriented either horizontally or vertically. A square with wavy lines indicates water and will not contain a ship. The numbers at the edge of the diagram indicate how many squares in that row or column contain parts of ships. When all 10 ships are correctly placed in the diagram, no two of them will touch each other, not even diagonally.

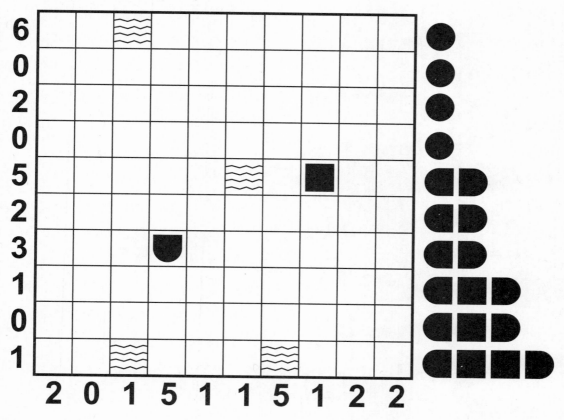

CLUELESS CROSSWORD

Complete the crossword with common uncapitalized seven-letter words, based entirely on the letters already filled in for you.

★★ Triad Split Decisions

In this clueless crossword puzzle, each answer consists of two words whose spellings are the same, except for the consecutive letters given. All answers are common words; no phrases or hyphenated or capitalized words are used. Some of the clues may have more than one solution, but there is only one word pair that will correctly link up with all the other word pairs.

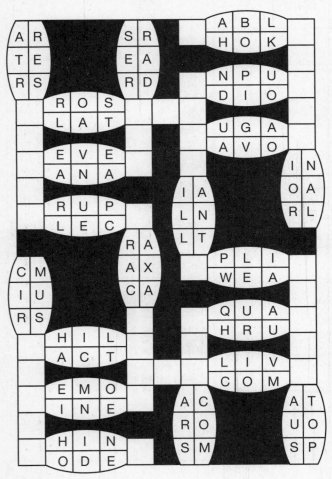

EQUATION CONSTRUCTION

Arrange these signs and numbers to form a correct number sentence. Numbers may be placed together to form a greater number (for example, a *1* and an *8* can be combined to form *18* or *81*). It is not necessary to use all the signs and numbers. No parentheses are needed.

$$7 , 0 , 8 , 9 , 11 , 10 , + , \times , +$$

[   ] = [   ]

★★ Parting Words by Robert H. Wolfe

ACROSS

1 Elevator path
6 Written agreement
10 Ceremonial splendor
14 Luminous stars
15 Annoy
16 Pennsylvania port
17 La Scala production
18 A nose catches it
19 Olin or Horne
20 Cut in half
22 "Bye!"
24 Word to Silver
26 Coast on the runway
27 Not wild
30 Painter Jean
32 Romanov rulers
36 Eve's second
37 One who works hard
40 Procedure
41 "Bye!"
44 Bustling commotion
45 Symbol of home
46 Approximately
47 Taylor of *The Nanny*
49 Male heir
50 Notable achievement
51 Wine-barrel bottom
54 Little bites
56 "Bye!"
60 Cookware material
64 Emulate Ebert
65 Destruction
67 Serta rival
68 Eye part
69 Capri, e.g.
70 Intuit
71 "Hey, you!"
72 Right on a map
73 Advances slowly

DOWN

1 Arrogant one
2 Shoshonean Indian
3 Birds: Lat.
4 "Bye!"
5 Head a class
6 Non-amateur
7 Elton John musical
8 Influence
9 Earth, in sci-fi
10 Where the ilium is
11 Popular cookie
12 Small thing
13 Juicy fruit
21 Perfectly
23 Crowd-scene performer
25 A nose catches it
27 Certain Mongolian
28 Put up with
29 Juicy fruit
31 Docking places
33 Conscious
34 Bring up
35 Church council
38 Give away
39 Racial
42 Ancient invention
43 "Bye!"
48 Firstborn
52 Out of this world
53 March man
55 Western group
56 Lose one's balance
57 Boat movers
58 Elevator man
59 Artist's materials
61 Sudden twinge
62 Additional
63 Bread choices
66 Gross less deductions

★★★ Kakuro

Fill in the blank white boxes of the diagram with digits from 1 to 9 so that
each group of numbers adds up to the shaded number above it (for a column)
or to the left of it (for a row). Each group of numbers must contain all different
digits. That is, no digit may be repeated within a particular sum.

WORD WIT

Adding the letters UN to the beginning of a word usually produces a word with the opposite
meaning. What common one-word baseball term becomes a two-word term with the same meaning when the letters UN are added at the end?

_____

★★★ Circular Reasoning

Connect all of the circles by drawing a single continuous line through every square of the diagram. All right-angle turns of your line must alternate between boxes containing a circle and boxes not containing a circle. You must make a right-angle turn out of every square that contains a circle. Your line must end in the same square that it begins, and it cannot enter any square more than once.

COMMON SENSE

What eight-letter word can be found in the dictionary definitions of all of these words: SIGHT-SEEING, NEWSLETTER, INVEST and ALLIANCE?

— — — — — — — —

★★ Money, Money, Money by Randall J. Hartman

ACROSS

1 "I want to be alone" sayer
6 Bistro
10 Got to town
14 Vocally
15 Track shape
16 Grandson of 23 Across
17 Tea biscuit
18 Highly offensive
19 Wine and __
20 Some steamers
23 Garden of Eden resident
24 Paleozoic or Cenozoic
25 Ticked off
27 British soldier of yore
30 Allowance source
32 __ Aviv
33 Coal scuttle
34 Call for help
35 Actress Hatcher
36 Yummy treats
39 Elvis __ Presley
41 Do lunch
42 Actress Gardner
43 Scatter, as seed
44 Hwy.
45 Gets testy toward
49 Winfrey's company
51 "__ 'em!"
52 Lennon's love
53 NBA team
58 "Livin' La __ Loca"
59 Garden flower
60 Wanted poster name
61 Don Juan's mother
62 Malicious gossip
63 Entrap
64 Home of the Taj Mahal
65 "¿Cómo __ usted?"
66 Buffet choice

DOWN

1 Hilarious joke
2 Nook
3 Installed shingles
4 Baseball ploy
5 Pindar works
6 Secret
7 Walled city near Madrid
8 "The __ of the House of Usher"
9 It's measured in kWh
10 Fragrant wood
11 Brings life to
12 Dr. Frankenstein's creation
13 U-turn from WNW
21 Telephone part
22 Blow the __ off (expose)
26 Yale student
28 Spot for a Vandyke
29 Alley-__
30 Old West Holliday
31 With suspicion
34 H.S. seniors' exam
35 Golf hazard
36 Kind of customized car
37 West of Hollywood
38 Zsa Zsa's sister
39 Fire residue
40 Word on a cell-phone bill
44 Spreadsheet division
45 Nap, in Monterrey
46 Sunday get-together
47 Capital of Turkey
48 Chucked
50 __ Suite
51 Midi, for one
54 Right-hand person
55 Exodus author
56 Guitar range
57 Humerus neighbor
58 By way of

★★★ Celtic Knot Maze

This design is based on Celtic knot patterns. Find a path that starts on any gem and then returns to it after passing through the other seven gems. Paths will cross over and under, but you may not retrace a path or visit an intersection more than once. The solution is left-right symmetric. That is, the part of the path in the left half of the circle will be the mirror image of the path in the right half of the circle.

THREE OF A KIND

Find the three hidden words in the sentence that, read in order, go together in some way.

A policeman screamed in panic on every false alarm.

bRaIn BReaTHer POTATO POWER

And you thought potatoes were for *eating*. Turns out that for the frugal-minded, there are many surprising uses for spuds.

Here are a few:

Remove stains on hands

Hard-to-remove stains on hands from peeling carrots or handling pumpkins come right off if you rub your hands with a potato.

Remove a broken lightbulb

Unplug the lamp. Cut a potato widthwise and place it over the broken bulb. Twist, and the rest of the lightbulb should come out easily.

Remove tarnish on silverware

Boil a bunch of potatoes, then remove them from the water. Place your silverware in the remaining water and let sit for an hour. Then remove the silverware and wash.

Keep ski goggles clear

You can't keep a good lookout for trees and other skiers through snow goggles that fog up during your downhill descent. Rub raw potato over the goggles before you get on the ski lift, and the ride down should be crystal clear.

Make a hot or cold compress

Potatoes retain both heat and cold well. The next time you need a hot compress, boil a potato, wrap it in a towel, and apply to the area. Refrigerate the boiled potato if you need a cold compress.

End puffy morning eyes

If you wake up and your eyes are puffy or swollen, apply slices of raw, cold potatoes to your peepers to make the puffiness go away.

Feed new geraniums

A raw potato can give a fledgling geranium all the nutrients it could desire. Carve a small hole in a potato. Slip a geranium stem into the hole. Plant the whole thing, potato and all.

Hold a floral arrangement in place

If you have a small arrangement of flowers that you'd like to stabilize but have none of that green floral foam on hand to stick the flower stems in, try a large baking potato. Cut it in half lengthwise and place it cut side down. Poke holes where you want the flowers and then insert the stems.

Restore old, beaten-up shoes

Before you give your favorite old shoes the brush-off, cut a potato in half and rub them with raw potato. After that, polish them; they should come out nice and shiny.

Lure worms out of houseplants

Place slices of raw potato around the base of the plant to act as a lure for the worms. They'll crawl up to eat, and you can grab them and toss them out.

★★★ Three or More

Enter the missing numbers from 1 to 9 into the diagram in such a way that all pairs of numbers connected by a line have a difference of three or more.

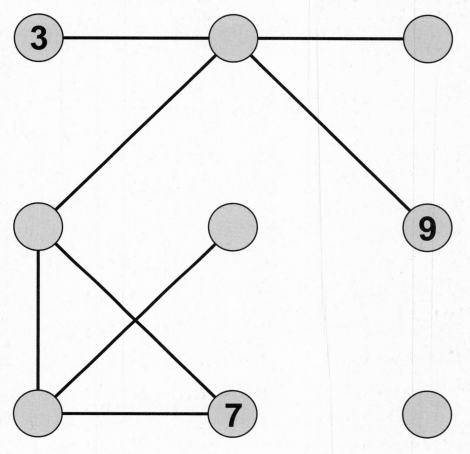

TRANSDELETION

Delete one letter from the word SUBTERRANEAN and rearrange the rest, to get a type of food.

_____

★★ Hyper-Sudoku

Fill in the blank boxes so that every row, column, 3×3 box, *and* each of the four 3×3 gray regions contains all of the numbers 1 to 9.

					1	6		
6	9			7		2		3
	1	3		2				5
		2			6			
		8		1			9	
3		7	2	6			4	
			1					
	8			9		3	5	

WORD WIT

The familiar two-word name of what major U.S. university contains only the letters in the word ANTES?

_____

★★★ Return to Oz by Fred Piscop

ACROSS

1 Have staying power
5 Merry mo.
8 Cue-ball shape
14 Job conditions org.
15 Forum greeting
16 Curiosity-arousing ad
17 Dangerous spot
19 Make beloved
20 Altar agreement
21 Dessert wine
22 Feel regret over
23 Aquarium dweller
25 Yellow-brown gem
30 State positively
32 Singer Orbison
33 Ginza gelt
34 Euro preceder, in Spain
37 Thin nail
38 Character associated with this puzzle's key words
41 *Serpico* author
43 Disco dance
44 Antiquated
45 Fill with wonder
47 Trouble persistently
51 Carries a weapon
55 On the briny
56 SSTs crossed it
57 Keynes subj.
59 Animator's unit
60 Goober
63 Eddie Fisher tune
65 Egg on
66 AEF conflict
67 Mimicked
68 Prom attendee
69 Watched Junior
70 Cold War foes

DOWN

1 Nabokov novel
2 Stage whispers
3 Snaps
4 Light brown
5 Pedestal part
6 Goolagong rival
7 Metric prefix
8 Sound system
9 Extreme want
10 Mythical underworld
11 Language suffix
12 Actor Stephen
13 Go wrong
18 Less meaty
24 Seized autos
26 Civil War soldiers
27 Brontë character
28 Pro vote
29 Phase out
31 General __'s chicken
35 Clear sky
36 Turkey day: Abbr.
37 Consecrated
38 Arp's art
39 Muscle car letters
40 Capital on the Hudson
41 Riotous bunch
42 Hoppy quaff
45 Sharp as a tack
46 Fictional Mitty
48 Break loose
49 Flowed slowly
50 Caesar and Greek
52 Apprehended
53 Siamese sounds
54 Inverted "e"
58 Skip over
60 Orchestra's place
61 Suffix with ethyl
62 Golfer's dream
64 Duffer's dream

★★★ One-Way Streets

The diagram represents a pattern of streets. P's are parking spaces, and the black squares are stores. Find the route that starts at a parking space, passes through all stores exactly once, and ends at the other parking space. Arrows indicate one-way traffic for that block only. No block or intersection may be entered more than once.

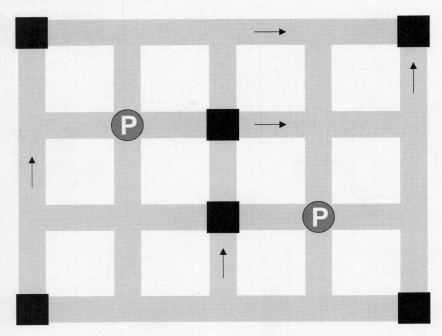

EQUATION CONSTRUCTION

Use the digits 9, 9, 8, and 4 plus standard symbols and operations of arithmetic, to create a mathematical expression that equals the number 1. All the digits must be used.

$$\boxed{} = \boxed{1}$$

★★★ Star Search

Find the stars that are hidden in some of the blank squares. The numbered squares indicate how many stars are hidden in the squares adjacent to them (including diagonally). There is never more than one star in any square.

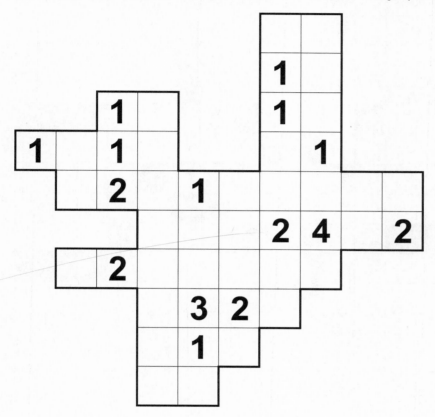

MIXAGRAMS

Each line contains a five-letter word and a four-letter word that have been mixed together (the order of the letters in each word has not been changed). Unmix the two words on each line and write them in the spaces provided. When you're done, find a two-word answer to the clue by reading down the letter columns in the answers.

CLUE: Schwarzenegger, for one

MALOIBION = _ _ _ _ _ + _ _ _ _

AIRNCPUTH = _ _ _ _ _ + _ _ _ _

LEONARGLY = _ _ _ _ _ + _ _ _ _

KESHAPKIY = _ _ _ _ _ + _ _ _ _

★★★ Sew What by Robert H. Wolfe

ACROSS

1 Ink stain
5 Skater Sonja
10 Mistake maker's word
14 Shade of blue
15 Madrid month
16 March Madness org.
17 Stylish elegance
18 Atomic number 18
19 By way of, for short
20 Really care
22 *GWTW* name
23 __ of Capricorn
24 Really odd
25 Deer relative
28 Blasting letters
29 Fertile soil
31 Treat a winter windshield
33 Did some carpentry
37 Role for Jodie
38 Taters
40 Ibsen character
41 Amaze
43 Wing it
44 RCA alternative
45 Jacket spec: Abbr.
47 USN officer
48 Head tops
51 Clergyman
54 Investment
55 Speak hesitantly
59 Beeper
60 Morse et al.
61 Cartoonist Goldberg
62 Contra- kin
63 Taps player
64 Indication
65 Cardinal point
66 Leaves in, in editing
67 Put down one's cards

DOWN

1 Blood type: Abbr.
2 Caron film
3 Big name in Norway
4 Religious doctrine
5 Like some collisions
6 Wholly absorbed
7 Silents actress Pola
8 Without loopholes
9 Very long time
10 Getting better
11 Earthy pigment
12 Serial starter
13 Fry a bit

21 Comic Johnson
22 Paper quantity
25 Writer Ferber
26 Levis alternatives
27 Tartan skirt
30 Mantra sounds
32 Like some families
33 "What was that?"
34 Thespian's quest
35 Limerick's land
36 Hair-cream portions
38 Wrong act
39 Intimidate, in a way
42 Wine aroma

43 Opposed, nonstandardly
45 Thaw anew
46 Rubs out
48 Old-style exclamation
49 Make up (for)
50 Bakery buys
52 Windowsill
53 Computer adjunct
56 Actor Cronyn
57 First shepherd
58 Make (one's way)
60 *Survivor* network

★★ Möbius Maze

If the three ants are following each other in a continuous loop, mark the path they are following. Draw a dark line to represent the side that is visible, and a lighter line to represent the unseen side.

AND SO ON

Unscramble the letters in the phrase APPLE PRINCE to form two words that are part of a common phrase that has the word *and* between them.

_____ and _____

★★★ Sudoku

Fill in the blank boxes so that every row, column, and 3×3 box contains all of the numbers 1 to 9.

5							3	
				5		4		1
		7		6				
7	4		5	9				8
						7		
	3			2	6		5	
3		2		7				
		1	6		8	3		5
		4				8		7

EQUATION CONSTRUCTION

Use the digits 9, 9, 8, and 4 plus standard symbols and operations of arithmetic, to create a mathematical expression that equals the number 36. All the digits must be used.

$$\boxed{} = \boxed{36}$$

★★★ Last Three by Robert H. Wolfe

ACROSS

1 One who stares
6 Rejuvenation stations
10 Permits
14 Lasso element
15 Far from jumpy
16 Song for one
17 Kennel cries
18 Aware of
19 Jeff's friend
20 Penetrating pictures
23 Bit of cereal
24 Pink flower
25 Stone workers
29 Lose energy
32 Map holder
33 Earring shape
34 '40s White House pet
38 Pardner's agreement
41 Copies
42 Not pro
43 Snow pile
44 Garcia or Griffith
45 Chin hair
46 How some bonds are sold
50 Eur. country
51 Fanny Brice vehicle
59 Kind of lift
60 Send out
61 Stately bird
62 England neighbor
63 Swenson of *Benson*
64 Ran off with
65 Lawyer's work
66 Try out
67 Tear up

DOWN

1 Variety of quartz
2 One on the move
3 *Damn Yankees* character
4 Catch sight of
5 Debate statement
6 Move quickly
7 Breathe fast
8 Sax range
9 Air pollution
10 Tibetan priests
11 Blow, like Etna
12 Church levy
13 Bacchus attendant
21 Possesses
22 Cleaning cloth
25 Ancient Yucatán inhabitant
26 Over
27 Turn sharply
28 Boat movers
29 Tennis score
30 Burt ex
31 Mentally quick
33 Dealer's dealing
34 __ song (inexpensively)
35 Busy
36 Existence
37 Pay for play
39 Rather of news
40 Without smell
44 Kennel cry
45 It means "world"
46 Stone calendar maker
47 Leg bone
48 Juicy fruits
49 Be compatible
50 Note above F
52 Give out
53 Road division
54 Is into
55 Strip of wood
56 Fictional assistant
57 Fashion magazine
58 Plant source

★★★ Split Decisions

In this clueless crossword puzzle, each answer consists of two words whose spellings are the same, except for the consecutive letters given. All answers are common words; no phrases or hyphenated or capitalized words are used. Some of the clues may have more than one solution, but there is only one word pair that will correctly link up with all the other word pairs.

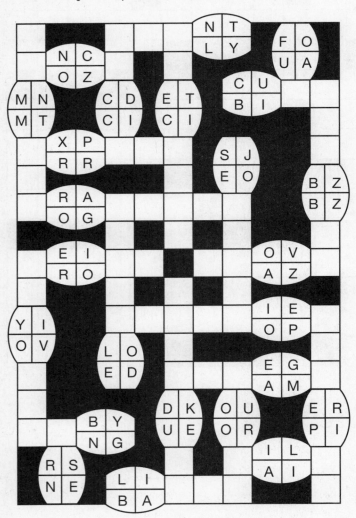

WORD WIT

The words CRABCAKE and INDEFINITE each contain three adjacent consecutive letters of the alphabet. What common uncapitalized word contains four adjacent consecutive letters of the alphabet?

_____

★★★ Islands

Shade in some of the white squares in the diagram with "water," so that each remaining white box is part of an island. Each island will contain exactly one numbered square, indicating how many squares that island contains. Each island is separated from the other islands by water but may touch other islands diagonally. All water is connected, but there are no 2×2 regions of water in the diagram.

	2			3	
	4			2	
4					
				3	

TELEPHONE TRIOS

1	ABC 2	DEF 3
GHI 4	JKL 5	MNO 6
PRS 7	TUV 8	WXY 9
*	0	#

Using the numbers and letters on a standard telephone, what three seven-letter words from the same category can be formed from these telephone numbers?

342-6663   _ _ _ _ _ _ _

628-2466   _ _ _ _ _ _ _

797-2643   _ _ _ _ _ _ _

★★★ Off the Ground by Doug Peterson

ACROSS

1 Fall from grace
6 "Rule, Britannia" composer
10 Oliver's request
14 Grads
15 Boxer Max
16 Shangri-la
17 Movie cowboy
20 Not imaginary
21 Basketball great Jerry
22 Bearlike beast
23 Impolite look
25 Dealer's bullets
27 Half of a magician's phrase
29 Forehead
30 Star Wars initials
33 Wisdom tooth, e.g.
34 Besmirch
35 "Say __!"
36 Dine and dash
39 Guns the motor
40 Croupier's tool
41 Boxcar riders
42 Historic lead-in
43 Evening bugle call
44 Type of race
45 Farmer's place
46 "You are __"
47 Love, in Lille
50 Practice blade
52 Role for Costner
56 Square one
59 "I cannot tell __"
60 Baseball ploy
61 Open courtyards
62 Like some AARP members
63 Opie's dad
64 Lachrymose

DOWN

1 Cowardly Lion portrayer
2 Lotion ingredient
3 Insect stage
4 Speculative stocks
5 Recent immigrant's class: Abbr.
6 "Li'l" guy
7 Janitor's supply
8 Smooth-skinned fruit
9 Epoch
10 Tablelands
11 Chief Norse god
12 Comedian Foxx
13 New Age singer
18 Is in the hole
19 Gush violently
24 Mark's successor
26 Popular beverage
27 Bluffer's game
28 Popeye's gal
29 Makes a reservation
30 Biblical queen's home
31 Undercover cop, at times
32 Autographs
33 Automobile ad abbr.
34 Upholsterer's tool
35 Oval on a staff
37 Asian mountain range
38 Sonny ex
43 Actress Garr
44 Coral chain
45 Bamboozled
46 Big and strong
47 Slightly open
48 Woman's slipper
49 Exclude
51 Place for water lilies
53 Birthplace of 13 Down
54 Use a scissor
55 Spend some time
57 76ers' org.
58 Handle clumsily

★★★ ABC

Enter the letters A, B, and C into the diagram so that each row and column has exactly one A, one B, and one C. The letters outside the diagram indicate the first letter encountered, moving in the direction of the arrow. Keep in mind that after all the letters have been filled in, there will be two blank boxes in each row and column.

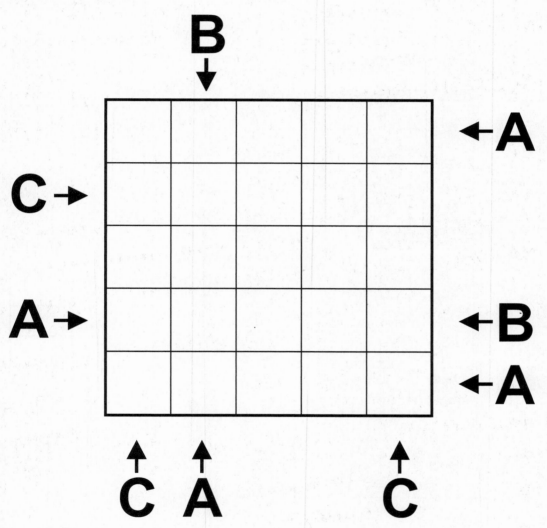

WORD WIT

What Oscar-winning actress's first and last names are the surnames of two famous adversaries from American history?

_____   _____

★★ All-Star Game

Draw four different paths that enter and exit the maze that do not intersect or retrace each other, according to these rules:

A) Enter at the bottom opening at left, pass through one star, then exit.
B) Enter at the left opening at the top, pass through three stars, then exit.
C) Enter at the top opening at right, pass through seven stars, then exit.
D) Enter at the left opening at bottom, pass through nine stars, then exit.

INITIAL REACTION

The "equation" below contains the initials of words that will make it correct, forming a numerical fact. Solve the equation by supplying the missing words.

300 = P.G. in B. _____

★★ Line Drawings

Draw two straight lines, each from one edge of the square to another edge, so that the letters in each of four regions spell a word of a different length.

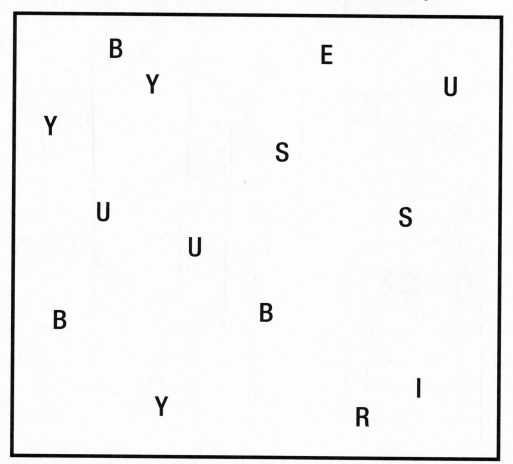

MIXAGRAMS

Each line contains a five-letter word and a four-letter word that have been mixed together (the order of the letters in each word has not been changed). Unmix the two words on each line and write them in the spaces provided. When you're done, find a two-word answer to the clue by reading down the letter columns in the answers.

CLUE: Dogwood's sound

JHOERUSBT = _ _ _ _ _ + _ _ _ _

FAINUREAR = _ _ _ _ _ + _ _ _ _

COZHONARE = _ _ _ _ _ + _ _ _ _

SLIPANREK = _ _ _ _ _ + _ _ _ _

★★★ All in Place by Bob Frank

ACROSS

1 "¿Qué __?"
5 Sell seats shadily
10 Heedless
14 Grad
15 Fiber-__ cable
16 "Golly, Guv'nor!"
17 What stars get
19 Irving character
20 Caruso or Fermi
21 Lattice-crust dessert
23 Vast waters
24 __ for Evidence (Grafton book)
26 Amo, amas, __
27 Tilt to one side
28 Go back to square one
32 Said yes
36 Pitch
37 Complaint
38 With 35 Down, "in the middle" descriptor
41 The Time Machine race
42 Comedienne Butler
44 The Miracle Worker star
46 Sponges up
49 Ancient Persian
50 "Way cool!"
51 Unit-cost word
52 Fr. holy woman
55 Desists from
59 __ baked beans
61 Falstaff feature
62 Low-lying farmsite
64 Reheats, in a way
65 "Now that sounds like __!"
66 Choir voice
67 Otherwise
68 All together
69 Snow pusher

DOWN

1 Party spreads
2 Unaccompanied
3 Above: Lat.
4 Prefix for "both"
5 Musicians playing 2 Down
6 PFC superior
7 "Take __ from me!"
8 One-dimensional
9 Electronic entertainment
10 Pointer's words
11 P.D.Q.
12 Delhi wrap
13 Publicity, and then some
18 Strand, perhaps
22 Start fishing
25 Pipe part
27 Ballfield runners
29 Woody's son
30 Do some shingling
31 Pain in the neck
32 "Dancing Queen" quartet
33 Belgrade resident
34 Pays a call on
35 See 38 Across
39 Troop quarters
40 Patella
43 Family chart
45 AOL freebie
47 Black sheep's plaint
48 Barbershop sharpeners
52 Play for time
53 Lone Ranger's sidekick
54 Provide with long-term funding
55 Daunt
56 Unwritten test
57 Taylor and Torn
58 Normandy town
60 Rebuke
63 Brown shade

★★★ Find the Ships

Determine the position of the 10 ships listed to the right of the diagram. The ships may be oriented either horizontally or vertically. A square with wavy lines indicates water and will not contain a ship. The numbers at the edge of the diagram indicate how many squares in that row or column contain parts of ships. When all 10 ships are correctly placed in the diagram, no two of them will touch each other, not even diagonally.

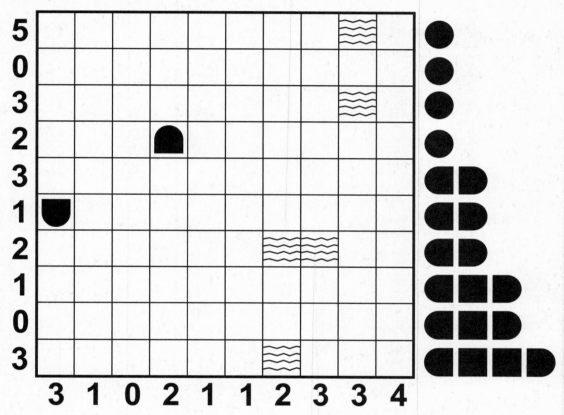

EQUATION CONSTRUCTION

Arrange these signs and numbers to form a correct number sentence. Numbers may be placed together to form a greater number (for example, a *1* and an *8* can be combined to form *18* or *81*). It is not necessary to use all the signs and numbers. No parentheses are needed.

3 , 4 , 13 , 6 , 5 , 0 , + , × , ×

★★★ Hyper-Sudoku

Fill in the blank boxes so that every row, column, 3×3 box, *and* each of the four 3×3 gray regions contains all of the numbers 1 to 9.

					9		1	
5				3	6	8		
1			4		5			
				9	3			4
	9					7	6	
	6		7	2				
	1							
4								8
			3	6		2	5	

WORD WIT

Most English nouns that end with a consonant form their plurals by adding one letter (S) at the end. The plural of what common five-letter noun that ends with a consonant is formed by adding three letters at the end, none of which is an S?

— — — — —

★★★ Winning Hands by Doug Peterson

ACROSS

1 T, to telegraphers
5 Woodwind instrument
9 *Enterprise* medical officer
14 Discontinue
16 Windy City hub
17 Suit buyer's incentive
19 Chinese principle
20 One who served
21 Broadcast
22 Invest with authority
24 Junior, for example
29 Tippler
30 Kuwaiti VIP
31 Periphery
32 "That __" (closing words)
35 Poet's contraction
36 Rose of baseball
37 He doesn't mince words
40 Outline
41 Aphrodite's son
42 Like the sound of a 5 Across
43 Pub quaff
44 Grace finisher
45 They replaced LPs
46 Fruit pests
48 Saudi Arabian capital
52 It might be negative
53 Daystar
54 Homer Simpson's bartender
55 Home of the U.S. Open
61 Major vessel
62 They're tightened before a march
63 Nirvana
64 Vital parts
65 '96 also-ran

DOWN

1 "Same here!'"
2 Nobelist Sadat
3 Was a straphanger
4 In the know
5 Marco Polo's destination
6 Loni's ex
7 Special __ (elite military division)
8 DDE's command
9 More down in the dumps
10 Cooks too long
11 Make preserves
12 Table morsel
13 Thumbs-up
15 Trattoria entree
18 Withhold nourishment
23 C.S. Lewis character
24 Wayne and Isaac
25 Pile up
26 Rugged ridge
27 Cashed a forged check
28 Manicurist's __ board
32 Religion of 48 Across
33 Steps over a wall
34 Ready for battle
35 Babe Ruth's number
36 Donne's work
38 Program preceding Apollo
39 3rd or 4th
44 Hilo hellos
45 Vessels filled with oil
47 Dukes
49 Company that merged with BP
50 Wooden peg
51 *Steppenwolf* author
53 Angelenos' bane
55 Adjective for the Beatles
56 Online guffaw
57 Mentalist Geller
58 *Fear Factor* network
59 Sticky substance
60 The old man

★★★ Circular Reasoning

Connect all of the circles by drawing a single continuous line through every square of the diagram. All right-angle turns of your line must alternate between boxes containing a circle and boxes not containing a circle. You must make a right-angle turn out of every square that contains a circle. Your line must end in the same square that it begins, and it cannot enter any square more than once.

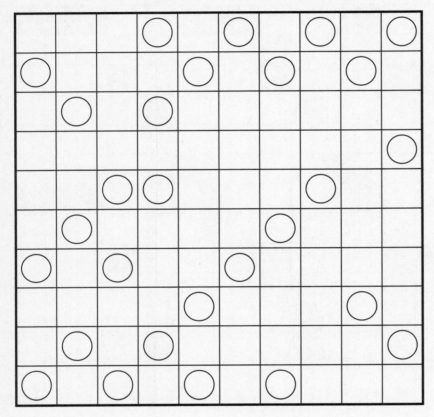

WORD SQUARE JIGSAW

Place the given pieces into the 4×4 blank diagram to form eight common words, four reading across and four reading down.

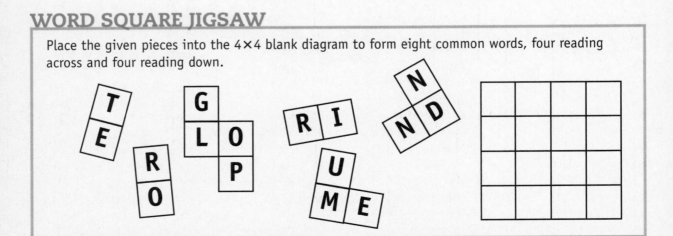

★★ Solitaire Poker

Group this deck of cards into ten poker hands of five cards each, so that each hand contains two pairs or better. The cards in each hand must be connected by an adjacent horizontal or vertical side. The correct groupings include two hands with a straight, two with a flush, and one with a full house.

CITY SEARCH

Use the letters in AMARILLO to form common uncapitalized five-letter words. We found five of them. How many can you find?

_____ _____ _____

_____ _____

★★★ Islands

Shade in some of the white squares in the diagram with "water," so that each remaining white box is part of an island. Each island will contain exactly one numbered square, indicating how many squares that island contains. Each island is separated from the other islands by water but may touch other islands diagonally. All water is connected, but there are no 2×2 regions of water in the diagram.

		3		2		4
5						
						4
			1			
					3	
		2				
						5

COMMON SENSE

What six-letter word can be found in the dictionary definitions of all of these words: PINKING SHEARS, WRAP, CRUDE and STUCCO?

— — — — — —

★★★ Soundalikes by Fred Piscop

ACROSS

1 Triangle or circle
6 Annoying one
10 Annoying one
14 *Casablanca* actor
15 Singer McEntire
16 __ cost (free)
17 Michigan national park
19 Young fellas
20 General __ chicken
21 Cowgirl Evans
22 *Dallas* matriarch
23 "As __ on TV"
25 Left early, slangily
26 *Return of the Jedi* critters
29 Chaucer's __ Inn
32 Premier Khrushchev
34 Put into piles
35 Schuss or wedel
38 Noncommittal response
41 Narc's org.
42 Toledo's lake
43 Hill hundred
44 Lieus
46 Pertinent, in law
47 Canine tooth
50 Scale down
52 Bit of clowning
53 No longer valid
55 Perlman of *Cheers*
59 Sax man Getz
60 Air travelers' assignments
62 Bias-ply, for one
63 Secluded valley
64 Hispaniola part
65 Film locations
66 Commotions
67 Book of maps

DOWN

1 Thin opening
2 Ponderosa son
3 Folksy Guthrie
4 Promo package
5 Bard's "always"
6 Gumbel of TV
7 "It's been __!"
8 Fit for the job
9 __ kwon do
10 Far from ruddy
11 To any extent
12 Low-budget film, often
13 __ around (was a snoop)
18 Work of praise
22 Like a wide grin
24 Having a sense of style
25 Biting remarks
26 Novelist Bagnold
27 __ E. Coyote
28 Sooner State: Abbr.
30 Sought information
31 Jungle crusher
33 Was broadcast
35 Walk of Fame implant
36 Franklin's flier
37 Agenda bit
39 Actress Vardalos
40 Have too little
44 Backbones
45 Tanker mishaps
47 Play rosters
48 Loosen, in a way
49 Kick off
51 Summer quaff
53 Contended
54 Scandinavian capital
56 Flag down
57 Sundance's gal
58 Tag-sale caveat
60 Tooth-care grp.
61 __ Na Na

★★★ Kakuro

Fill in the blank white boxes of the diagram with digits from 1 to 9 so that each group of numbers adds up to the shaded number above it (for a column) or to the left of it (for a row). Each group of numbers must contain all different digits. That is, no digit may be repeated within a particular sum.

WORD WIT

The full name of cartoonist Rube Goldberg has entered the language as an adjective meaning "complex and impractical." The full name of what cartoon character has entered the language as an adjective meaning "worthless" or "petty"?

_____

★★★ Split Decisions

In this clueless crossword puzzle, each answer consists of two words whose spellings are the same, except for the consecutive letters given. All answers are common words; no phrases or hyphenated or capitalized words are used. Some of the clues may have more than one solution, but there is only one word pair that will correctly link up with all the other word pairs.

EQUATION CONSTRUCTION

Use the digits 1, 8, 3, and 3 plus standard symbols and operations of arithmetic, to create a mathematical expression that equals the number 26. All the digits must be used.

$$\boxed{} = \boxed{26}$$

★★★ Suit Yourself by Doug Peterson

ACROSS

1 Arcing shots
5 __ Tranquility (lunar area)
10 Drainage container
14 "__ Ben Adhem"
15 Provide (with)
16 Director Kazan
17 Flashy 19th-century financier
20 Cryptogram solvers
21 Qom residents
22 Hosp. ward
23 Scissors sound
24 Lunch triple-deckers
31 Charged towards
32 Schlock
33 PD broadcast
35 Osbourne of rock
36 Court TV focus
38 Dixie Chicks, for one
39 Shar-__
40 Elvis' middle name
41 Command to Fido
42 *The Maltese Falcon* agency
46 Christopher of the Senate
47 Leave dumbstruck
48 Tentacled mollusks
51 Fender benders
56 Elvis' first #1 song
58 Greater
59 Loyal subject
60 Stare amazedly
61 JFK jets, once
62 Pa Clampett portrayer
63 Lose fur

DOWN

1 *Shane* star
2 Theater award
3 Airline's former name
4 Japanese wrestling
5 Iroquois tribe
6 Evasive maneuver
7 Pts. of speech
8 Avignon assent
9 Like some Spanish nouns
10 High-ranking angel
11 __ Bator
12 Skirt style
13 Ponies up
18 Keats or Shelley
19 Wall component
23 Did the backstroke
24 Arise, with "up"
25 Lounges around
26 Open, as a tote bag
27 Sheltered water
28 Bottled spirit
29 Our world
30 Flavorful additive
34 Danish physicist
36 On good authority
37 Line on a map
38 Either half of 42 Across
40 Start a family, perhaps
41 Just picked
43 Is gaga for
44 Mess up
45 Heed the alarm clock
48 Units of resistance
49 Boardroom VIPs
50 Bakery buy
51 Matches a bet
52 Takes all for oneself
53 Beehive State
54 Toon skunk Le Pew
55 Iditarod vehicle
57 Josh

★★★ Three or More

Enter the missing numbers from 1 to 9 into the diagram in such a way that all pairs of numbers connected by a line have a difference of three or more.

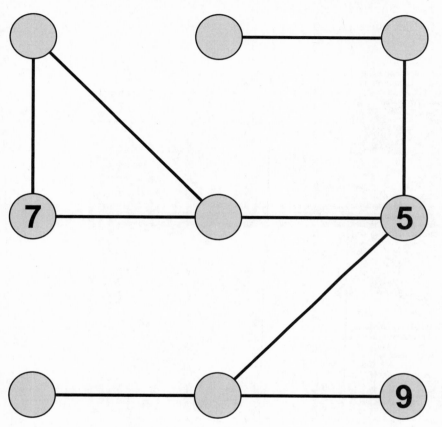

CLUELESS CROSSWORD

Complete the crossword with common uncapitalized seven-letter words, based entirely on the letters already filled in for you.

P						
	■	X	■		■	Q
	H			E		
C	■		■	G	■	
	P	I				
	■		■	S	■	
O	V					X

★★★ Animals of Africa

Enter the maze at the top left, visit all the African animals, and then exit at the bottom right without retracing your path. Note that there are only two openings to each of the six chambers (one to enter and the other to exit), so start by drawing the portions of the path that must lead in and out of the chambers.

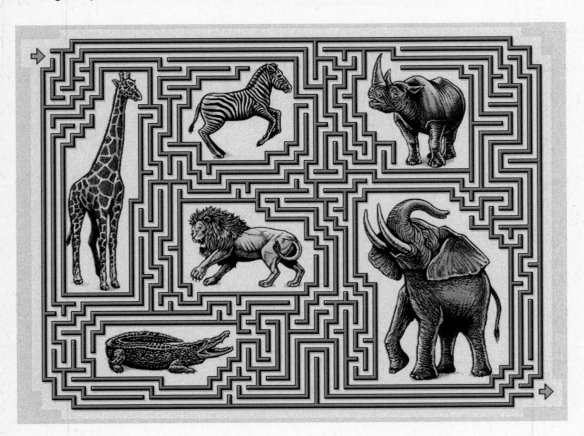

WORD WIT

What two three-letter homophones (uncapitalized words that have the same pronunciation in American English) have no letters in common with each other?

_____ and _____

★★★ Star Search

Find the stars that are hidden in some of the blank squares. The numbered squares indicate how many stars are hidden in the squares adjacent to them (including diagonally). There is never more than one star in any square.

	4		**5**		**4**	
						1
1	**1**		**1**		**2**	**1**
			4		**2**	**1**
1		**2**			**2**	
						3
		2		**3**		

TELEPHONE TRIOS

Using the numbers and letters on a standard telephone, what three seven-letter words from the same category can be formed from these telephone numbers?

272-4379   _ _ _ _ _ _ _

269-5464   _ _ _ _ _ _ _

274-2538   _ _ _ _ _ _ _

★★★ Gamesters' Woes by Fred Piscop

ACROSS

1 Lion group
6 Monastery superiors
11 Astor's business
14 Goes it alone
15 Superman portrayer
16 Santa __ winds
17 Video effect
19 JFK served in it
20 Statement of belief
21 Did some cobbling
23 Poet Hughes
24 Napoleon or turnover
25 Flat dweller
29 Grew like a weed
31 Cuzco people
32 In one piece
33 Hasty escape
36 Satirist Sahl
37 Monstro, in *Pinocchio*
38 Sitarist Shankar
39 Mad __ hatter
40 "Done at last!"
41 Like some booms
42 *Bounty* port of call
44 Rip off
45 Artist of visual
   paradoxes
47 Adversary
48 Iranian faith
49 Boat hangers-on
55 Have dinner
56 Club-soda garnish
58 SFO listing
59 Apartment sign
60 Dine at home
61 Rorem or Beatty
62 Mushers' vehicles
63 Resided

DOWN

1 Attention getter
2 Tug-of-war need
3 Misfortunes
4 __-yourselfer
5 Fancy homes
6 Bow-shaped
7 Swiss capital
8 Red veggie
9 She raised Cain
10 Having feeling
11 Geological break site
12 Racing family name
13 Hurler Johnson
18 Hook henchman
22 Buckeyes' sch.
24 Vaulter's need
25 Peru's capital
26 Son of Seth
27 Place to doodle
28 Took a load off
29 Puppeteer Lewis
30 Putter's target
32 Sharpen
34 Tel __
35 Nursery rhyme trio
37 Propeller sound
38 *Reine*'s spouse
40 Supreme Being
   believers
41 Bundled, as straw
43 "Caught ya!"
44 __ avail
45 Haley replaced him
   as the Tin Man
46 Brown in a pan
47 Guitar ridges
49 Liver product
50 Got 100 on
51 Lobster's weapon
52 Lo-cal
53 Oscar winner
   Jannings
54 Shipped off
57 Cyber-guffaw

★★★ Sudoku

Fill in the blank boxes so that every row, column, and 3×3 box contains all of the numbers 1 to 9.

				7		5		
		2	8		4	7		
		7		6		8		
		5		2	8			4
7								
9		1		3			2	8
3		6				4	1	
			5		6	9	3	

AND SO ON

Unscramble the letters in the phrase TART BUD BEER, to form two words that are part of a common phrase that has the word *and* between them.

_____ and _____

★★★ One-Way Streets

The diagram represents a pattern of streets. A and B are parking spaces, and the black squares are stores. Find the route that starts at A, passes through all stores exactly once, and ends at B. Arrows indicate one-way traffic for that block only. No block or intersection may be entered more than once.

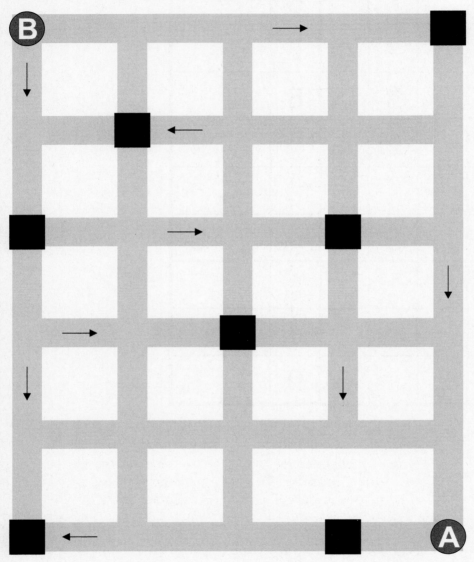

COMMON SENSE

What five-letter word can be found in the dictionary definitions of all of these words: CIVIL WAR, LOCAL, EURO and SPLICE?

__ __ __ __ __

★★★ ABC

Enter the letters A, B, and C into the diagram so that each row and column has exactly one A, one B, and one C. The letters outside the diagram indicate the first letter encountered, moving in the direction of the arrow. Keep in mind that after all the letters have been filled in, there will be two blank boxes in each row and column.

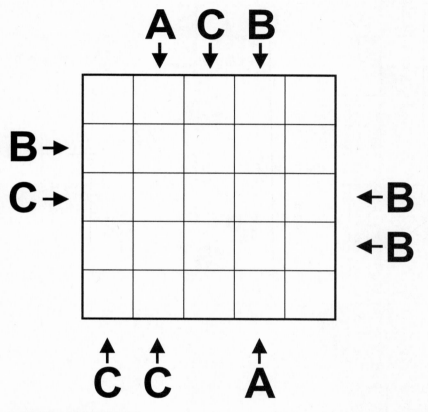

MIXAGRAMS

Each line contains a five-letter word and a four-letter word that have been mixed together (the order of the letters in each word has not been changed). Unmix the two words on each line and write them in the spaces provided. When you're done, find a two-word answer to the clue by reading down the letter columns in the answers.

CLUE: Long arms

EGASIGDSE = _ _ _ _ _ + _ _ _ _

WHOUSINTE = _ _ _ _ _ + _ _ _ _

GROGNUEAT = _ _ _ _ _ + _ _ _ _

EATSHERKS = _ _ _ _ _ + _ _ _ _

★★★ Colors of the Day by Doug Peterson

ACROSS

1 Gander or drake
5 Monty Python specialty
10 Gymnast Korbut
14 "Zounds!"
15 Ancient marketplace
16 Zen paradox
17 W.C. Handy tune
20 Urban concern
21 Erik of *CHiPs*
22 Thumbs up
23 Aurora alias
25 Middling grade
26 Seedless fruit
32 "Fat chance!"
35 Considers
36 Yosemite Sam, e.g.
37 Dressing choice
40 Oscar role for Julia
41 Host a roast
43 Thick soups
45 Sparkling teeth, slangily
48 Freelancer's enc.
49 151, in old Rome
50 Egg cells
53 Three-horse sleighs
57 Type of patch
59 Hardy fowl
61 Abacus component
62 Gettysburg general
63 Salad veggie
64 Public houses
65 Chorus section
66 "Oh! What __ Was Mary"

DOWN

1 In need of tidying
2 Slack-jawed
3 Hibernation spots
4 __ St. Vincent Millay
5 Topple
6 In the past
7 No gentleman
8 Mazola alternative
9 Spring holiday
10 Tex. neighbor
11 Like some ties
12 Earth goddess
13 Ques. response
18 Small adjustment
19 Atkins Diet no-no
24 Emmy winner Ward
26 West Coast footballer
27 *Blue Velvet* director
28 Food and water
29 *Chicago* star
30 Kuwaiti ruler
31 Nine-digit IDs
32 Miners' sch.
33 Alaska city
34 Like Ricky Martin's "Vida"
38 All the rage
39 Many 800 numbers
42 Borden spokescow
44 Off-the-wall
46 City southeast of Seattle
47 Mink relative
50 Get the better of
51 Screwdriver need
52 Photographer Adams
53 At that time
54 Reddish-brown
55 Tote-board info
56 Wood strip
58 Killer whale
59 Stat for A-Rod
60 Brouhaha

★★★ One Solution

These four mazes have very similar patterns. By eliminating the white tiles that are not found in all four, find the path to the center of each maze that is identical in all four.

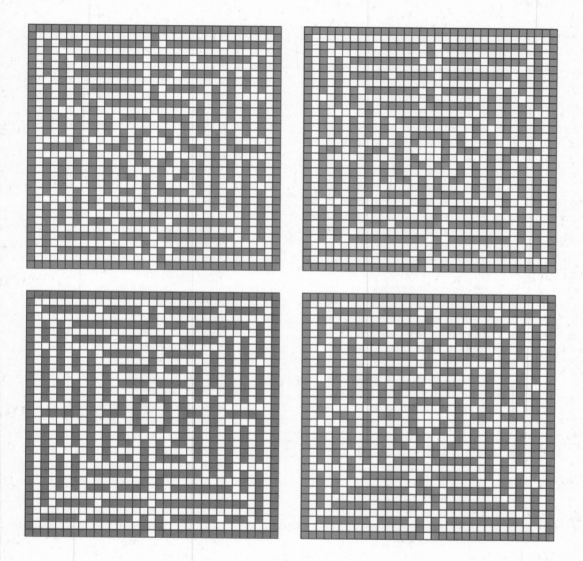

WORD WIT

Rearrange the letters in the word CHOREOGRAPH to form two words, both of which are the names of animals.

_____   _____

★★★★ Find the Ships

Determine the position of the 10 ships listed to the right of the diagram. The ships may be oriented either horizontally or vertically. A square with wavy lines indicates water and will not contain a ship. The numbers at the edge of the diagram indicate how many squares in that row or column contain parts of ships. When all 10 ships are correctly placed in the diagram, no two of them will touch each other, not even diagonally.

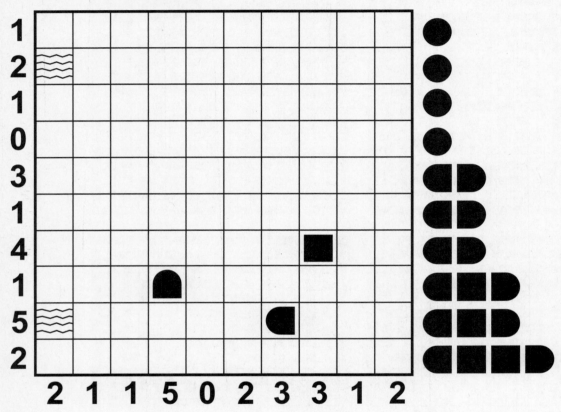

EQUATION CONSTRUCTION

Use the digits 1, 8, 3, and 3 plus standard symbols and operations of arithmetic, to create a mathematical expression that equals the number 1. All the digits must be used.

★★★★ Kakuro

Fill in the blank white boxes of the diagram with digits from 1 to 9 so that each group of numbers adds up to the shaded number above it (for a column) or to the left of it (for a row). Each group of numbers must contain all different digits. That is, no digit may be repeated within a particular sum.

IN OTHER WORDS

The abbreviation SST is short for "supersonic transport." Not counting the exclamation PSST, the shortest common word that contains the consecutive letters SST has seven letters in all. What is that word?

— — — — — — —

bRain BREatHer
INGENIOUS KITCHEN FIXES

We love clever solutions to everyday problems. And if there's a place where problems pop up every day, it's the kitchen. We bet you can use one of these tips tonight:

BURNED-ON FOOD WON'T COME OFF MY POT.
Put a few inches of water into the pot, add a few drops of dishwashing soap, bring the water to boil, turn off the heat, then let sit for at least 15 minutes. The food should come off easily now with a plastic scraper.

I CAN'T GET MY CHEESE GRATER CLEAN.
Use an old, hard-bristled toothbrush that's been wetted.

MY PLASTIC CUTTING BOARD IS GRIMY.
Spray on a 50-50 water-and-bleach solution and wipe it off with a paper towel.

THERE'S A BAD ODOR IN THE KITCHEN.
Get rid of the source, then boil some orange peels and cinnamon in water for a few minutes so that the sweet-smelling steam spreads through the area. Leave the open pot on the stove.

I SPILLED VEGETABLE OIL ALL OVER THE COUNTER.
Sop up what you can with paper towels. Sprinkle sugar over what's left, wait a few moments, and then wipe (sugar absorbs the oil). Finally, use a sponge and dish detergent to remove the remaining oily film.

THE BUTTER IS TOO HARD TO SPREAD.
Put the butter on a dish and microwave for 15 seconds. No more than that!

THE SPAGHETTI SAUCE IS WATERY.
Stir in tomato paste, a tablespoon at a time, until it's the right thickness.

THE SOUP IS FATTY.
Put ice cubes in a metal ladle and run it along the surface of the soup. Fat will stick to the cold metal; wipe off with paper towels and repeat.

THE VEGETABLES ARE MUSHY.
Throw them into a blender and purée. Return them to the cooking pot and add an equal amount of canned chicken or vegetable broth. Stir and add salt and seasonings to taste. Serve as a soup.

THE SOUP IS SALTY.
Add cooked potatoes, noodles, or rice. Starchy foods like these will absorb the excess salt.

THE MEAT OR VEGETABLES ARE SALTY.
Sprinkle a light pinch of sugar over the food. The extra sweetness actually does mask the saltiness.

I BIT INTO SOMETHING PAINFULLY SPICY.
Don't drink water, beer, or a soft drink—that will spread the pain. Instead, eat a quick serving of salt. You can also use milk, yogurt, cheese, bread, crackers, or tortillas to absorb the spice chemical, capsaicin.

★★★★ **Whoa!** by Bob Frank

ACROSS

1 Wipes lightly
5 Menu
10 Maturing agent
14 The lowdown
15 Like college walls
16 Broadway aunt
17 Paris' hometown
18 Camcorder battery
19 Jai __
20 "Whoa!"
23 Speaker's spot
24 Edgar __ Poe
25 Pub order
26 Scrapbook activity
31 Summer in Versailles
32 Passover feast
34 Party thrower
35 Ranked competitor
36 "Whoa!"
39 Baby bed
42 Triple-decker treat
43 Saint __ Square, Venice
47 Author Deighton
48 African capital
50 Time
51 Sneezer's sound
53 Of value
55 "Whoa!"
60 Sulk
61 Attribute
62 Current fashion
64 Scottish Gaelic
65 Chili con __
66 " ... __ a man with seven wives"
67 Like Easter eggs
68 High-strung
69 Architect Saarinen

DOWN

1 Onetime pesticide: Abbr.
2 Pet-carrier vent
3 Sulked
4 LP needles
5 Movie theatre
6 Tel __
7 Hundreds of things for dinner
8 Eye drop
9 Whirling water
10 __ and the Night Visitors
11 Biblical sea
12 Send forth
13 Had power
21 Barbizon School painter
22 Playground game
23 Faux __
27 Puppeteer Lewis
28 One not serious
29 Childish comeback
30 Ultimate degree
33 Period of decline
35 B&O stop
37 Mauna __
38 Plain-living group
39 Held firmly
40 Priest's house
41 Not subcontracted
44 Pose again, as a question
45 Elm Street villain
46 Gal of song
48 Fish-fowl connector
49 Churned product
52 Chose, with "for"
54 Shiver-inducing
56 Longing
57 Noted anatomist
58 Lampshade holder
59 Fork prong
63 WWII battle area

★★★ Circular Reasoning

Connect all of the circles by drawing a single continuous line through every square of the diagram. All right-angle turns of your line must alternate between boxes containing a circle and boxes not containing a circle. You must make a right-angle turn out of every square that contains a circle. Your line must end in the same square that it begins, and it cannot enter any square more than once.

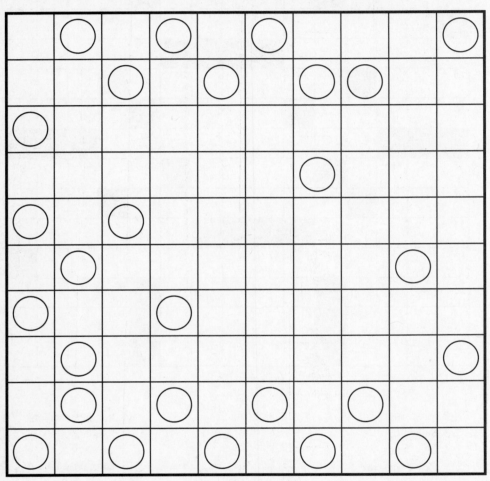

AND SO ON

Unscramble the letters in the phrase PREACHER VEST, to form two words that are part of a common phrase that has the word *and* between them.

_____ and _____

★★★ Islands

Shade in some of the white squares in the diagram with "water," so that each remaining white box is part of an island. Each island will contain exactly one numbered square, indicating how many squares that island contains. Each island is separated from the other islands by water but may touch other islands diagonally. All water is connected, but there are no 2×2 regions of water in the diagram.

		5					
			3				**1**
		3					
					3		
3							
					4		
							7

EQUATION CONSTRUCTION

Arrange these signs and numbers to form a correct number sentence. Numbers may be placed together to form a greater number (for example, a *1* and an *8* can be combined to form *18* or *81*). It is not necessary to use all the signs and numbers. No parentheses are needed.

$$3 \, , \, 5 \, , \, 11 \, , \, 12 \, , \, 13 \, , \, 14 \, , \, \div \, , \, \times$$

	=	

★★★★ Sweet Cinema by Richard Silvestri

ACROSS

1 Suffused with light
6 Border on
10 Will Smith's wife
14 Tropical fruit
15 Press one's luck
16 List extender
17 Sweet cartoon character?
19 Eighteen-wheeler
20 Springer __
21 Spock's lack
23 New Jersey five
25 Rigatoni relative
26 Hair protectors
30 Work a party
33 Squashed circle
34 __ plexus
35 3 to 5, per hole
38 Sweet serial predicaments?
42 Before, to Browning
43 Goldbricks
44 Himalayan sighting
45 "You Send Me" singer
46 Land on the Baltic
48 Put off
51 Gloomy
53 Pays and Plummer
56 Separate by zip code
61 Sonoma neighbor
62 Sweet Oscar-winning film?
64 Made a bow
65 Mrs. Casey Stengel
66 To the point
67 Actress Raines
68 Withstand scrutiny
69 Vermeer contemporary

DOWN

1 "... and children of all __"
2 Big swig
3 Lhasa holy man
4 Range part
5 Pennsylvanians bandleader
6 Fully developed
7 Rotten
8 Cheer (on)
9 Overflow
10 Court figure
11 Had leftovers, perhaps
12 Famous friend
13 Dress design
18 Service charges
22 *Louise* or *Norma*
24 Mocked
26 Scoop
27 Egg order
28 Steak order
29 "Rumble in the Jungle" victor
31 Yodeler's place
32 Pitch
34 Overcharge
35 Parti-colored
36 Initial payment
37 Bit attachment
39 *Safety Last* star
40 Great Lakes' __ Canals
41 Industrial cleaner
45 NAFTA signatory
46 Beyond a doubt
47 Takes by force
48 Florentine poet
49 PC postings
50 Pin place
52 *O* Magazine head
54 Two or three
55 Pop
57 Proof annotation
58 Grimm beast
59 Trick
60 Revenuers
63 Hosp. personnel

★★★ Pentagram

Find a path that enters the maze, passes through each of the five "arms" of the pentagram, and then exits. Assume that the path continues in a straight line in any unseen part of the pentagram.

WORD WIT

Think of the name of a world city where a Summer Olympics was once held. If you change the last letter, then reverse the order of the letters, you'll get the name of a well-known U.S. company in the food business. What are the city and company?

_____

★★★ Hyper-Sudoku

Fill in the blank boxes so that every row, column, 3×3 box, *and* each of the four 3×3 gray regions contains all of the numbers 1 to 9.

6	4					7		
2	3				7	1		
	5				6	4		
7	9							1
		3		9	5			
	6		3		1	2		
						9		
							7	
4					9			3

TELEPHONE TRIOS

1	ABC 2	DEF 3
GHI 4	JKL 5	MNO 6
PRS 7	TUV 8	WXY 9
*	0	#

Using the numbers and letters on a standard telephone, what three seven-letter words from the same category can be formed from these telephone numbers?

234-6642   – – – – – – –

527-6463   – – – – – – –

738-8642   – – – – – – –

★★★ Three or More

Enter the missing numbers from 1 to 9 into the diagram in such a way that all pairs of numbers connected by a line have a difference of three or more.

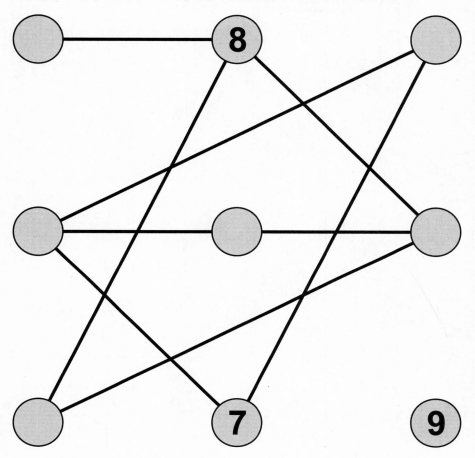

TRANSDELETION

Delete one letter from the word CONSTRAINS and rearrange the rest, to get a type of food.

_____

★★★★ Political Give-Ups by Bob Frank

ACROSS

1 Church areas
6 Fire residue
9 Letter starter
13 Obnoxious one
14 Where Bartletts grow
16 Quit on Election Night
18 Comic Philips
19 Watergate prosecutor
20 Help in a holdup
21 Wine cooler
24 Lawn invaders
28 "She Loves You" drummer
29 '60s protest
32 Zodiac beast
33 Midwest st.
35 Clear drink
36 Government agent
37 Let a colleague speak
41 *Around the World in Eighty Days* producer
42 Statuary and murals
43 Not 'neath
44 20th cen. conflict
45 "Gray __ are gonna clear up ..."
47 Bakery treats
51 Pond growth
53 Type of track finish
55 Big dogs
58 Altar agreement
59 *Roma*'s hill count
60 Try again, in a legislature
64 Call number
65 Feature of some oranges
66 Vale
67 Letters on a car battery
68 Throws off

DOWN

1 Password's purpose
2 Timely
3 Married lady of Madrid
4 Common Market letters
5 Phantomlike
6 Highest points
7 Defeat, in bridge
8 Prankster's laugh
9 Spread by scattering
10 Really steamed up
11 VCR button
12 Match, as a bet

15 1860s combatant
17 Egg qty.
22 Annoyed
23 Made amends for
25 Red Muppet
26 High-priced
27 Michael, to Kirk
30 Make a clove hitch
31 Data
34 Mont. neighbor
36 Sabbath reading
37 Let loose a holler
38 "Got you!"
39 Pod prefix

40 Bummers
41 PanAm rival
45 Naval recruit
46 Fish nets
48 Come to
49 Tagged after
50 Movie ad photos
52 *Seascape* playwright
54 Summer drink
56 Scripto alternative
57 Red sign word
60 Give in to gravity
61 WWW address
62 Fuss
63 Word of scorn

★★ Triad Split Decisions

In this clueless crossword puzzle, each answer consists of two words whose spellings are the same, except for the consecutive letters given. All answers are common words; no phrases or hyphenated or capitalized words are used. Some of the clues may have more than one solution, but there is only one word pair that will correctly link up with all the other word pairs.

EQUATION CONSTRUCTION

Use the digits 1, 8, 3, and 3 plus standard symbols and operations of arithmetic, to create a mathematical expression that equals the number 2. All the digits must be used.

$$\boxed{} = \boxed{2}$$

★★★ One-Way Streets

The diagram represents a pattern of streets. A and B are parking spaces, and the black squares are stores. Find the route that starts at A, passes through all stores exactly once, and ends at B. Arrows indicate one-way traffic for that block only. No block or intersection may be entered more than once.

WORD WIT

PETROL is the British word for gasoline. The full name of what famous actor from the British Isles uses only six different letters—the letters in PETROL?

_____

★★★★ Catch-All by Fred Piscop

ACROSS

1 Fashions
6 Provo's state
10 Catches on to
14 Turn outward
15 "__ of your beeswax!"
16 Tater topper
17 A spy might crack it
19 Exploitative type
20 Fly ball's path
21 Wiener holder
22 Most calamitous
24 Abstract sculpture
26 Shut loudly
27 The whole shebang
28 Some time or another
32 Oil-bearing rock
35 "__ on first?"
36 Actress Reid
37 Comet part
38 Erstwhile cataloguer
39 Film fragment
40 Parisian pronoun
41 Patriot Nathan
42 Linen item
43 Put off
45 Lawyer's charge
46 Mongrel dogs
47 Young lobo
51 Make a bust, maybe
54 River in England
55 Barbary beast
56 Singer Turner
57 Military youth group
60 Granola bits
61 Elec., for one
62 Rental sign
63 Courts
64 Watch over
65 Practices with a pug

DOWN

1 Flat formations
2 In the open
3 Bing's label
4 Make a mistake
5 Germ-free
6 Quitter's cry
7 Adz or awl
8 What's more
9 Unmindful
10 Truffles preparer
11 "If all __ fails ..."
12 Drivers' aids
13 Washday step
18 Motorist's payout
23 Actor Holm
25 Dance studio offering
26 Sand castle site
28 *Pinocchio* beast
29 Low-lying area
30 HOMES body
31 Wholly absorbed
32 Dance move
33 Angelic topper
34 Has a bug
35 Withdraws, in a way
38 Time saver
42 Picks out
44 Young seal
45 Knox or Dix
47 Use skillfully
48 Rhea's *Cheers* role
49 High berth
50 Outdoes
51 Store away
52 "See ya!"
53 Golden Rule word
54 Score after deuce
58 Had lunch
59 *Alley* __

★★★ Train Maze

A train enters the maze at the top left and exits at the bottom left, and a second train enters at the bottom right and exits at the top right. If the routes of both trains form the same pattern and do not intersect each other at any point, find the paths of the two trains.

TRANSDELETION

Delete one letter from the word RUMINATIONS and rearrange the rest, to get a two-word Biblical place.

_____

★★★★ Star Search

Find the stars that are hidden in some of the blank squares. The numbered squares indicate how many stars are hidden in the squares adjacent to them (including diagonally). There is never more than one star in any square.

			1	1			
	1		4		3		
2					4		
						1	
4		3	4		2		1
					1		
2		3		3		2	2
	1						
	1	1	1	1	1		

MIXAGRAMS

Each line contains a five-letter word and a four-letter word that have been mixed together (the order of the letters in each word have not been changed). Unmix the two words on each line and write them in the spaces provided. When you're done, find a two-word answer to the clue by reading down the letter columns in the answers.

CLUE: It doubles your money

SOBURESFE = _ _ _ _ _ + _ _ _ _

CHOIDBEOR = _ _ _ _ _ + _ _ _ _

FORLAUTLE = _ _ _ _ _ + _ _ _ _

LULASMEAD = _ _ _ _ _ + _ _ _ _

★★★★ Sudoku

Fill in the blank boxes so that every row, column, and 3×3 box contains all of the numbers 1 to 9.

	2	9	7	4				
	4			8	3	5	1	
8			9		1			
7		3	6					
				5			8	
2		4						5
			1	9				
	7					2		
					4	7		

THREE OF A KIND

Find the three hidden words in the sentence that, read in order, go together in some way.

The enemy of airlines these days is the fuel malady.

★★★★ The Ex-Files by Lee Glickstein & Nancy Salomon

ACROSS

1 Date source
5 Tune from *Guys and Dolls*
10 Not much
14 Author Wiesel
15 Skylit lobbies
16 Bathroom square
17 Laundry fuzz
18 Flipper's choice
19 Not in gear
20 Overnight Fluffy?
23 Wynonna's mom
24 2002 British Open champion
25 Part of some portfolios
28 Hovel addition?
32 Current unit
35 '50s pop singer Wooley
36 Fit for a king
37 Summary statistic
39 Ordeals
42 __ log
43 Borden character
45 Author Hoffer
47 UK heads
48 "The escape hatch is stuck!"?
52 Cash cache: Abbr.
53 "See __ care!"
54 Picture cards
57 Dental offices?
62 Earned
64 Crack squad
65 Capital of Yemen
66 2000 role for Julia
67 Mediterranean republic
68 Boxer's stat
69 Jayhawks' org.
70 German steel city
71 All there

DOWN

1 Ill-gotten gains
2 Beyond one's ken
3 TV reporter Ellerbee
4 Space streaker
5 Waited patiently
6 Beehive State
7 Sal's canal
8 Exploited
9 Hands down
10 Bickering
11 Doing some housework
12 The works
13 *A Summer Place* star
21 Shortened holiday
22 Old overlord
26 Kingdom
27 Car bars
29 "Fancy that!"
30 Clampett portrayer
31 Marshal under Napoleon
32 The end
33 Spartan serf
34 Television and radio
38 Medical research agcy.
40 Three, in Sicily
41 Basketball substitute
44 Splice frames
46 "See you later!"
49 Chalet shape
50 Rodeo ropes
51 Buster's targets
55 Honshu port
56 Mortise insert
58 Warrior Princess of TV
59 Disney frames
60 English art philanthropist
61 Freelancer's enc.
62 What boys will be
63 Hook-shot trajectory

★★★★ ABC

Enter the letters *A*, *B*, and *C* into the diagram so that each row and column has exactly one *A*, one *B*, and one *C*. The letters outside the diagram indicate the first letter encountered, moving in the direction of the arrow. Keep in mind that after all the letters have been filled in, there will be two blank boxes in each row and column.

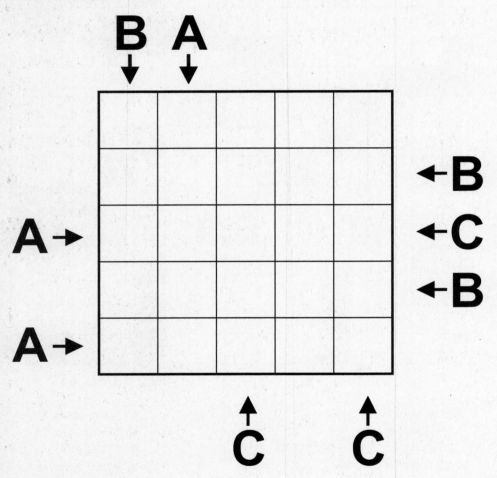

EQUATION CONSTRUCTION

Use the digits 1, 8, 3, and 3 plus standard symbols and operations of arithmetic, to create a mathematical expression that equals the number 15. All the digits must be used.

$$\boxed{} = \boxed{15}$$

★★★★ Find the Ships

Determine the position of the 10 ships listed to the right of the diagram. The ships may be oriented either horizontally or vertically. A square with wavy lines indicates water and will not contain a ship. The numbers at the edge of the diagram indicate how many squares in that row or column contain parts of ships. When all 10 ships are correctly placed in the diagram, no two of them will touch each other, not even diagonally.

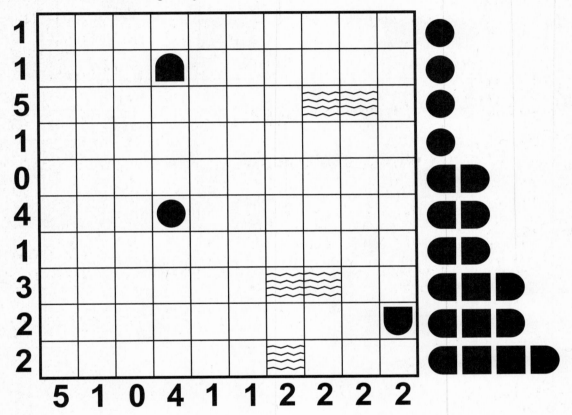

WORD WIT

What common five-letter English word becomes the plural of a French word with the same meaning often seen in crosswords (not counting any accent marks), when the word is spelled backwards?

— — — — —

★★★★ Shirt Stuff by Merle Baker

ACROSS

1 One of the Spice Girls
5 *La vita nuova* poet
10 Wharton degrees
14 Former Atlanta arena
15 New York city
16 Lichen symbiote
17 Manner of walking
18 Game surface
19 San __, PR
20 Exact
23 Terminate
24 Poet banished from Rome
25 Scamp
27 Agreeable sorts
30 Aware of
32 Strange
33 Golfer Tom
34 *Desire Under the __*
37 Cover
38 Phonograph part
41 "Lighthorse Harry"
42 PC owner
44 Was captured
45 Author Asimov
47 Made cereal, maybe
49 Not fragile
50 Pertaining to life
52 Last word of the Bible
53 Mandela's org.
54 A pitcher might tear one
60 Well-being
62 Put a mark on
63 Land in the ocean
64 Pitcher
65 Sphere of influence
66 *Familia* members
67 "Why don't we?"
68 Colorful horses
69 Side with turkey

DOWN

1 Walt Kelly's possum
2 Yemen neighbor
3 Nasty mood
4 Affected personally
5 Work horse
6 Not whispered
7 "Groovy!"
8 Fruity dessert
9 Advocate
10 Mil. rank
11 Like Joe Sixpack
12 Guam capital's former name
13 Financial inst.
21 One might be blessed
22 Aberdeen negative
26 __-Foy, Quebec
27 River to the Yellow Sea
28 Whiffenpoofs
29 Pool-table feature
30 Exercise
31 Romance lang.
33 Start for deep or high
35 Samoa studier
36 Cabinet off.
39 Not proper
40 Bishop topper
43 Track
46 Arizona retirement center
48 Black Forest tree
49 Migrating salmon
50 Swiss city
51 Dumbstruck
52 Ordered pizza, perhaps
55 South Seas staple
56 Eban of Israel
57 Former cultural exchange org.
58 Flim-__
59 Admit all, with "up"
61 Sounds of hesitation

★★★ Four Kings

Find a path that enters the maze, passes through all four kings, and then exits the maze all without retracing a path. Note that there are only two openings to each of the four chambers (one to enter and the other to exit), so start by drawing the portions of the path that must lead in and out of the chambers.

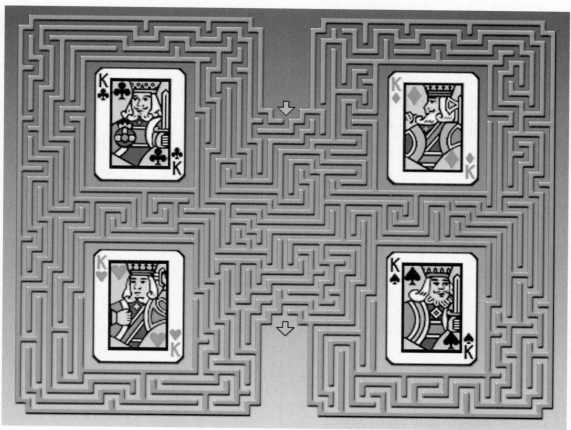

TELEPHONE TRIOS

1	ABC 2	DEF 3
GHI 4	JKL 5	MNO 6
PRS 7	TUV 8	WXY 9
*	0	#

Using the numbers and letters on a standard telephone, what three seven-letter words from the same category can be formed from these telephone numbers?

248-8639   _ _ _ _ _ _ _

538-2487   _ _ _ _ _ _ _

687-8273   _ _ _ _ _ _ _

★★★★★ Kakuro

Fill in the blank white boxes of the diagram with digits from 1 to 9 so that each group of numbers adds up to the shaded number above it (for a column) or to the left of it (for a row). Each group of numbers must contain all different digits. That is, no digit may be repeated within a particular sum.

COMMON SENSE

What five-letter word can be found in the dictionary definitions of all of these words: AQUA, ECLIPSE, FOAM RUBBER and REFLECT?

— — — — —

★★★★ Circular Reasoning

Connect all of the circles by drawing a single continuous line through every square of the diagram. All right-angle turns of your line must alternate between boxes containing a circle and boxes not containing a circle. You must make a right-angle turn out of every square that contains a circle. Your line must end in the same square that it begins, and it cannot enter any square more than once.

EQUATION CONSTRUCTION

Arrange these signs and numbers to form a correct number sentence. Numbers may be placed together to form a greater number (for example, a 1 and an 8 can be combined to form 18 or 81). It is not necessary to use all the signs and numbers. No parentheses are needed.

0 , 1 , 7 , 9 , 13 , 18 , ÷ , −

★★★★ Thievery by Merle Baker

ACROSS

1 Poker choice
5 Second showing
10 Sorry alternative
14 "Rule, Britannia" composer
15 Outcast
16 Bjorn contemporary
17 Suffice
19 Karate school
20 Initially
21 Photographic, as memory
23 Minty herb
24 As compared to
26 Blackens
28 Attest
32 Newsman Sevareid
36 Tempe sch.
37 Like some arms
38 Lomond, for one
39 Lines in a circle
41 Multicolored
42 Special Forces units
44 User or product leader
45 Agatha contemporary
46 Publications
47 Mex. misses
49 Have a liking for
51 Earthenware pots
56 Lambastes
59 Most peculiar
61 Et ___
62 Delayed reaction
64 Credulous one
65 D'Artagnan's creator
66 Uniform
67 Spunky quality
68 Dramatize
69 Make over

DOWN

1 Mubarak predecessor
2 One's word
3 Bring together
4 Jeans material
5 Agents
6 Emigrant's document
7 ___ Tin Tin
8 Worriers' risk
9 Radar's orders
10 Oblique blow
11 Heaps
12 30 Down discovery
13 Antidiscrimination agcy.
18 Son of Zeus
22 Partial darkness
25 They slip by
27 Sculling gear
29 Osman, for one
30 Explorer Tasman
31 Took a cab
32 Oater actor Jack
33 Repetitive learning
34 Topped the cake
35 Skier's way up
37 Slave of opera
40 Sewed up
43 West and Clarke
47 Don't take part in
48 Put out
50 Diane and Cheryl
52 Soda size
53 Take off
54 Set, as a price
55 Court reporter
56 Used a doorbell
57 Banned apple spray
58 Four on some faces
60 Otherwise
63 John's *Pulp Fiction* costar

★★★ Hyper-Sudoku

Fill in the blank boxes so that every row, column, 3×3 box *and* each of the four 3×3 gray regions contains all of the numbers 1 to 9.

		4	2	7			5	3
5			8					
	9			4	2			
			6	1		2		9
7			3			6		
					1	8		
				2		5		
	3		5					7

WORD WIT

What chemical element becomes the name of a garden flower when one letter is deleted?

_____

★★★ Split Decisions

In this clueless crossword puzzle, each answer consists of two words whose spellings are the same, except for the consecutive letters given. All answers are common words; no phrases or hyphenated or capitalized words are used. Some of the clues may have more than one solution, but there is only one word pair that will correctly link up with all the other word pairs.

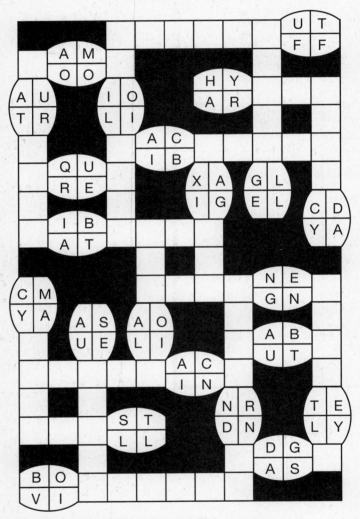

EQUATION CONSTRUCTION

Use the digits 4, 9, and 5 plus standard symbols and operations of arithmetic, to create a mathematical expression that equals the number 1. All the digits must be used.

★★★★ Just Desserts by A.J. Santora

ACROSS

1 Bona __
5 Like Batman
10 Israeli port
14 Piccadilly statue
15 Spry
16 Pants spec
17 Speak well of
18 Provokes
19 Hide, as a coin
20 H.S. subject
21 Illusory promises
23 Beachcomber find
25 ENT cases
26 Simpleton
27 Giant Hall of Famer
28 Prof.'s field
29 Nautical response
33 G.I. guy
36 Ex-G.I. guy
37 Head, so to speak
38 Clean air grp.
39 Feminine ending
40 Hinged (on)
41 *Heidi* locale
42 Sheep sound
43 Metallic combo
44 Goes forward
49 Convinces
50 "No problem!"
52 NBA official
54 Listen closely
55 Stingless bee
56 Commotion
57 *Picnic* playwright
58 Chilling
59 Shania Twain, for one
60 It could be a good thing
61 Food fish
62 Escutcheon spoiler

DOWN

1 Celebrate
2 Old __ (*U.S.S. Constitution*)
3 On-deck circle devices
4 Superlative suffix
5 Find fault
6 '69 Mets star
7 Sprite
8 Actress Verdugo
9 Kaput
10 Interpretation
11 Conflict
12 Austrian poet
13 TV trophies
21 Thickness
22 What "-phobe" means
24 Business letter abbr.
26 Actress Campbell
29 Phone-number starters
30 He played Mongkut
31 Inventor Whitney
32 Flagon filler
33 Ferdinand Morton's moniker
34 Against
35 One way to take it
37 *Red Badge of Courage* author
41 According to
42 Gave support to
43 Wonderment
44 Plant pest
45 Photographer Arbus
46 Brink
47 Violinist Zimbalist
48 Tally
49 Shooting game
51 Indigo
53 __ the bill
56 Bill

★★★ Labyrinth Cube

The diagram represents a paper cube that has been unfolded to form a flat surface. Visualize what the cube would look like if refolded, and draw a path that uses all the pink, yellow and blue tiles. Use the white space to connect the path between two adjacent faces of the cube that are apart while unfolded. Note that the two faces of each color are opposite each other in the folded cube.

WORD WIT

Think of a common two-word phrase for a type of musician. Move the second word of the phrase before the first word (don't rearrange any letters), and you'll get the name of a musical instrument that renders the musician unnecessary. What are the two phrases?

_____   _____

★★★★ Three or More

Enter the missing numbers from 1 to 9 into the diagram in such a way that all pairs of numbers connected by a line have a difference of three or more.

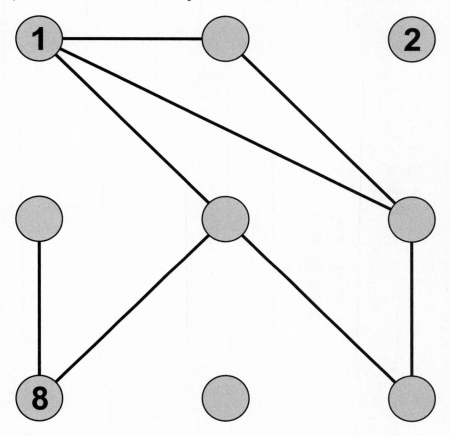

MIXAGRAMS

Each line contains a five-letter word and a four-letter word that have been mixed together (the order of the letters in each word has not been changed). Unmix the two words on each line and write them in the spaces provided. When you're done, find a two-word answer to the clue by reading down the letter columns in the answers.

CLUE: She wears little clothing

BEDERCHAW = _ _ _ _ _ + _ _ _ _

OAFTWERLS = _ _ _ _ _ + _ _ _ _

LOBECREOT = _ _ _ _ _ + _ _ _ _

LYAINKEUS = _ _ _ _ _ + _ _ _ _

★★★★ One-Way Streets

The diagram represents a pattern of streets. P's are parking spaces, and the black squares are stores. Find the route that starts at a parking space, passes through all stores exactly once, and ends at the other parking space. Arrows indicate one-way traffic for that block only. No block or intersection may be entered more than once.

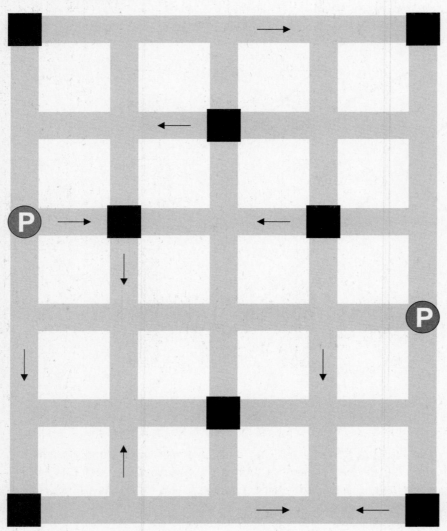

AND SO ON

Unscramble the letters in the phrase TOTE SOAP TEAM, to form two words that are part of a common phrase that has the word *and* between them.

_____ and _____

★★★★ Play-On Words by Merle Baker

ACROSS

1 Short pencil
5 Finish line
9 Drying ovens
14 Banderillero opponent
15 Put __ writing
16 Center of Florida
17 Mediterranean port
18 CPR pros
19 English teacher's concern
20 Bit of the Bahamas
21 Olympic shooting gear
23 One with equal billing
25 Get wind of
26 Yemeni neighbor
28 Ornament
33 Skilled
36 Opposed to
38 Morlocks' victims
39 They're obvious
41 Turnpike accesses
43 Artist Chagall
44 List ender
46 Medicinal plants
47 Like lox
49 Big blow
51 Government center
53 Say nothing
57 Flutters
62 Chowderhead
63 Arum family lily
64 Doing nothing
65 Arcing shots
66 White gold, for one
67 "Go ahead!"
68 Arena shouts
69 Cozy places
70 Objects
71 Boat trailer

DOWN

1 Unflappable
2 Many a sculpture
3 Europe-Asia divider
4 Beef
5 __ del Fuego
6 "Don't throw bouquets __"
7 Cooperate
8 Follow
9 Work, to Le Clerc
10 Church section
11 Strikebreaker
12 Deli option
13 Worry
22 1994 Peace Nobelist
24 Quantities: Abbr.
27 Democratic donkey creator
29 Set back
30 One of the Muppets
31 Contend
32 Warm welcome
33 20s dispensers
34 Pharmacist's weight
35 New money
37 Chime
40 Euripides tragedy
42 Julia on screen
45 Affected
48 Op-Ed pieces
50 Chamber groups
52 Put up with
54 Money
55 Tashkent native
56 Western group
57 Look over
58 Greens ingredient
59 Slings and arrows
60 Connect graph points
61 What you might put on it

★★★★ Sudoku

Fill in the blank boxes so that every row, column, and 3×3 box contains all of the numbers 1 to 9.

2	3							
			6			3	8	
					1	9		4
5								
		9		8	2		4	1
			9					
	5					7		6
		4	7					8
6			5				9	2

TRANSDELETION

Delete one letter from the word MISNOMER and rearrange the rest, to get a type of book.

_____

★★★★ Star Search

Find the stars that are hidden in some of the blank squares. The numbered squares indicate how many stars are hidden in the squares adjacent to them (including diagonally). There is never more than one star in any square.

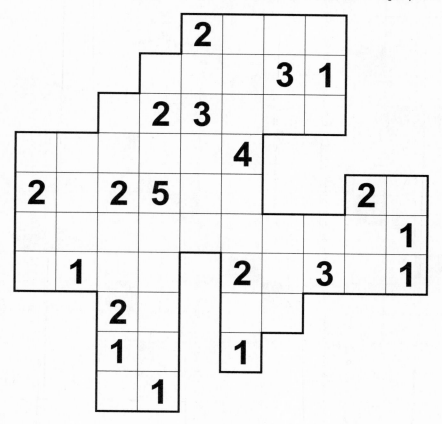

EQUATION CONSTRUCTION

Use the digits 4, 9, and 5 plus standard symbols and operations of arithmetic, to create a mathematical expression that equals the number 89. All the digits must be used.

[   ] = 89

★★★★ 0 K's by Fred Piscop

ACROSS

1 Green gem
5 Bus-sta. posting
10 Novelist Hunter
14 21 and 65
15 Josh Gibson contemporary
16 Zhivago's love
17 Clairvoyants, as a voting group?
19 "... way to skin __"
20 Small spaces, to a 28 Across
21 Borscht veggie
22 ICU hookup
24 Pittsburgh gridder
26 Parting word
27 Ginza cash
28 Print-shop worker
31 Clip-on device
34 Aquarium dweller
35 Relative of ante-
36 Burden of proof
37 Massenet opera
38 Go belly-up
39 Lateral lead-in
40 Acts the worrywart
41 Making all stops
42 Diamondbacks
44 "Luck __ Lady"
45 Came up
46 Closed loudly
50 Mason's assistant
52 Senior member
53 Bard's "before"
54 Haydn nickname
55 M.D. moonlighting as a mover?
58 Keep __ (persist)
59 Worn away
60 Turturro of *The Sopranos*
61 Somewhat indelicate
62 Blank look
63 Highlander

DOWN

1 Frank or Jesse
2 Bond or Smart
3 Tightly packed
4 Ft. Lauderdale hrs.
5 Vent one's __
6 Scots toss it
7 Sword handle
8 Sense of self
9 Outcome determiners
10 Tickles pink
11 D.C. appliance lobby?
12 Spirited steed
13 Cager Archibald
18 More fit
23 MasterCard rival
25 Potato features
26 *Ars gratia* __
28 Bog mosses
29 Diva's delivery
30 1994 role for Jodie
31 Serve drinks
32 Oscar winner Paquin
33 Photo in a rock mag?
34 "Out yonder!'"
37 Track supporters
38 Brewski topper
40 Arctic ice sheet
41 Country singer Rimes
43 Hostilities ender
44 1884 loser to Cleveland
46 Passover meal
47 Radio and TV
48 Crumble away
49 Model stick-on
50 Train in the ring
51 Parting syllables
52 Floppy filler
56 Granola tidbit
57 Rib-tickler

★★★ Poker Chips

Starting in the third row with the black chip on the blue tile, trace a path that visits every tile exactly once and ends in the fifth row with the white chip on the black tile. Each tile you visit must be the same color as the chip on the previous tile. You may move horizontally or vertically, but not diagonally.

WORD WIT

Rearrange the letters in the phrase RIVER CRUISE to get the last names of two famous American business partners.

_____   _____

★★ Line Drawings

Draw two straight lines, each from one edge of the square to another edge, so that the letters in each of three regions spell a word of a different length.

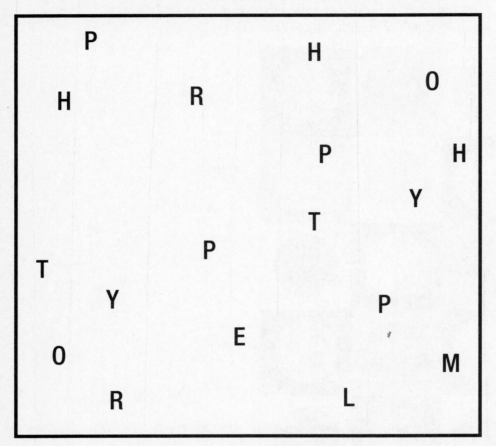

MIXAGRAMS

Each line contains a five-letter word and a four-letter word that have been mixed together (the order of the letters in each word has not been changed). Unmix the two words on each line and write them in the spaces provided. When you're done, find a two-part answer to the clue by reading down the letter columns in the answers.

CLUE: Gin, but not rye

CORGULEST = _ _ _ _ _ + _ _ _ _

LABOARUKT = _ _ _ _ _ + _ _ _ _

ROAMUGEHN = _ _ _ _ _ + _ _ _ _

DAMESILHY = _ _ _ _ _ + _ _ _ _

★★★★ ABCD

Enter the letters *A*, *B*, *C*, and *D* into the diagram so that each row and column has exactly one *A*, one *B*, one *C*, and one *D*. The letters outside the diagram indicate the first letter encountered, moving in the direction of the arrow. Keep in mind that after all the letters have been filled in, there will be two blank boxes in each row and column.

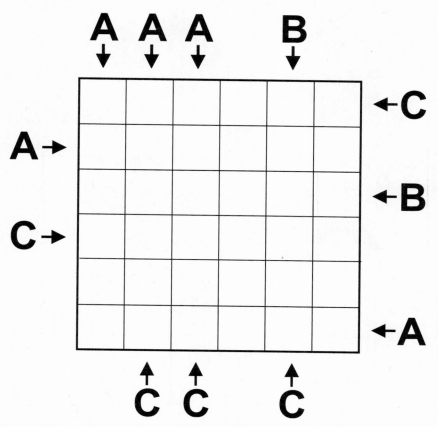

CLUELESS CROSSWORD

Complete the crossword with common uncapitalized seven-letter words, based entirely on the letters already filled in for you.

★★★★★ Themeless Toughie by Daniel R. Stark

ACROSS

1 Strikes out
7 CNN show
15 Carroll Baker title role
16 Unimaginative one
17 Steam
18 Government building
19 Touch up
20 Bill balance
22 They might come by air
23 Tries to learn more
24 Pipe fitting
25 Stories, for short
26 Grazing area
27 Fair-hiring letters
29 Spurs
31 Is, in Taxco
33 Camp drills
35 Name of nine popes
37 Indicative
41 Wise one
43 FitzGerald's poet
44 Capsize
47 Leaf vein
48 Noun starter
49 Teen's denial
50 Coral habitat
52 Gathering spots
53 Sudden downpour
56 Medieval menial
57 Senator Cranston
58 Hidden
60 Be sociable
62 __ mile
63 Noisy fan
64 Bushes
65 Way out

DOWN

1 Coaxes

2 Most convenient
3 Water
4 Ladies' casuals
5 Horror film cliché
6 Nobel, for one
7 More like Jack
8 Discharge
9 Take it
10 Mix
11 *Domicilio*
12 Invader of Gaul
13 Unsavory
14 Rendezvous

21 Bess' predecessor
28 What 10 may mean
29 Semisolid substance
30 '52 Winter Olympics locale
32 Arched recess
33 Honey, to a druggist
34 Brooder
36 Current
38 Blunt, perhaps
39 Gives an accounting of

40 Bad puns
42 Tight
44 Not celebrated
45 Willow relative
46 Work of art
51 Blazing
52 Kindness
54 Philippe's pate
55 Patrick's milieu
56 Hit the heights
59 Sublimation state
61 Egg ender

bRaIn BReatHer DEAR OL' BEN

Benjamin Franklin is arguably the most beloved of America's Founding Fathers. He was accomplished, charming, and absolutely filled with wisdom. Here are a few of his more memorable comments:

Those who would give up essential liberty to purchase a little temporary safety deserve neither liberty nor safety.

To lengthen thy life, lessen thy meals.

If you would not
be forgotten,
As soon as you are
dead and rotten,
Either write things
worthy reading,
Or do things worth
the writing.

An investment in knowledge always pays the best interest.

If your head is wax, don't walk in the sun.

Be civil to all; sociable to many; familiar with few; friend to one; enemy to none.

Having been poor is no shame, but being ashamed of it is.

Well done is better than well said.

BUT IN THIS WORLD NOTHING CAN BE SAID TO BE CERTAIN, EXCEPT DEATH AND TAXES.

He that falls in love with himself will have no rivals.

Three may keep a secret, if two of them are dead.

★★★★ Find the Ships

Determine the position of the 10 ships listed to the right of the diagram. The ships may be oriented either horizontally or vertically. A square with wavy lines indicates water and will not contain a ship. The numbers at the edge of the diagram indicate how many squares in that row or column contain parts of ships. When all 10 ships are correctly placed in the diagram, no two of them will touch each other, not even diagonally.

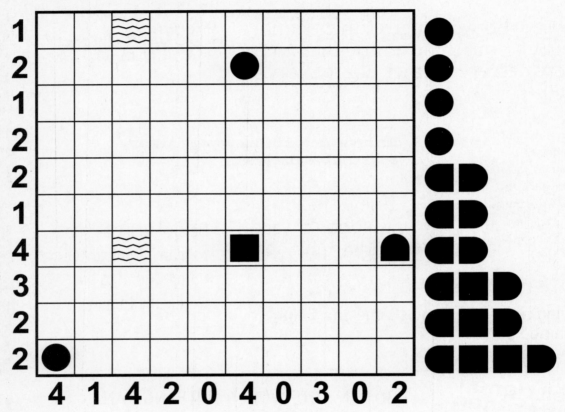

WORD WIT

What six-letter adjective becomes its antonym when its first letter (a consonant) is deleted?

— — — — — —

★★★★ Hyper-Sudoku

Fill in the blank boxes so that every row, column, 3×3 box *and* each of the four 3×3 gray regions contains all of the numbers 1 to 9.

			3	5			8	
3						2	4	5
7		8				6		
			7			1		
								2
			5					
			2					
		4			6		1	7
	8					4		3

CITY SEARCH

Using the letters in MILWAUKEE, we were able to form only one common uncapitalized five-letter word. Can you find it?

_____

★★★★★ Themeless Toughie by S.N.

ACROSS

1 No team player
8 Clad
15 "Tea for Two" singer
16 Absolutely
17 She portrayed Hoss Cartwright's mother
18 Afrin alternative
19 "Seriously!"
21 Shriver et al.
22 Literature Nobelist of '47
23 Emotional situation
24 Thine: Fr.
25 Skinflinty
26 Ebbed
28 Many ETS customers
29 Former German state
30 Frolicsome
31 Scientific calculator button
32 "__ Latest Flame" (Elvis tune)
33 Westerns Channel sister station
36 Station
39 F1 neighbor
42 Luke's companion
44 Maple genus
45 Edible seeds
46 Tar order
47 "OK!"
48 Goes for the gold
49 Hot stuff
51 Vehicle on runners
53 Skelton catchphrase
54 U.S., to Mexicans
55 Pond swimmer
56 __ City, CA
57 Provided direction

DOWN

1 Streamers
2 Not as graceful
3 Some American Revolution scouts
4 Present
5 Minute
6 Asked for nothing
7 Like some teachers
8 Gut
9 Khan follower
10 Cycle starter
11 Positively
12 Muscle, up or down
13 Energise with love
14 Physics calculation
20 Archibald of basketball
27 Throw out
29 Pain in the neck
31 Stringed instrument
32 Derided
33 Comparatively foolish
34 Schmaltz
35 Done
36 True
37 Plaintiff list abbr.
38 Attention getters of a sort
39 Land on the Pacific
40 Cringing
41 Made up
43 Schumer predecessor
44 Tilting
50 Predicament
52 Start of Montana's motto

★★★ Egyptian Maze

Find a path that enters the maze, passes through all three Egyptian scenes, and then exits the maze, all without retracing your path. Note that there are only two openings to each of the three chambers (one to enter and the other to exit), so start by drawing the portions of the path that must lead in and out of the chambers.

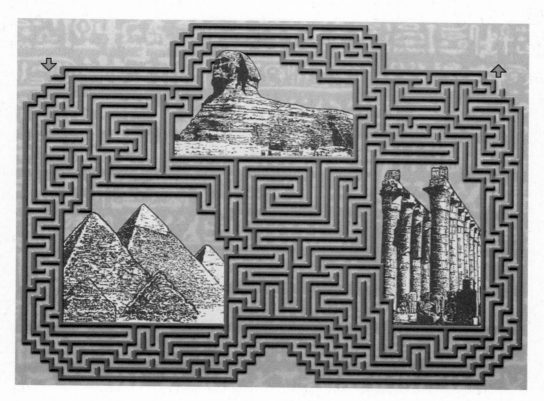

EQUATION CONSTRUCTION

Arrange these signs and numbers to form a correct number sentence. Numbers may be placed together to form a greater number (for example, a *1* and an *8* can be combined to form *18* or *81*). It is not necessary to use all the signs and numbers. No parentheses are needed.

0 , 5 , 8 , 12 , 14 , 4 , ÷ , ×

	=	

★★★★ Circular Reasoning

Connect all of the circles by drawing a single continuous line through every square of the diagram. All right-angle turns of your line must alternate between boxes containing a circle and boxes not containing a circle. You must make a right-angle turn out of every square that contains a circle. Your line must end in the same square that it begins, and it cannot enter any square more than once.

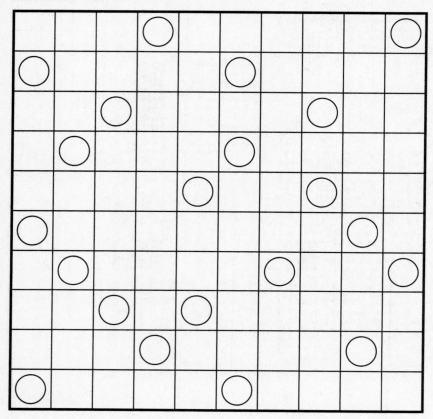

TELEPHONE TRIOS

1	ABC **2**	DEF **3**
GHI **4**	JKL **5**	MNO **6**
PRS **7**	TUV **8**	WXY **9**
*	**0**	#

Using the numbers and letters on a standard telephone, what three seven-letter words from the same category can be formed from these telephone numbers?

374-4283   _ _ _ _ _ _ _

466-3652   _ _ _ _ _ _ _

884-2628   _ _ _ _ _ _ _

★★★★★ Themeless Toughie by Daniel R. Stark

ACROSS

1 How some dine
9 J.R.'s town
15 *Glengarry Glen Ross* figure
16 Make adjustments to
17 Cherish
18 Lorre role
19 Constantly
20 Heaters
22 Pansy's boy
23 Lost no time
25 Precariously balanced
27 Tentacle
28 Removed the pits
30 Early 11th-century date
31 *Star Trek* counselor
32 Works a do
34 Archeologist's find
35 Physics Nobelist of 1909
39 One way to travel
41 Firer's need
42 Quit
44 Deion Sanders' nickname
45 *Errare humanum __*
46 Shut tight
51 Fly's path
52 Mine entrances
54 Extra
55 Netlike fabrics
57 Part of NOW
59 11th-grade exam
60 Mexican herbivore
62 Glacial fissure
64 Computer network need
65 More warm
66 Say for sure
67 Like some records

DOWN

1 Sunflower kin
2 Butterflies-to-be
3 Raw wool
4 Brought up
5 Hairpin curve
6 Too sure
7 Solitaire unit
8 Former
9 Lisbon honorific
10 Matrix
11 Nesting place
12 *Catch Me If You Can* name
13 Reception area
14 With anger
21 Skyline features
24 Geometric style
26 Forecaster's duo
29 Moved on the floor
31 It won't rust
33 Shows a connection
35 "Many dreams have been brought" to her doorstep
36 Finds the means
37 Keeps happening
38 King's realm
40 Southey selections
43 Throws mud
47 Fill with dismay
48 Laird's daughter
49 Tapes over
50 Impedes
52 '80s Screen Actors Guild president
53 Remove paint
56 Chalet feature
58 He switched jobs with Couric for a day in May, 2003
61 Canvas product
63 Computer monitor: Abbr.

★★★★★ Kakuro

Fill in the blank white boxes of the diagram with digits from 1 to 9 so that each group of numbers adds up to the shaded number above it (for a column) or to the left of it (for a row). Each group of numbers must contain all different digits. That is, no digit may be repeated within a particular sum.

WORD WIT

The name of actress LAUREN BACALL contains ABC, three consecutive letters of the alphabet, with other letters in between. What actor's first and last names contain five consecutive letters of the alphabet (with other letters in between)?

_____

★★★★ Islands

Shade in some of the white squares in the diagram with "water," so that each remaining white box is part of an island. Each island will contain exactly one numbered square, indicating how many squares that island contains. Each island is separated from the other islands by water but may touch other islands diagonally. All water is connected, but there are no 2×2 regions of water in the diagram.

	6								
		1			2				
				2		5			
					5				
5							4		
				4			2		
			6						

IN OTHER WORDS

The shortest common word that contains the consecutive letters IOE has seven letters in all. What is that word?

_____

★★★★★ Themeless Toughie by Merle Baker

ACROSS

1 Judges, at times
9 Muddy
15 Sheridan character
16 Sent down
17 Swagger
19 Good __
20 Alvy's love
21 Sight: Fr.
22 Frat letters
23 Plant bane
24 Utilitarianism expounder
25 Draw upon
26 Get all of
27 Office practice, perhaps
28 Doesn't go straight
30 Brewer et al.
32 Like carillon bells
34 Latin American language group
35 Hoity-toity
37 "The Venice of America"
40 Prohibitions
41 Vasco __ de Balboa
43 Shuttle engine intake
44 Some bill-paying transactions: Abbr.
45 Olympic vessel
46 Lose strength
47 Molokai dish
48 Tampico toast
49 Cocteau collaborator
50 Peace process?
53 Senator Fong et al.
54 Critical trial
55 Confound
56 Goes by again

DOWN

1 Repercussions
2 Arrange effectively
3 Full-power
4 The Wild Bunch actor
5 Utter angrily
6 Mod attachment
7 Like a cam
8 Prolong
9 Spread, as news
10 Handle with care
11 Mrs. Andy Gump
12 They're bound to happen
13 Sports section feature
14 "Three Precious Words" singers
18 Without a commitment
23 Railroad flare
24 Pulitzer category
26 Leanings
27 Big Red Machine member
29 Flat-bottomed boats
31 Street show
33 Alaska Range peak
35 Try
36 Crescent-shaped
38 Leafy
39 Stretches
40 Low points
42 "Fuggedaboutit!"
45 Demonstration impetus
46 British hymn writer
48 Gazetteer stat.
49 Thompson of Pollock
51 '60s war zone
52 Energy

★★★★ Three or More

Enter the missing numbers from 1 to 9 into the diagram in such a way that all pairs of numbers connected by a line have a difference of three or more.

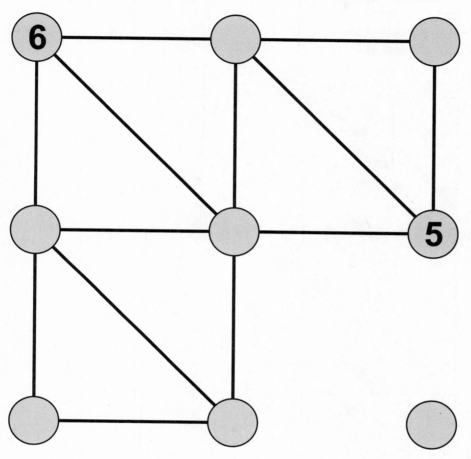

COMMON SENSE

What four-letter word can be found in the dictionary definitions of all of these words: TRICKLE, MINUET, LOITER and ERODE?

— — — —

★★★ Monkeys and Bananas

Enter the maze at left, passing through every chamber with monkeys and bananas exactly once, then exit the maze at the bottom. You must "pick up" the bananas as you reach them, and feed one banana to every monkey you visit. You must always have enough bananas to feed the monkeys as you visit them. Following the correct path, you will have one banana left over at the end for yourself.

Hint: The correct path moves horizontally and vertically only, and does not use any of the diagonal sections.

WORD SQUARE JIGSAW

Place the given pieces into the 4×4 blank diagram to form eight common words, four reading across and four reading down.

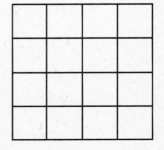

★★★★★ Themeless Toughie by Daniel R. Stark

ACROSS

1 Russian dressing ingredient
8 Like some fists
14 Beersheba native
15 Look forward to
16 Dental procedure
17 Not kosher
18 Fluid holder
19 Gallivant
21 Calculator key
22 Long tales
24 Quilt filler
26 Jane Fonda film role
27 Artist Lalique
28 Art medium
29 Not flighty
31 Like earthworms
34 Not flat
35 Facilitate
36 Ancient Greek coin
38 Signified
41 Café serving
46 Long overcoat
48 *Café* serving
49 Pasta partner, perhaps
50 No longer changeable
51 Become edible
53 *Hombre*'s address
54 Home of Irish kings
56 Bag
58 Guitarist Wood
59 Liquor ingredient
61 Overturn
63 Animal order
64 Blotter listing
65 Doesn't 15 Across
66 Least confused

DOWN

1 Mugs
2 The one that got away
3 Copy of a sort
4 Therm fract.
5 Whodunit suspects
6 Humerus neighbor
7 Colorful
8 Fracases
9 Apiece
10 Snacks in white paper
11 Sound
12 Give forth
13 Struck out
15 Undetermined, in some games
20 Human-powered vehicle
23 Unite
25 Move a fern
28 Election winners
30 Expand
32 What "-phage" means
33 Black Friar
37 Corn holder
38 Deli freebie
39 Henry II's wife
40 On a horse
42 Motorcycle hero
43 Early morning
44 Naps
45 Heartfelt
47 Holds firmly
52 Protects, in a way
53 Photo tint
55 Lost
57 Pelletier's skating partner
60 Loaf's heel
62 Posed

★★★ Split Decisions

In this clueless crossword puzzle, each answer consists of two words whose spellings are the same, except for the consecutive letters given. All answers are common words; no phrases or hyphenated or capitalized words are used. Some of the clues may have more than one solution, but there is only one word pair that will correctly link up with all the other word pairs.

WORD WIT

Combine and rearrange the 11 letters in the words GOPHER and SWINE to get the names of another two types of animals.

_____   _____

★★★★ Sudoku

Fill in the blank boxes so that every row, column, and 3×3 box contains all of the numbers 1 to 9.

		7			9		8	
			2				3	
	2	6						
4			7		1			3
	7		9		2			
		3	8			2		9
				5				
8						9		4
							6	

AND SO ON

Unscramble the letters in the phrase ENGLAND TEE SLIME, to form two words that are part of a common phrase that has the word *and* between them.

_____ and _____

★★★★★ Themeless Toughie by S.N.

ACROSS

1 Head creations
9 It's below D
15 Integrated
16 *Poltergeist* director
17 Mix over
18 *Trail to San* __ (Autry film)
19 Bors' uncle
20 City south of Fort Myers
21 Charms
23 Unitary principle
24 Taking pot luck, maybe
28 Shade of gray
31 Rushed
34 Takes over
36 Clapping candidates
37 Sweater protectors
39 Stuck
40 Hit
41 Bunyan's blacksmith
42 Current controls
50 Release people
53 Frank
54 Change at Moose Jaw
55 Chant
56 Couples
57 Pencil product
58 Sneak protector
59 Grammarian's bane

DOWN

1 His theme was "Sunrise Serenade"
2 City on the Allegheny
3 Approach
4 Onetime CBS owner
5 Andretti rival
6 Funds
7 Join the club
8 Pioneer, perhaps
9 *The House Without a Key* hero
10 Mozart selections
11 '70s fashion
12 "Sorry!"
13 Odo portrayer
14 MVB or JKP
22 Overindulges
25 Libel or slander
26 Hungarian name
27 Hotbed
28 101 concepts
29 Haggis ingredient
30 Type of ferry
31 Tricky business
32 Pap's boy
33 Last choice, often
35 Attack
38 I.B. Singer story
43 Sony competitor
44 Secret stuff
45 Took
46 Restorative
47 Sultan subject
48 They may be going
49 Dog of the comics
50 Speak up for
51 *Miss* __ (gossipy autobiography)
52 It won't hold water

★★★★ One-Way Streets

The diagram represents a pattern of streets. P's are parking spaces, and the black squares are stores. Find the route that starts at a parking space, passes through all stores exactly once, and ends at another parking space. Arrows indicate one-way traffic for that block only. No block or intersection may be entered more than once.

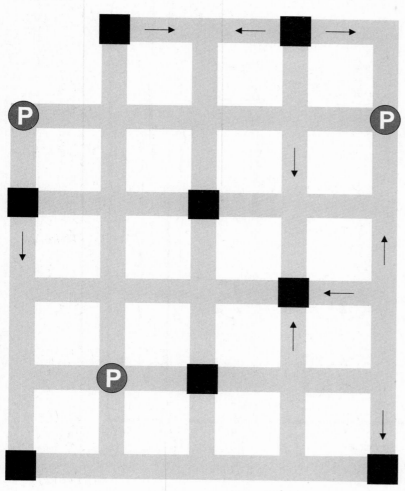

EQUATION CONSTRUCTION

Use the digits 4, 9, and 5 plus standard symbols and operations of arithmetic, to create a mathematical expression that equals the number 65. All the digits must be used.

★★ Line Drawings

Draw two straight lines, each from one edge of the square to another edge, so that there is the same amount of money in each of three regions.

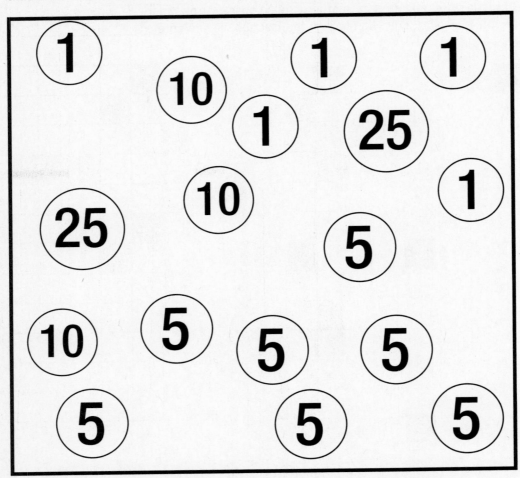

TRANSDELETION

Delete one letter from the word UNTRACEABLE and rearrange the rest, to get a type of building.

_____

★★★★★ Themeless Toughie by Daniel R. Stark

ACROSS

1 Like a wagon trail
7 Is conciliatory
15 Zip
16 Most intense
17 Like
18 Tenor's asset
19 Sharp flavor
21 One in the lead
22 Garlic juicer
23 Stein line ender
25 Dog days in Dijon
26 Attention
27 Wooden wedges
29 Balboa foe
31 Microbiology gel
33 Social connections
34 PDA entry
35 Formality
37 Jeered at
41 Master of the macabre
42 "Le Jazz ___" (Mancini song)
43 Audition tape
44 "Go ahead!"
47 Uses rattan
49 Bozo
50 Bandleader Weems
51 Carroll beast
53 Directs a hoedown
55 Grandson of Cronus
57 Pretty plant
59 Great fall
61 Natural
62 Gets rid (of)
63 Walked unsteadily
64 Broadcasts
65 Determine

DOWN

1 Come back
2 Minor
3 Poster paints
4 Game-show prizes
5 Way out
6 *The Power of Intention* author
7 Upholds
8 Saloon amenities
9 Trapper commodity
10 Pause fillers
11 *Easy* ___ (old-time radio show)
12 Parlor furnishing
13 Tycoon's digs
14 Packed away
20 "This is Mrs. Norman ___"
24 Brown shade
28 Queen's quarters
30 Watermelon part
32 Nonpayer's risk
34 Kismet
36 Deteriorates
37 Hasbro division
38 Revealing
39 Acts like
40 Wheelless vehicles
42 Bring under control
44 Groups of trees
45 Larger than life
46 Black Sea port
47 Jack-o'-lantern artist
48 Public tiffs
52 Sleep disturber
54 Boleyn and Baxter
56 Equinox mo.
58 Pulsar in Cetus
60 Half an umlaut

★★★ Block Maze

Start at the block with the skeleton's feet, visit all the block tops exactly once, then hop down one level to exit the structure. From any position, your next move must be to an adjacent block on the same level, or to an adjacent block one level higher or lower. No diagonal moves are permitted.

THREE OF A KIND

Find the three hidden words in the sentence that, read in order, go together in some way.

Who told the chairman that his unruly outburst surprises no one?

★★★★ Star Search

Find the stars that are hidden in some of the blank squares. The numbered squares indicate how many stars are hidden in the squares adjacent to them (including diagonally). There is never more than one star in any square.

1				3			
	2	5			1	2	
2				3			
		3		5		3	2
							1
2		3		2		5	1
						2	
	1		1		1	2	

MIXAGRAMS

Each line contains a five-letter word and a four-letter word that have been mixed together (the order of the letters in each word has not been changed). Unmix the two words on each line and write them in the spaces provided. When you're done, find a two-word answer to the clue by reading down the letter columns in the answers.

CLUE: Paddling place

B I D O W A E S L = _ _ _ _ _ + _ _ _ _

A L S H O A N H E = _ _ _ _ _ + _ _ _ _

F I L R O U N E Y = _ _ _ _ _ + _ _ _ _

W H O I D R E S D = _ _ _ _ _ + _ _ _ _

★★★★★ Themeless Toughie by Anna Stiga

ACROSS

1 Unexpected assistance
8 Credit cards
15 Gulf of Guayaquil locale
16 Ingrid married him
17 Expertise
18 Hold
19 Face or lace starter
20 Roasting
22 *King Rat* actor
23 Pulls in
24 Central points
26 Swoosie's sister in *Sisters*
27 Former Ugandan name
28 Sennett genre
30 Hubbub
31 Capital founded circa 1610
33 Late
35 Means of escape
36 Norm
37 *Whip Hand* author
41 Impression
45 Concord, for one
46 Part of a row
48 Diagnostic technique
49 Inventor's middle name
51 Blabbermouth
52 Posture
53 Grand __
55 *Hip-Hop Countdown* network
56 Fire starter
57 Sentence that uses every letter
59 Newtonian subject
61 Nested district
62 Least thorny
63 Heinz Field player
64 Fields

DOWN

1 Most with June birthdays
2 "__! Our home and native land!"
3 Place for Rugby rubbish
4 Fills up
5 *Jekyll & Hyde* star
6 Also not
7 Wildcatter's bane
8 Fake it
9 Colleague of Boris and Bela
10 Basics
11 Hingis rival
12 Kind of play
13 Emphatic denial
14 *A Lincoln Portrait* writer
21 Metric homage
24 Swell stuff
25 Plan part
28 Not very impolite
29 Neologisms
32 Passel
34 Pendulum path
37 Cool treats
38 Trusting
39 Make headway
40 Less likely
41 They're not uniforms
42 Transistor part
43 Fixed
44 Soldier's toppers
47 Accept, with "in"
50 Devious purpose
52 One of the Dionne quints
54 __ history
56 Netting
58 Galba's greeting
60 Downy coating

★★★★ Islands

Shade in some of the white squares in the diagram with "water," so that each remaining white box is part of an island. Each island will contain exactly one numbered square, indicating how many squares that island contains. Each island is separated from the other islands by water but may touch other islands diagonally. All water is connected, but there are no 2×2 regions of water in the diagram.

				3					
	2						2		
3									2
			5		5				
		6							
	2								3
							4		
		1					4		

INITIAL REACTION

The "equation" below contains the initials of words that will make it correct, forming a numerical fact. Solve the equation by supplying the missing words.

9 = S.W. by L.V.B. _____

★★★ Anagram Crossword

To solve this unique crossword variety:

1. Fill in the answers to each of the six crossword clues in the spaces provided. Each answer is a common five-letter word. The clues are listed in random order.

2. Next, find a common word that is an anagram of each answer.

3. Then, arrange the six anagrammed words into the diagram. Note that some of the answer words have more than one common anagram, so your list of words may not fit on the first try.

4. One letter is filled in the diagram to help get you started.

CLUE	CLUE ANSWER	ANAGRAM OF ANSWER
Acting parts		
Big		
Heavenly being		
Smiles		
Strict		
Fork prongs		

★★★★★ Themeless Toughie by Daniel R. Stark

ACROSS

1 Literally, "divine favor"
9 Proof list
15 Logical link
16 Award for cartoonists
17 Small orbiter
18 Alabama school
19 "__ Thine That Special Face"
20 Plod along
22 *Like Water for Chocolate* character
23 Reference-book unit
25 Memsahibs' nannies
27 Ring toss, perhaps
28 Rodeo gear
30 Festive night
31 California county
32 Cassette tape portion
34 News item
35 Hid in the weeds
39 Ron Howard's production company
41 Fabio's pride
42 Chili bean
44 Mishmash
45 Help-wanted abbr.
46 Soap, for example
51 Crass one
52 Sign of annoyance
54 Diploma word
55 Chooser's option
57 Eleanor's mother-in-law
59 Side track
60 Was attentive
62 Tattler
64 Luxury wrap
65 Necessitated
66 Cloudy and damp
67 Not at all continuous

DOWN

1 Embroidery yarn
2 Western capital
3 Some radio announcements
4 Some bicycles
5 Morticia's cousin
6 Letter leadoff
7 Shekels
8 Sore
9 Time piece
10 Enlists again
11 Kadiddlehopper persona

12 Mideast capital
13 Maryland athlete
14 Explain, in a way
21 Relented
24 White's opposite
26 Mythical herald
29 Harry Potter's quidditch position
31 Wooden block
33 Farewells
35 Used a plane
36 African desert
37 Similar outfits
38 Guitarmaker Fender

40 Votes for
43 Chips in
47 Kadiddlehopper persona
48 African antelope
49 Charm
50 Rio Grande city
52 Jeff Goldblum ex
53 16th-century council city
56 Look at quickly
58 Opposite of *baja*
61 Computer key
63 Milk, in prescriptions

★★ Triad Split Decisions

In this clueless crossword puzzle, each answer consists of two words whose spellings are the same, except for the consecutive letters given. All answers are common words; no phrases or hyphenated or capitalized words are used. Some of the clues may have more than one solution, but there is only one word pair that will correctly link up with all the other word pairs.

EQUATION CONSTRUCTION

Use the digits 4, 9, and 5 plus standard symbols and operations of arithmetic, to create a mathematical expression that equals the number 5. All the digits must be used.

| | = | 5 |

★★★ Twilight Maze

Find a path that enters the maze, passes through the chambers containing the sun and the moon, and then exits the maze, all without retracing your path. Note that there are only two openings to each of the two chambers (one to enter and the other to exit), so start by drawing the portions of the path that must lead in and out of the chambers.

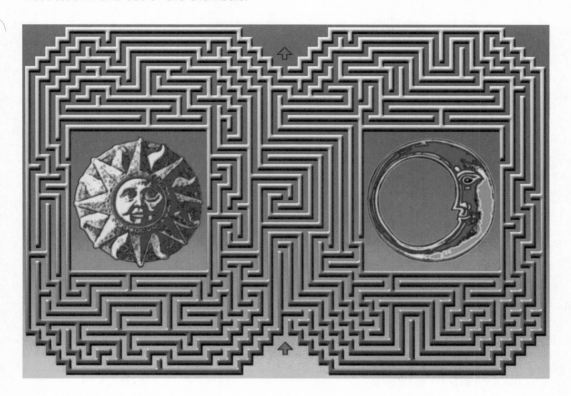

CLUELESS CROSSWORD

Complete the crossword with common uncapitalized seven-letter words, based entirely on the letters already filled in for you.

★★★★★ Themeless Toughie by S.N.

ACROSS

1 Mensch
9 Expression
15 Lemmon/Matthau film
16 Asian peninsula
17 Pool place
18 Knocks down
19 Hitchcockian quality
20 Not so 14 Down
21 Schooner contents
22 Paul Pry
24 *Will Rogers Follies* prop
27 Shift neighbor
28 Health agency
31 Performer
33 Chico, in *Animal Crackers*
36 Exploit
37 18th-century Russian ruler
38 "Suit of lights" wearers
39 Condition
40 Fleece source
41 Conservative
43 Fulfills
44 Star at Sarajevo
46 Needle producer
47 The Hermit and Temperance
50 Still
55 Mythical lyrist
56 Work underground
57 Polite declination
58 Faithful followers
59 Thin
60 *The Way of Perfection* writer

DOWN

1 Important components
2 Elaborate feast
3 Sources of funds
4 Quit
5 Ungracious type
6 Jointly
7 Board bigwigs
8 Least lively
9 Batman portrayer
10 Pax's equivalent
11 Bask in
12 Foster
13 Fancy layer
14 Tractable
23 One at Exeter
24 Foamy drink
25 Pointer
26 It may be blank
27 Expurgate
28 First two-time Nobelist
29 Thomas Jefferson, e.g.
30 Agency awards
32 Delicious
34 Post-WWII period
35 Emphatic denial
42 Turns back
44 Grinding
45 Moon of Saturn
46 Aspect
47 Turns brown
48 Per
49 Via Veneto locale
51 Go
52 Note
53 2001 Las Vegas Bowl champs
54 *Cabin in the Sky* name

PAGE 15

By the Book

M	A	N	O	R		R	E	U	P		G	R	I	T
I	N	A	W	E		A	L	S	O		R	A	S	H
L	I	F	E	J	A	C	K	E	T		O	S	L	O
E	S	T		O	G	E	E		P	A	U	P	E	R
S	E	A	B	I	R	D		S	I	G	N			
		O	N	E		Y	I	E	L	D	S	T	O	
	S	I	X		E	D	A	M		O	C	C	U	R
A	P	R	I	L		R	H	O		W	O	O	E	R
S	C	O	N	E		O	O	N	A		V	W	S	
K	A	N	G	A	R	O	O		B	E	E			
			T	R	A	P		B	O	A	R	D	E	R
B	I	K	I	N	I		I	O	U	S		R	A	E
E	D	I	T		S	E	N	A	T	E	P	A	G	E
T	E	L	L		I	R	K	S		L	O	P	E	D
S	A	N	E		N	E	S	T		S	E	E	R	S

PAGE 16

Scram

B	A	R	S		A	T	L	A	S		H	O	A	R
A	L	U	M		S	H	A	R	P		U	R	S	A
N	I	N	E		T	E	T	R	A		N	E	A	R
G	E	T	A	W	A	Y	C	A	R		G	O	N	E
S	N	O	R	E			H	Y	E	N	A			
			B	A	N			S	O	R	E	S	T	
F	A	C	E		L	E	A	D		M	I	N	E	O
L	E	A	V	E	I	T	T	O	B	E	A	V	E	R
E	R	R	O	R		S	E	L	L		N	Y	N	Y
D	O	L	L	A	R			E	T	A				
	U	S	U	R	P			I	T	E	M	S		
S	W	A	T		S	H	O	O	F	L	Y	P	I	E
T	A	X	I		H	O	R	N	E		P	O	L	E
O	S	L	O		E	D	G	E	R		E	X	A	M
W	H	E	N		D	A	Y	A	N		S	Y	N	S

PAGE 17

Fill 'Er Up

I	N	C	H		A	S	P	S		A	B	H	O	R
B	E	L	A		P	U	R	E		S	L	I	D	E
M	A	U	I		P	R	O	M		H	A	V	O	C
	R	E	L	I	E	F	P	I	T	C	H	E	R	
		S	R	A	S			H	A	S				
R	E	N	T	A	L		S	K	I	N		C	P	A
O	R	I	O	N		R	A	I	N		S	H	O	E
M	A	G	N	I	F	Y	I	N	G	G	L	A	S	S
A	S	H	E		R	A	N	G		L	A	S	S	O
N	E	T		S	E	N	T		B	O	P	E	E	P
			C	U	E			S	E	A	S			
	M	A	A	N	D	P	A	K	E	T	T	L	E	
P	U	R	R	S		O	M	I	T		I	O	T	A
A	S	I	D	E		S	E	L	L		C	R	O	C
L	E	A	S	T		E	R	L	E		K	E	N	T

PAGE 18

Tea Time

EQUATION CONSTRUCTION

$5/8 \times 24 = 15$

PAGE 19

A Puzzle

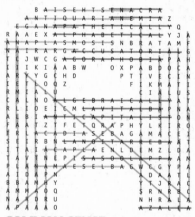

COMMON SENSE

HAIR

PAGE 20

Sudoku

9	3	7	8	1	6	5	4	2
4	6	5	9	2	7	3	8	1
8	2	1	3	4	5	9	6	7
1	7	8	5	9	3	6	2	4
3	4	2	6	8	1	7	9	5
6	5	9	4	7	2	8	1	3
7	9	4	2	5	8	1	3	6
5	8	3	1	6	4	2	7	9
2	1	6	7	3	9	4	5	8

MIXAGRAMS

SHORE LIFT
HUMOR TAIL
OCTET RANG
OKAYS MENU

PAGE 21

About Time

R	A	C	E	D		C	L	A	N		D	Y	E	S
A	C	H	O	O		L	O	U	T		E	E	L	S
T	H	I	N	G	S	O	F	T	H	E	P	A	S	T
S	E	C		P	L	U	T	O		G	O	R	E	S
			M	A	I	D		G	N	A	T			
A	B	B	O	T	T		B	R	E	D		A	M	P
B	R	O	N	C		C	R	A	B		A	L	O	E
B	I	R	T	H	D	A	Y	P	R	E	S	E	N	T
E	D	I	E		I	T	C	H		A	C	U	T	E
Y	E	S		D	O	S	E		B	R	O	T	H	S
			T	O	N	I		D	E	P	T			
A	R	S	O	N		T	O	W	E	L		P	O	W
B	A	C	K	T	O	T	H	E	F	U	T	U	R	E
B	R	A	Y		N	E	I	L		G	A	Z	E	S
R	E	N	O		T	R	O	T		S	N	O	O	T

PAGE 22

Circular Reasoning

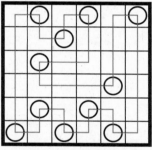

WORD SQUARE JIGSAW

O	U	T	S
D	R	O	P
O	G	R	E
R	E	E	D

PAGE 23

Line Drawings

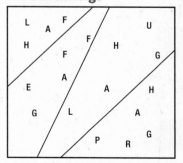

INITIAL REACTION

50 = STARS ON THE AMERICAN FLAG

PAGE 24

Z Puzzle

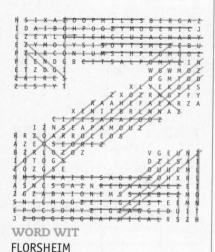

WORD WIT

FLORSHEIM

PAGE 25

In the Cards

B	E	A	M		A	M	E	S		T	S	A	R	S
U	R	S	A		T	Y	R	O		E	A	T	U	P
T	R	O	J	A	N	W	A	R		A	F	T	E	R
T	O	N		N	O	O	S	E		C	A	N	D	Y
E	L	E	A	N	O	R			O	A	R			
		L	O	N	D	O	N	B	R	I	D	G	E	
C	A	T	S			H	O	O	T		A	M	A	
O	R	E	O		B	R	A	V	E		A	L	A	S
A	L	E		S	O	A	R				S	E	N	T
L	O	N	E	L	Y	H	E	A	R	T	S			
			S	I	S		R	A	I	N	B	O	W	
R	E	A	C	T		S	P	E	N	T		U	N	I
A	L	L	A	H		C	O	T	T	O	N	G	I	N
S	L	O	P	E		A	S	H	E		A	L	O	E
P	E	T	E	R		R	E	A	D		P	E	N	S

PAGE 26

Islands

AND SO ON

FAST and LOOSE

PAGE 27

Loose Change

EQUATION CONSTRUCTION

$(4 \times 5) - (8 \times 2) = 4$

PAGE 28

The i's Have It

B	O	L	O	S		M	O	S	T		A	G	R	A
A	L	O	N	E		A	L	T	O		I	R	O	N
R	E	S	I	N		A	D	A	M		M	O	A	T
D	O	T	C	O	M	M	E	R	C	E		U	S	E
			E	R	E		T	A	L	E	N	T	S	
A	B	E		A	T	O	M		T	O	L	D		
P	U	P	S		R	A	I	N		P	A	R	T	S
P	O	I	N	T	O	F	N	O	R	E	T	U	R	N
T	Y	P	E	R		S	O	L	O		E	L	I	A
	H	E	A	T		T	O	U	R		E	G	G	
S	W	A	R	M	E	D		N	E	W				
T	I	N		P	E	R	I	O	D	P	I	E	C	E
A	L	I	T		T	A	R	A		E	L	B	O	W
G	L	E	E		E	M	I	T		A	D	O	R	E
E	A	S	E		R	A	S	H		L	E	N	D	S

PAGE 29

One-Way Streets

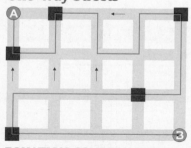

EQUATION CONSTRUCTION

$21 \div 3 = 7$

PAGE 30

Split Decisions

WORD WIT

TENOR (TENNER)

PAGE 31

Star Search

MIXAGRAMS

ADMIT SLUE
THEME IONS
INANE MAUL
BUTTE AFAR

PAGE 32

Smooth Sailing

TELEPHONE TRIOS

HUNDRED, SEVENTY, MILLION

PAGE 33

Cruising

S	T	R	I	P		C	L	O	C	K		S	A	D
O	H	A	R	A		P	E	R	O	N		U	S	E
W	A	V	E	G	O	O	D	B	Y	E		R	I	B
	T	E	N	E	T	S		S	E	E		F	A	T
			E	A	T		S	P	A	T				
O	A	F		N	E	T		S	T	A	S	H	E	D
U	N	O		T	R	U	S	T		D	E	E	R	E
S	T	A	B		S	N	O	O	T		A	W	O	L
T	I	M	E	R		I	N	L	A	W		E	D	T
S	C	R	E	A	M	S		E	R	E		B	E	A
		U	N	D	O				T	A	C			
J	A	B		I	D	A		S	A	L	A	M	I	
E	B	B		C	U	R	R	E	N	T	C	O	S	T
E	E	E		A	L	I	E	N		H	A	L	L	E
P	E	R		L	E	A	D	S		Y	O	D	E	L

PAGE 34

Hyper-Sudoku

1	4	5	9	3	6	7	2	8
9	2	7	5	8	4	1	3	6
3	8	6	1	7	2	9	5	4
5	9	3	4	2	7	8	6	1
2	6	1	8	5	9	3	4	7
8	7	4	6	1	3	2	9	5
7	1	9	3	6	5	4	8	2
4	5	8	2	9	1	6	7	3
6	3	2	7	4	8	5	1	9

TRANSDELETION
SAN ANTONIO

PAGE 35

Loops

WORD WIT
FORTY

PAGE 36

Kakuro

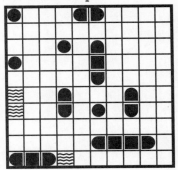

THREE OF A KIND
THE <u>TICKETS</u> WERE
A<u>T A CONCERT</u>O EVENT.

PAGE 37

Happy Day

G	N	A	S	H		B	A	R		E	G	R	E	T
R	O	M	E	O		E	T	A		E	L	A	T	E
A	S	P	E	N		A	L	I		R	A	I	T	T
D	E	L	I	G	H	T	E	D		I	D	L	E	S
E	D	E	N		A	L	A		R	E	D			
			L	I	E	S	T	O		E	T	O	N	
S	I	N	G	E	R		T	W	O		N	I	L	E
C	L	E	R	I	C	S		A	T	T	E	N	D	S
A	S	I	A		U	K	E		B	A	D	G	E	S
M	A	L	T		T	I	L	T	E	D				
		I	Q	S		E	E	E		H	E	R	A	
S	N	A	F	U		O	V	E	R	J	O	Y	E	D
L	O	U	I	E		R	A	P		A	N	I	T	A
I	N	T	E	R		A	T	E		D	E	N	I	M
M	O	O	D	Y		L	E	E		E	D	G	E	S

PAGE 38

ABC

B	A	C
C		A	B
A	B		C
	C	B	A

CLUELESS CROSSWORD

E	X	C	E	R	P	T
X		I		U		R
P	E	T	U	N	I	A
O		A		N		C
R	E	D	D	I	S	H
T		E		E		E
S	O	L	A	R	I	A

PAGE 39

Find the Ships

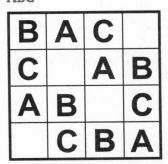

WORD WIT
IVORY COAST

PAGE 40

Buried Treasure

```
X R C H J H G I L U Z A L S I P A L T O
E I A W O O X R P Z C W L M Y K V L U G
L G M Q A H T O P A Z B K I D K S O R Y
F Y E Q B K W V F X H T J A J M A V Q B
U Y T A X V O V G F I Y S Q Z B P M U U
V X Y A U G G Z C D L A R E M E H E I E
W Y S Z X K F C P G Z A L G N L I E S E
P P T U I Z O E E N X T P R Z Q W B A J
S O P X C M M I A R Q I S J U Y E W B I
H I B E V N I P L W O J M Z E U F X R J
S A U N G B F J J D E C D U P K U L Q P
Z M L O N D F G A R N E T W S G W M M Q
P O G T K X S U V G V Y Y A S A D U T E H
F N F S Y U M N D A C V L I J Z S F E O
E D I N Q F Z X H Y L N A M B E R O B K
Q A Q O K E U J U V X T G R C S D M A
C D F Q Y T K T K K A E T R G A V N B I
J K W M L O Y X G C O N C A L E Z X X F
```

IN OTHER WORDS
NEIGHBOR

PAGE 41

Anthem Phrases

C	A	N	T		S	T	E	E	P		W	O	L	F
O	L	E	O		H	O	T	E	L		A	L	A	I
D	A	W	N	S	E	A	R	L	Y	L	I	G	H	T
A	S	S		C	A	S	E		M	O	L	A	R	S
			D	A	R	T		B	O	O	S			
A	C	T	O	R	S		T	A	U	T		V	C	R
P	H	O	N	E		C	O	S	T		S	A	R	I
P	R	O	U	D	L	Y	W	E	H	A	I	L	E	D
L	I	N	T		A	C	E	S		I	N	U	S	E
E	S	S		F	U	L	L		G	R	E	E	T	S
			C	A	G	E		C	U	B	S			
B	L	E	A	C	H		A	R	I	A		P	A	N
R	O	C	K	E	T	S	R	E	D	G	L	A	R	E
A	C	H	E		E	L	A	T	E		A	L	E	X
T	K	O	S		R	O	B	E	S		B	E	A	T

PAGE 42

Cash Drops

WORD WIT
YACHT (CATHY)

PAGE 43

Circular Reasoning

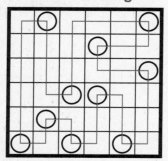

EQUATION CONSTRUCTION
58−42=16

PAGE 44

Three or More

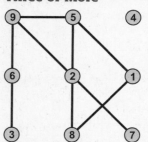

CITY SEARCH
ACROSS, CANCAN, CASINO,
CRANIA, FARINA, FIASCO, FRACAS,
SAFARI

PAGE 45

Cupfuls

T	O	D	O		B	I	D	E		R	E	C	A	P
A	L	I	T		A	S	I	A		E	R	O	D	E
L	I	S	T		U	S	E	S		W	A	F	E	R
C	O	C	O	A	B	U	T	T	E	R		F	E	M
		M	U	L	E	S		V	O	T	E	R	S	
P	E	T	A	L	E	D		R	E	T	I	E		
U	P	E	N	D	S		C	A	R	E	S	S	E	D
S	E	A			A	S	H			H	A	Y		
H	E	S	I	T	A	N	T		O	P	P	O	S	E
	E	V	E	R	T		D	R	O	O	P	E	D	
C	E	R	E	A	L		S	A	B	R	A			
L	X	V		S	O	U	P	K	I	T	C	H	E	N
O	P	I	N	E		S	O	O	T		H	I	L	O
D	E	C	O	R		M	I	T	E		E	R	L	E
S	L	E	D	S		C	L	A	D		D	E	A	L

PAGE 46

Split Decisions

EQUATION CONSTRUCTION
42+85=127

PAGE 47

Kakuro

	1	2	3				1	3	2
3	1	4	2			2	5	4	1
		5	1	2	4	3			
		4	2	3	1		4	1	5
3	1						3	9	
9	2	5		9	8	1	2		
		1	2	5	4	3			
3	4	2	1		9	6	5	7	
1	2	3				2	1	9	

AND SO ON
SONG and DANCE

PAGE 48

Oops!

S	W	A	P		S	P	E	C	K		O	W	E	D
A	R	C	H		L	I	T	H	E		N	I	L	E
P	O	T	A	T	O	C	H	I	P		A	S	S	N
S	N	O	R	E		K	I	L	T		D	E	E	S
	G	R	A	S	S		C	L	I	N	I	C		
			O	T	T	O		S	N	E	E	R	A	T
P	O	S	H		A	D	O			S	T	A	L	E
A	K	A		C	R	E	W	C	U	T		C	A	N
T	R	I	A	L		N	O	T		S	K	I	T	
H	A	N	G	A	R	S		W	A	G	E			
		T	I	D	I	E	D		H	A	V	O	C	
F	O	N	T		A	Q	U	A		R	E	P	O	T
A	R	I	A		L	U	N	C	H	B	R	E	A	K
T	A	C	T		T	I	E	R	S		A	R	L	O
E	L	K	E		O	N	S	E	T		L	A	S	S

PAGE 49

One-Way Streets

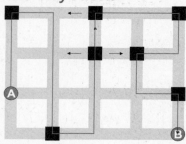

MIXAGRAMS
MANIA BURN
OTHER RUST
PRISM ANTE
READY TOIL

PAGE 50

Mixed Nuts

COMMON SENSE
NUT

PAGE 51

Star Search

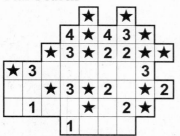

TELEPHONE TRIOS
BICYCLE, SCOOTER, TROLLEY

PAGE 52

Summer Is Here

A	L	A	N		S	H	E	L	F		R	O	S	E

(crossword grid)

A	L	A	N		S	H	E	L	F		R	O	S	E
R	O	M	E		P	A	T	I	O		E	R	A	S
C	O	M	B		A	L	T	A	R		A	S	I	S
S	T	O	R	E	C	L	E	R	K		G	O	N	E
		A	G	E	S				P	A	N	T	S
L	A	S	S	O	S		A	T	E	I	N	
A	M	O	K		S	T	E	A	L		S	I	P
S	O	L	A	R	C	A	L	C	U	L	A	T	O	R
T	S	E		A	L	L	A	H		P	A	T	E
	F	I	X	E	S		C	A	T	N	A	P
T	A	L	O	N		T	O	N	I	
O	M	A	R		A	C	C	O	U	N	T	A	N	T
N	O	T	E		C	H	U	M	P		U	T	A	H
I	R	I	S		R	E	B	E	L		D	O	M	E
C	E	N	T		E	R	A	S	E		E	P	E	E

PAGE 53

Grin and Wear It

WORD WIT
ILLINOIS (LAND OF LINCOLN)

PAGE 55

Line Drawings

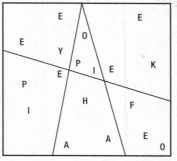

EQUATION CONSTRUCTION
$14 \times 5 = 7 \times 10$

PAGE 56

ABC

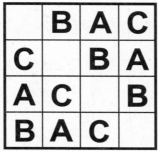

WORD WIT
OF

PAGE 57

Keeping Afloat

G	I	J	O	E		B	I	B	S		I	S	I	T
A	R	U	B	A		E	T	A	L		M	A	N	E
M	I	N	I	S		E	C	R	U		A	M	P	S
A	S	K		I	N	T	H	E	D	U	G	O	U	T
		B	O	N	E	S			G	R	E	A	T	S
S	P	O	N	G	E		P	I	E	S	
L	I	N	T		D	E	A	R		A	S	H	E	N
U	N	D	O		S	A	G	A	S		P	E	T	E
G	A	S	P	S		R	E	N	E		O	A	R	S
		A	S	P	S		E	R	O	D	E	S
A	C	C	E	N	T		S	T	I	L	L	
G	A	L	L	E	Y	P	R	O	O	F		I	S	A
A	B	A	T		R	E	I	N		L	O	N	E	R
T	A	R	O		O	R	C	A		E	R	E	C	T
E	L	A	N		N	E	A	R		S	O	R	T	S

PAGE 58

Sets of Three

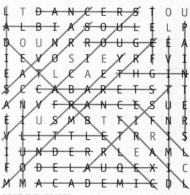

WORD WIT
DEEDED

PAGE 59

Mystery Guest
THE ARTIST TOULOUSE-LAUTREC.

WORD WIT
UNITED ARAB EMIRATES

PAGE 60

Find the Ships

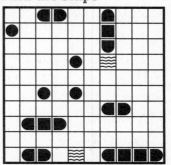

TRANSDELETION
CHARTREUSE

PAGE 61

Sudoku

9	4	6	8	1	2	7	3	5
7	5	1	6	3	9	4	8	2
8	2	3	7	4	5	1	6	9
3	9	4	2	7	6	5	1	8
2	1	8	9	5	3	6	7	4
5	6	7	1	8	4	2	9	3
1	7	5	3	2	8	9	4	6
4	8	9	5	6	7	3	2	1
6	3	2	4	9	1	8	5	7

MIXAGRAMS

SALAD CHEF
CHEST LURE
AFFIX TRUE
DATES ROUT

PAGE 62

Hit for the Cycle

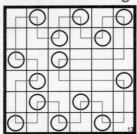

PAGE 63

Circular Reasoning

WORD SQUARE JIGSAW

C	A	T	S
A	R	E	A
R	I	N	K
E	A	S	E

PAGE 64

Triad Split Decisions

EQUATION CONSTRUCTION

25−7=18

PAGE 65

Kakuro

WORD WIT

SONY and SANYO

PAGE 66

The Green Stuff

PAGE 67

Islands

TRANSDELETION

VIN ROUGE

PAGE 68

Tire Maze

INITIAL REACTION

39 = BOOKS OF THE OLD
TESTAMENT

PAGE 69

Three or More

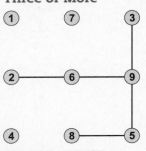

COMMON SENSE

CELLS

PAGE 70

Easy Going

I	D	T	A	G		U	M	P	S		E	D	E	N
N	E	R	V	E		P	E	A	L		A	R	C	O
F	L	O	A	T	P	L	A	N	E		T	I	R	E
E	T	O		R	O	A	N		E	Y	E	F	U	L
R	A	P	P	E	R	S		S	P	E	N	T		
		O	A	K	T	R	E	E	S			W	W	I
A	W	F	U	L		H	A	R	M		O	A	T	
W	A	L	T		P	O	E	T	S		F	O	N	T
A	D	O		L	O	U	T			B	U	D	D	Y
Y	E	W		S	P	I	T	F	I	R	E			
		C	L	A	S	S		I	S	O	L	A	T	E
T	A	H	I	T	I		M	E	N	U		W	O	N
I	R	A	N		C	O	A	S	T	G	U	A	R	D
N	E	R	D		L	I	S	T		H	A	R	T	E
T	A	T	A		E	L	S	A		T	W	E	E	D

PAGE 71

One-Way Streets

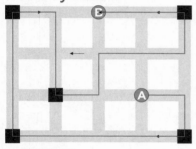

WORD WIT
BEGINS

PAGE 72

Hyper-Sudoku

7	4	8	3	1	6	2	9	5
5	2	3	4	7	9	1	8	6
1	9	6	5	8	2	7	3	4
9	7	1	8	3	4	5	6	2
3	6	5	9	2	7	4	1	8
2	8	4	6	5	1	9	7	3
6	5	9	1	4	3	8	2	7
8	3	2	7	9	5	6	4	1
4	1	7	2	6	8	3	5	9

TELEPHONE TRIOS
CYPRESS, DOGWOOD, HEMLOCK

PAGE 73

Star Search

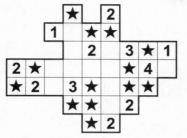

EQUATION CONSTRUCTION
$(5 \times 7) - 2 = 33$

PAGE 74

Comparatively Speaking

Z	E	B	R	A		T	O	A	D	S		C	O	B
A	G	L	E	T		A	P	R	O	N		A	R	E
G	O	O	D	T	I	M	E	C	H	A	R	L	I	E
	C	O	N	F	E	R			P	I	L	O	T	
A	S	K		I	R	A	N	I		B	E	L	L	
P	E	A	R	L		A	D	E		D	E	E		
O	R	D	A	I	N		E	V	A	D	E			
	B	E	T	T	E	R	B	E	H	A	V	E	D	
	S	H	R	U	B		O	M	E	L	E	T		
S	M	L		E	D	S		S	N	E	E	R		
T	A	O	S		S	H	A	R	I		P	R	Y	
A	T	S	E	A		R	A	D	I	S	H			
B	E	S	T	F	O	O	T	F	O	R	W	A	R	D
L	Y	E		A	U	D	I	T		M	A	N	O	R
E	S	S		R	I	D	E	S		A	N	T	E	S

PAGE 75

ABC

C		B	A
	B	A	C
A	C		B
B	A	C	

AND SO ON
TRACK and FIELD

PAGE 76

Bookworm

FIVE INCHES
WORD WIT
INGRID (RIDING)

PAGE 77

Sudoku

1	8	9	5	6	7	3	4	2
5	6	2	3	1	4	7	8	9
4	3	7	9	2	8	5	6	1
3	9	8	1	7	5	6	2	4
2	4	1	8	3	6	9	7	5
6	7	5	2	4	9	8	1	3
9	2	6	4	8	3	1	5	7
7	5	4	6	9	1	2	3	8
8	1	3	7	5	2	4	9	6

MIXAGRAMS
SCANT RIDE
TIDAL BLUE
OTTER LIMO
LYRIC DUPE

PAGE 78

Thoroughfares

	S	W	I	S	H		F	T	C		R	O	O	M
G	O	A	T	E	E		O	R	A	T	I	O	N	S
A	R	R	E	A	R		R	I	C	O	C	H	E	T
P	R	I	M	R	O	S	E	P	A	T	H			
E	E	L	S			H	I	L	O			A	H	A
S	L	Y		I	M	A	G	E		D	O	L	E	D
			D	O	W	N	T	H	E	R	O	A	D	
P	E	A	R	L	S				E	I	D	E	R	S
O	N	T	H	E	S	T	R	E	E	T				
L	I	M	O	S		R	E	D	D	Y		A	S	H
E	D	S		S	I	T	E			A	S	I	A	
	B	O	W	L	I	N	G	A	L	L	E	Y		
I	N	F	E	R	I	O	R		O	U	T	A	G	E
S	C	A	V	E	N	G	E		S	T	O	N	E	S
R	O	S	Y		E	Y	E		H	O	S	T	S	

PAGE 79

Line Drawings

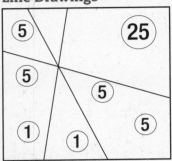

EQUATION CONSTRUCTION
$8 \times 2 - 15 = 1$

PAGE 80

Find the Ships

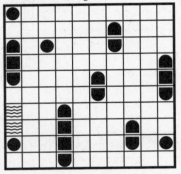

CLUELESS CROSSWORD

Q	U	I	Z	Z	E	S
U		M		O		T
I	M	P	R	O	V	E
B		R		M		R
B	E	E	H	I	V	E
L		S		N		O
E	N	S	I	G	N	S

PAGE 81

Circular Reasoning

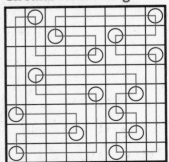

WORD WIT
BRENDA LEE

PAGE 82

Continental Breakfast

PAGE 83

Four-Letter Word Routes

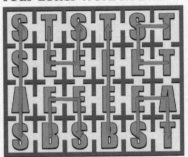

CITY SEARCH
BRIGHT, HUBRIS, PURIST, THIRST, THRUST

PAGE 84

Kakuro

3	9		7	9	8		2	1
2	8		1	7	5		5	3
1	5			3	1	4	2
	3	4	1	2		3	1
	5	3	1	2	4		
	7	9		3	6	2	1
5	6	8	9			6	2
4	8		5	1	7		2	4
7	9		8	6	9		3	1

TRANSDELETION
GILA MONSTER

PAGE 85

Islands

Grid puzzle with numbered cells: 3, 1, 1, 3, 3, 3, 1, 1

WORD WIT
BAHAMAS

PAGE 86

Social Settings

M	A	R	E	S		C	A	N	O	E		I	N	S
O	B	E	Y	S		A	R	E	N	A		S	I	T
C	E	M	E	N	T	M	I	X	E	R		L	E	E
S	T	E	W		R	E	S	T	S		F	A	C	E
	S	T	A	T	U	R	E		L	I	O	N	E	L
		S	E	E	A		T	I	R	E	D			
M	O	C	H	A		N	I	C	E		H	A	M	
E	A	U		C	H	A	N	N	E	L		O	W	E
G	R	R		A	I	D	E		A	S	P	E	N	
		V	E	R	G	E		B	O	N	A			
S	L	E	U	T	H		G	R	A	D	U	A	L	
N	E	B	R		S	T	O	A	T		S	U	E	S
A	V	A		S	E	A	R	C	H	P	A	R	T	Y
G	I	L		R	A	N	G	E		A	G	A	I	N
S	N	L		A	S	K	E	D		N	E	S	T	S

PAGE 87

Apple Tree Maze

EQUATION CONSTRUCTION
$52 - 7 = 45$

PAGE 88

Split Decisions

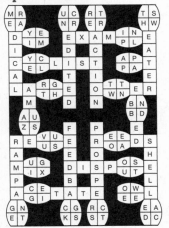

COMMON SENSE
PLOT

PAGE 89

Hyper-Sudoku

1	3	7	5	4	9	6	8	2
8	2	5	7	1	6	9	4	3
4	6	9	3	2	8	1	5	7
5	1	4	8	9	7	2	3	6
9	8	6	2	3	1	4	7	5
2	7	3	6	5	4	8	9	1
3	4	8	1	7	2	5	6	9
6	5	2	9	8	3	7	1	4
7	9	1	4	6	5	3	2	8

MIXAGRAMS
ACORN WHIP
CAMEO HORN
ALARM SMOG
CRAZE NEON

PAGE 90

Going Solo

PAGE 91

Three or More

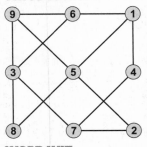

WORD WIT
LESLIE NIELSEN

PAGE 93

One-Way Streets

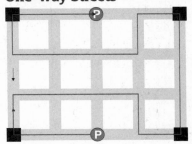

TRANSDELETION
NAVIGATION

PAGE 94

Be Calm

P	A	R	T		A	M	I	S	H		Y	A	M	S
E	S	A	I		R	O	D	E	O		E	T	A	T
S	I	M	M	E	R	D	O	W	N		R	A	R	E
T	A	P	E	R		E	L	S	E		T	R	I	M
		W	A	I	L			A	L	I	A	S		
A	S	T	A		N	A	S	T	A	S	E			
S	T	E	R	N	S		C	A	P	P		I	R	K
K	E	E	P	Y	O	U	R	S	H	I	R	T	O	N
S	R	S		E	L	S	A		I	C	I	C	L	E
		S	T	E	E	P	E	D		P	H	E	W	
A	P	L	U	S			A	S	H	E				
M	E	I	N		A	L	O	T		A	N	N	U	L
I	N	N	S		T	A	K	E	I	T	E	A	S	Y
S	A	G	E		T	W	I	R	L		S	P	A	R
S	L	O	T		A	N	E	Y	E		S	A	F	E

PAGE 95

Labyrinth Walk

AT NO TIME WILL THE WALKERS PASS ON ADJACENT PATHS.

THREE OF A KIND
THE FOOD WAS B<u>LAND</u>, UNS<u>EA</u>SONED, AND BARELY F<u>AIR</u>.

PAGE 96

Star Search

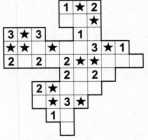

TELEPHONE TRIOS
CAPTAIN, COLONEL, PRIVATE

PAGE 97

Triad Split Decisions

EQUATION CONSTRUCTION
$(7-2) \times 5 = 25$

PAGE 98
Burning Issues

E	L	L	S		P	R	O	P		T	A	M	E	R
M	O	O	T		R	E	B	O		I	T	A	L	O
I	B	A	R		E	V	E	N		B	E	T	S	Y
R	O	M	A	N	C	A	N	D	L	E		C	I	A
		P	O	O	R		S	A	T	C	H	E	L	
H	A	P		T	O	N	E		P	A	L	S		
E	P	I	C		K	I	N	G		N	A	T	A	L
R	E	L	A	X		S	T	Y		S	P	I	R	E
S	T	O	R	M		H	E	R	B		S	C	O	T
	T	E	A	M		R	O	L	E		K	O	S	
F	E	L	T	S	A	D		S	O	B	S			
A	R	I		C	O	R	N	C	O	B	P	I	P	E
M	A	G	N	A		D	O	O	M		U	S	E	D
E	T	H	E	R		R	O	P	E		D	A	N	G
D	O	T	E	D		E	K	E	D		S	Y	N	E

PAGE 101
Quiet on the Set

L	E	S	S		F	E	A	R		A	L	O	O	F
A	T	T	A		R	E	B	A		C	A	C	T	I
T	H	E	B	O	O	K	O	F	L	I	G	H	T	S
I	N	T	E	R	N		F	E	D		S	O	T	
N	O	S		S	T	O	G	I	E					
		M	O	I	R	A		S	A	L	A	D	S	
A	R	E	A		E	A	S	E		L	E	G	I	T
M	U	G	F	O	R	T	H	E	C	A	M	E	R	A
P	L	A	I	N		E	I	R	E		A	R	T	Y
S	E	D	A	T	E		N	I	L	L	Y			
			A	N	G	E	L	A		S	A	X		
U	R	I		F	R	I		M	I	S	U	S	E	
M	I	S	S	I	N	G	I	N	A	C	T	I	O	N
P	A	L	E	S		E	D	I	T		A	T	N	O
S	L	E	E	K		L	A	K	E		B	E	E	N

PAGE 104
Circular Reasoning

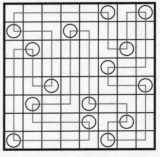

EQUATION CONSTRUCTION

$49 \div 7 = 7$

PAGE 99
ABC

A	C	B		
B		A	C	
C	B			A
A	C			B
	B	A	C	

IN OTHER WORDS

OFFHAND

PAGE 100
Find the Ships

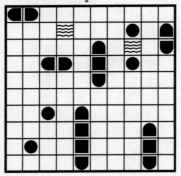

AND SO ON

FLESH and BLOOD

PAGE 102
Knife, Fork, Spoon

WORD WIT

U-HAUL and LUAU

PAGE 103
Sudoku

2	6	5	4	3	9	7	1	8
7	9	8	1	2	5	6	3	4
3	4	1	8	7	6	9	5	2
5	3	4	2	6	8	1	7	9
9	7	2	5	4	1	3	8	6
1	8	6	7	9	3	4	2	5
8	5	9	3	1	4	2	6	7
6	2	3	9	5	7	8	4	1
4	1	7	6	8	2	5	9	3

MIXAGRAMS

GHOST RARE
ROUSE ARMY
ANNEX FEUD
YOUTH DAIS

PAGE 105
Hookups

C	U	S	P	S		J	E	L	L	O		B	A	T
A	L	L	O	T		O	R	I	O	N		U	N	O
S	N	A	P	O	U	T	O	F	I	T		C	A	R
T	A	V	E	R	N		S	E	T		S	K	I	T
			D	E	R	R		R	E	P	U	L	S	E
G	O	T	O	S	E	E	D		R	A	R	E		
W	H	I	M		A	C	I	D		L	E	D	G	E
E	N	E		A	L	A	M	O	D	E		O	R	G
N	O	B	E	L		P	E	L	E		S	W	I	G
	R	A	I	D		D	E	S	C	E	N	T	S	
C	H	E	S	T	E	R		D	I	R	E			
H	E	A	T		V	I	A		L	E	N	D	M	E
I	N	K		Z	I	P	P	L	U	S	F	O	U	R
L	I	E		A	C	U	T	E		T	I	N	C	T
D	E	R		P	E	P	S	I		S	T	A	K	E

PAGE 106
Islands

COMMON SENSE

TIE

PAGE 107

Split Decisions

TRANSDELETION
SCREECH

PAGE 108

Hold It

S	P	A	S		V	A	L	I	D		O	P	A	L
H	O	R	N		A	B	A	S	E		Z	E	R	O
A	L	A	I		C	A	C	T	I		O	N	U	S
W	O	L	F	P	A	C	K		T	E	N	A	N	T
			T	A	N	K		P	I	X	E	L		
O	B	J	E	C	T		I	S	E	E		T	A	B
P	O	U	R	S		B	R	A	S	S		Y	M	A
T	O	S	S		A	I	L			T	B	A	R	
I	T	T		P	R	I	S	M		F	R	O	Z	E
C	H	I		L	A	T	H		C	O	A	X	E	D
	N	O	O	N	S		M	I	N	I				
A	S	C	O	T	S		B	U	N	D	L	E	U	P
U	T	A	H		O	R	A	T	E		E	T	R	E
R	U	S	E		M	O	D	E	M		R	O	S	E
A	B	E	D		S	O	U	S	A		S	N	A	P

PAGE 109

Three or More

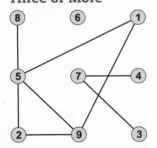

INITIAL REACTION
10 = AMENDMENTS IN THE BILL
OF RIGHTS

PAGE 110

Weather Maze

AND SO ON
ARTS and CRAFTS

PAGE 111

Governmental

D	I	R	T	Y		A	M	O	K		A	W	O	L
A	R	I	E	S		N	E	H	I		P	E	K	E
L	O	C	A	L	A	N	E	S	T	H	E	S	I	A
E	N	O	S		L	I	T		B	A	S	T	E	R
			E	L	B	E		T	A	S				
M	A	I	T	A	I		H	I	G	H	T	A	I	L
A	C	C		S	N	O	O	T			A	N	N	A
S	T	A	T	E	O	F	T	H	E	U	N	I	O	N
S	O	N	S			F	L	E	A	S		T	I	C
E	N	T	E	R	K	E	Y		R	E	G	A	L	E
			O	A	R		A	W	R	Y				
I	S	O	B	A	R		F	R	I		P	A	S	T
F	E	D	E	R	A	L	R	E	G	I	S	T	E	R
F	L	O	E		T	E	E	N		D	U	N	N	E
Y	A	R	N		S	T	E	T		S	M	O	T	E

PAGE 112

One-Way Streets

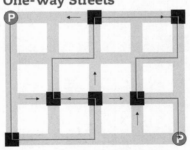

EQUATION CONSTRUCTION
$84-(9\times9)=3$

PAGE 113

Kakuro

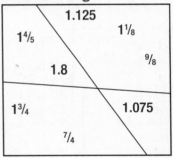

TELEPHONE TRIOS
ARSENIC, MERCURY, URANIUM

PAGE 114

Line Drawings

1.125

$1^4/_5$ $1^1/_8$

$9/_8$

1.8

$1^3/_4$ 1.075

$7/_4$

WORD WIT
TACO (COAT)

PAGE 115

Sticking Points

G	R	A	S	P	S		F	I	T	S		S	T	D
D	I	A	L	U	P		O	S	H	A		P	O	I
S	O	R	O	R	I	T	Y	P	I	N		A	C	S
			V	E	R	I	T	Y		T	A	C	O	S
P	A	P	E	R	E	R		S	A	V	E	M	E	
E	R	I	N		E	L	A	L		O	N	E	S	
R	I	C	E	R	S		E	L	A	I	N	E		
P	A	K		A	T	A	V	I	S	T		E	P	S
	L	E	G	U	M	E		H	O	L	D	I	T	
P	R	E	P		N	Y	E	T		I	L	K	A	
L	O	S	I	N	G			H	A	S	B	E	E	N
A	S	P	C	A		S	E	E	T	H	E			
T	I	E		B	R	O	K	E	N	A	R	R	O	W
T	E	A		O	B	O	E		O	R	I	O	L	E
E	R	R		B	I	N	S		S	E	A	T	E	D

PAGE 116
Star Search

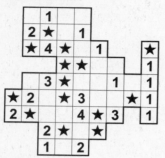

MIXAGRAMS

GROPE HAWK
IGLOO REIN
PEARL NINE
MONTH IDEA

PAGE 117
Twelve-Letter Word

EQUATION CONSTRUCTION
$(9 \times 4) \div (9 \times 8) = 1/2$

PAGE 118
Arctic Natives

E	T	A	L		E	L	I	S	E		A	G	R	A
M	I	M	I		S	A	D	A	T		S	U	E	S
S	E	A	L	I	T	W	I	T	H	A	K	I	S	S
	C	R	A	N	E			R	A	N		N	E	E
C	L	I	C	K		J	E	A	N	E		E	A	T
H	A	L		S	C	A	M	P		M	E	A	T	S
I	S	L	E		U	M	P		P	I	E			
	P	O	L	A	R	B	E	A	R	C	L	U	B	
		A	P	T		R	I	O		S	N	U	G	
S	C	E	N	E		W	O	R	D	S		I	C	I
H	A	Y		R	O	A	R	S		P	I	C	K	S
O	N	E		C	U	R		T	O	N	Y	S		
W	A	L	R	U	S	M	O	U	S	T	A	C	H	E
E	D	E	N		T	U	L	S	A		P	L	O	W
D	A	T	A		S	P	E	A	R		T	E	T	E

PAGE 119
Hyper-Sudoku

7	5	1	4	9	2	6	8	3
4	2	6	7	3	8	5	1	9
8	9	3	1	5	6	2	4	7
2	4	8	5	1	7	9	3	6
1	6	7	3	2	9	4	5	8
5	3	9	6	8	4	7	2	1
3	7	5	2	6	1	8	9	4
9	1	4	8	7	5	3	6	2
6	8	2	9	4	3	1	7	5

WORD SQUARE JIGSAW

S	H	O	T
P	O	U	R
A	L	T	O
T	E	S	T

PAGE 120
ABC

A	B	C		
C			B	A
B	A			C
	C	B	A	
		A	C	B

IN OTHER WORDS
BUCKWHEAT

PAGE 121
Hat Shop

B	U	G	S		P	S	S	T		C	A	B	I	N
O	H	I	O		A	C	H	E		O	H	A	R	A
S	U	L	U		T	R	I	M		W	A	G	E	D
C	H	A	R	T	T	O	P	P	E	R		I	N	E
			O	I	D			S	I	S	T	E	R	
O	F	L	A	T	E		B	E	S	E	T			
L	L	A	M	A		S	O	R	E		E	B	A	N
D	E	M	O	L	I	T	I	O	N	D	E	R	B	Y
S	A	B	E		N	E	S	S		A	L	I	E	N
		B	L	A	M	E		F	R	E	E	L	Y	
A	S	S	A	I	L		S	R	I					
V	I	A		B	L	A	S	T	I	N	G	C	A	P
I	N	T	E	R		P	I	E	D		R	O	M	E
A	G	I	T	A		E	Z	R	A		U	R	I	S
N	E	E	D	S		D	E	N	Y		B	E	S	T

PAGE 122
This Way

CITY SEARCH
MARGIN

PAGE 123
Find the Ships

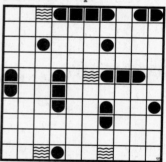

CLUELESS CROSSWORD

P	A	J	A	M	A	S
E		A		I		A
P	U	Z	Z	L	E	D
P		Z		I		D
E	P	I	S	T	L	E
R		E		I		N
S	U	R	P	A	S	S

PAGE 124

Triad Split Decisions

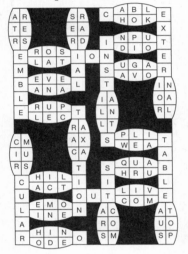

EQUATION CONSTRUCTION

$9 \times 11 + 8 = 107$

PAGE 125

Parting Words

S	H	A	F	T		P	A	C	T		P	O	M	P
N	O	V	A	E		R	I	L	E		E	R	I	E
O	P	E	R	A		O	D	O	R		L	E	N	A
B	I	S	E	C	T		A	U	R	E	V	O	I	R
			W	H	O	A		T	A	X	I			
T	A	M	E		A	R	P			T	S	A	R	S
A	B	E	L		T	O	I	L	E	R		W	A	Y
T	I	L	L	W	E	M	E	E	T	A	G	A	I	N
A	D	O		H	E	A	R	T	H		O	R	S	O
R	E	N	E	E		S	O	N		D	E	E	D	
			L	E	E	S		N	I	P	S			
T	O	O	D	L	E	O	O		C	O	P	P	E	R
R	A	T	E		R	U	I	N		S	E	A	L	Y
I	R	I	S		I	S	L	E		S	E	N	S	E
P	S	S	T		E	A	S	T		E	D	G	E	S

PAGE 126

Kakuro

WORD WIT

HOMER + UN

PAGE 127

Circular Reasoning

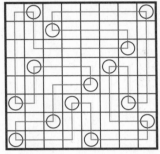

COMMON SENSE

INTEREST

PAGE 128

Money, Money, Money

G	A	R	B	O		C	A	F	E		C	A	M	E
A	L	O	U	D		O	V	A	L		E	N	O	S
S	C	O	N	E		V	I	L	E		D	I	N	E
S	O	F	T	S	H	E	L	L	C	L	A	M	S	
E	V	E		E	R	A			I	R	A	T	E	
R	E	D	C	O	A	T		D	A	D		T	E	L
		H	O	D		S	O	S		T	E	R	I	
	L	I	P	S	M	A	C	K	E	R	S			
A	R	O	N		E	A	T		A	V	A			
S	O	W		R	T	E		S	N	A	P	S	A	T
H	A	R	P	O		S	I	C		O	N	O		
	M	I	L	W	A	U	K	E	E	B	U	C	K	S
V	I	D	A		I	R	I	S		A	L	I	A	S
I	N	E	Z		D	I	R	T		S	N	A	R	E
A	G	R	A		E	S	T	A		S	A	L	A	D

PAGE 129

Celtic Knot Maze

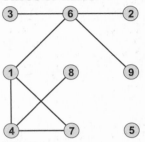

THREE OF A KIND

A POLICEMAN SCREAMED IN PANIC ON EVERY FALSE ALARM.

PAGE 131

Three or More

TRANSDELETION

SAUERBRATEN

PAGE 132

Hyper-Sudoku

7	2	5	9	3	1	6	8	4
6	9	4	8	7	5	2	1	3
8	1	3	6	2	4	9	7	5
9	7	2	5	4	6	8	3	1
5	3	1	7	8	9	4	2	6
4	6	8	3	1	2	5	9	7
3	5	7	2	6	8	1	4	9
2	4	9	1	5	3	7	6	8
1	8	6	4	9	7	3	5	2

WORD WIT

TENNESSEE STATE or EAST TENNESSEE

PAGE 133

Return to Oz

L	A	S	T		D	E	C		S	P	H	E	R	E
O	S	H	A		A	V	E		T	E	A	S	E	R
L	I	O	N	S	D	E	N		E	N	D	E	A	R
I	D	O		P	O	R	T		R	U	E			
T	E	T	R	A		T	I	G	E	R	S	E	Y	E
A	S	S	E	R	T		R	O	Y		Y	E	N	
			P	E	S	E	T	A			B	R	A	D
		D	O	R	O	T	H	Y	G	A	L	E		
M	A	A	S		H	U	S	T	L	E				
O	L	D		A	W	E		O	B	S	E	S	S	
B	E	A	R	S	A	R	M	S		A	T	S	E	A
			A	T	L		E	C	O	N		C	E	L
P	E	A	N	U	T		O	H	M	Y	P	A	P	A
I	N	C	I	T	E		W	W	I		A	P	E	D
T	E	E	N	E	R		S	A	T		R	E	D	S

PAGE 134

One-Way Streets

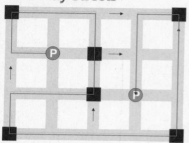

EQUATION CONSTRUCTION

8/4−9/9=1

PAGE 135

Star Search

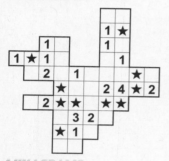

MIXAGRAMS

ALIBI MOON
INPUT ARCH
EARLY LONG
KHAKI ESPY

PAGE 136

Sew What

B	L	O	T		H	E	N	I	E		O	O	P	S
N	I	L	E		E	N	E	R	O		N	C	A	A
E	L	A	N		A	R	G	O	N		T	H	R	U
G	I	V	E	A	D	A	R	N		R	H	E	T	T
		T	R	O	P	I	C		E	E	R	I	E	
E	L	K		T	N	T		L	O	A	M			
D	E	I	C	E		H	A	M	M	E	R	E	D	
N	E	L	L		S	P	U	D	S		N	O	R	A
A	S	T	O	N	I	S	H		A	D	L	I	B	
		S	O	N	Y		R	E	G		E	N	S	
P	A	T	E	S		C	L	E	R	I	C			
S	T	A	K	E		H	E	M	A	N	D	H	A	W
H	O	R	N		C	O	D	E	S		R	U	B	E
A	N	T	I		B	U	G	L	E		O	M	E	N
W	E	S	T		S	T	E	T	S		M	E	L	D

PAGE 137

Möbius Maze

AND SO ON

PENCIL and PAPER

PAGE 138

Sudoku

5	1	9	4	8	7	6	3	2
8	6	3	2	5	9	4	7	1
4	2	7	3	6	1	5	8	9
7	4	6	5	9	3	2	1	8
2	9	5	8	1	4	7	6	3
1	3	8	7	2	6	9	5	4
3	8	2	9	7	5	1	4	6
9	7	1	6	4	8	3	2	5
6	5	4	1	3	2	8	9	7

EQUATION CONSTRUCTION

(9×8)−(9×4)=36

PAGE 139

Last Three

O	G	L	E	R		S	P	A	S		L	E	T	S
N	O	O	S	E		C	A	L	M		A	R	I	A
Y	E	L	P	S		O	N	T	O		M	U	T	T
X	R	A	Y	P	H	O	T	O	G	R	A	P	H	Y
		O	A	T							A	S	T	E	R
M	A	S	O	N	S		F	L	A	G				
A	T	L	A	S		H	O	O	P		F	A	L	A
Y	O	U	R	E	D	A	R	N	T	O	O	T	I	N
A	P	E	S		A	N	T	I		D	R	I	F	T
			A	N	D	Y		G	O	A	T	E	E	
A	T	P	A	R			G	E	R					
Z	I	E	G	F	E	L	D	F	O	L	L	I	E	S
T	B	A	R		M	A	I	L		E	A	G	L	E
E	I	R	E		I	N	G	A		S	T	O	L	E
C	A	S	E		T	E	S	T		S	H	R	E	D

PAGE 140

Split Decisions

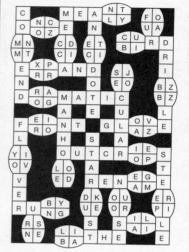

WORD WIT

UNDERSTUDY or OVERSTUFFED

PAGE 141

Islands

TELEPHONE TRIOS

DIAMOND, OCTAGON, PYRAMID

PAGE 142

Off the Ground

L	A	P	S	E		A	R	N	E		M	O	R	E
A	L	U	M	S		B	A	E	R		E	D	E	N
H	O	P	A	L	O	N	G	C	A	S	S	I	D	Y
R	E	A	L		W	E	S	T		P	A	N	D	A
		L	E	E	R		A	C	E	S				
P	O	C	U	S		B	R	O	W		S	D	I	
M	O	L	A	R		S	O	I	L		W	H	E	N
S	K	I	P	O	U	T	O	N	A	C	H	E	C	K
R	E	V	S		R	A	K	E		H	O	B	O	S
P	R	E		T	A	P	S		R	E	L	A	Y	
		D	E	L	L		H	E	R	E				
A	M	O	U	R		E	P	E	E		N	E	S	S
J	U	M	P	I	N	G	O	F	F	P	O	I	N	T
A	L	I	E		B	U	N	T		A	T	R	I	A
R	E	T	D		A	N	D	Y		W	E	E	P	Y

PAGE 143

ABC

	B		C	A
	C	A		B
B	A			C
A		C	B	
C		B	A	

WORD WIT
LEE GRANT

PAGE 144

All-Star Game

INITIAL REACTION
300 = PERFECT GAME IN BOWLING

PAGE 145

Line Drawings

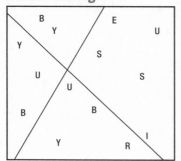

MIXAGRAMS
JOUST HERB
FINER AURA
OZONE CHAR
SPARE LINK

PAGE 146

All in Place

P	A	S	A		S	C	A	L	P		R	A	S	H
A	L	U	M		O	P	T	I	C		I	S	A	Y
T	O	P	B	I	L	L	I	N	G		G	A	R	P
E	N	R	I	C	O		P	E	A	C	H	P	I	E
S	E	A		E	I	S		A	M	A	T			
		L	I	S	T		R	E	S	T	A	R	T	
A	S	S	E	N	T	E	D			T	H	R	O	W
B	E	E	F		S	M	A	C	K		E	L	O	I
B	R	E	T	T			B	A	N	C	R	O	F	T
A	B	S	O	R	B	S		M	E	D	E			
		N	E	A	T		P	E	R			S	T	E
F	O	R	B	E	A	R	S			B	O	S	T	O	N
A	R	I	A		B	O	T	T	O	M	L	A	N	D
Z	A	P	S		A	P	L	A	N		A	L	T	O
E	L	S	E		A	S	O	N	E		P	L	O	W

PAGE 147

Find the Ships

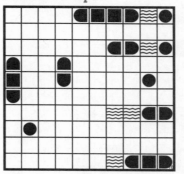

EQUATION CONSTRUCTION
$3 \times 4 \times 5 = 60$

PAGE 148

Hyper-Sudoku

8	4	6	2	7	9	3	1	5
5	7	9	1	3	6	8	4	2
1	3	2	4	8	5	9	7	6
7	5	8	6	9	3	1	2	4
2	9	1	5	4	8	7	6	3
3	6	4	7	2	1	5	8	9
6	1	3	8	5	2	4	9	7
4	2	5	9	1	7	6	3	8
9	8	7	3	6	4	2	5	1

WORD WIT
CHILD

PAGE 149

Winning Hands

D	A	S	H		O	B	O	E		M	C	C	O	Y
I	N	T	E	R	R	U	P	T		O	H	A	R	E
T	W	O	P	A	I	R	S	O	F	P	A	N	T	S
T	A	O		V	E	T		A	I	R				
O	R	D	A	I	N		N	A	M	E	S	A	K	E
		S	O	T		E	M	I	R		R	I	M	
I	S	A	L	L		T	W	A	S		P	E	T	E
S	T	R	A	I	G	H	T	S	H	O	O	T	E	R
L	I	M	N		E	R	O	S		R	E	E	D	Y
A	L	E		A	M	E	N		C	D	S			
M	E	D	F	L	I	E	S		R	I	Y	A	D	H
			I	O	N		S	U	N		M	O	E	
F	L	U	S	H	I	N	G	M	E	A	D	O	W	S
A	O	R	T	A		B	O	O	T	L	A	C	E	S
B	L	I	S	S		C	O	G	S		D	O	L	E

PAGE 150

Circular Reasoning

WORD SQUARE JIGSAW

G	R	I	T
L	O	R	E
U	P	O	N
M	E	N	D

PAGE 151

Solitaire Poker

CITY SEARCH
ALARM, AROMA, LLAMA, MOLAR, MORAL

PAGE 152

Islands

COMMON SENSE

FINISH

PAGE 153

Soundalikes

S	H	A	P	E		B	R	A	T		P	A	I	N
L	O	R	R	E		R	E	B	A		A	T	N	O
I	S	L	E	R	O	Y	A	L	E		L	A	D	S
T	S	O	S		D	A	L	E		E	L	L	I	E
		S	E	E	N			B	A	I	L	E	D	
E	W	O	K	S		T	A	B	A	R	D			
N	I	K	I	T	A		S	O	R	T		S	K	I
I	L	L	T	H	I	N	K	A	B	O	U	T	I	T
D	E	A		E	R	I	E		S	E	N	A	T	E
		S	T	E	A	D	S		A	D	R	E	M	
C	U	S	P	I	D			P	A	R	E			
A	N	T	I	C		V	O	I	D		R	H	E	A
S	T	A	N		A	I	S	L	E	S	E	A	T	S
T	I	R	E		D	E	L	L		H	A	I	T	I
S	E	T	S		A	D	O	S		A	T	L	A	S

PAGE 154

Kakuro

WORD WIT

MICKEY MOUSE

PAGE 155

Split Decisions

EQUATION CONSTRUCTION

(81−3)÷3=26

PAGE 156

Suit Yourself

L	O	B	S		S	E	A	O	F		S	U	M	P
A	B	O	U		E	N	D	U	E		E	L	I	A
D	I	A	M	O	N	D	J	I	M	B	R	A	D	Y
D	E	C	O	D	E	R	S		I	R	A	N	I	S
			I	C	U		S	N	I	P				
C	L	U	B	S	A	N	D	W	I	C	H	E	S	
R	A	N	A	T		J	U	N	K		A	P	B	
O	Z	Z	Y		C	R	I	M	E		T	R	I	O
P	E	I		A	R	O	N		F	E	T	C	H	
	S	P	A	D	E	A	N	D	A	R	C	H	E	R
		D	O	D	D		A	W	E					
O	C	T	O	P	I		S	M	A	S	H	U	P	S
H	E	A	R	T	B	R	E	A	K	H	O	T	E	L
M	O	R	E		L	I	E	G	E		G	A	P	E
S	S	T	S		E	B	S	E	N		S	H	E	D

PAGE 157

Three or More

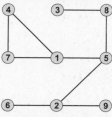

CLUELESS CROSSWORD

P	R	E	C	E	D	E
I		X		L		Q
C	H	A	T	E	A	U
C		M		G		I
O	P	I	N	I	O	N
L		N		S		O
O	V	E	R	T	A	X

PAGE 158

Animals of Africa

WORD WIT

YOU and EWE

PAGE 159

Star Search

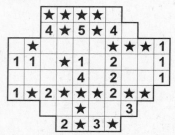

TELEPHONE TRIOS

ARCHERY, BOWLING, CRICKET

PAGE 160

Gamesters' Woes

P	R	I	D	E		A	B	B	E	S		F	U	R
S	O	L	O	S		R	E	E	V	E		A	N	A
S	P	L	I	T	S	C	R	E	E	N		U	S	N
T	E	S	T	A	M	E	N	T		S	O	L	E	D
			T	E	D			P	A	S	T	R	Y	
L	E	S	S	E	E		S	H	O	T	U	P		
I	N	C	A	S		W	H	O	L	E		L	A	M
M	O	R	T		W	H	A	L	E		R	A	V	I
A	S	A		T	H	E	R	E		S	O	N	I	C
	T	A	H	I	T	I		T	H	I	E	V	E	
E	S	C	H	E	R			F	O	E				
B	A	H	A	I		B	A	R	N	A	C	L	E	S
S	U	P		S	L	I	C	E	O	F	L	I	M	E
E	T	A		T	O	L	E	T		E	A	T	I	N
N	E	D		S	L	E	D	S		D	W	E	L	T

PAGE 161

Sudoku

8	6	3	1	7	9	5	4	2
1	9	2	8	5	4	7	6	3
4	5	7	3	6	2	8	9	1
6	3	5	9	2	8	1	7	4
7	2	8	6	4	1	3	5	9
9	4	1	7	3	5	6	2	8
5	7	9	4	1	3	2	8	6
3	8	6	2	9	7	4	1	5
2	1	4	5	8	6	9	3	7

AND SO ON
BREAD and BUTTER

PAGE 162

One-Way Streets

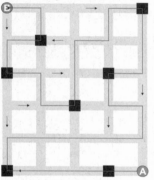

COMMON SENSE
UNION

PAGE 163

ABC

B	A			C
	B	C		A
	C	A	B	
A			C	B
C		B	A	

MIXAGRAMS
ASIDE EGGS
WHINE OUST
ROGUE GNAT
ETHER ASKS

PAGE 164

Colors of the Day

PAGE 165

One Solution

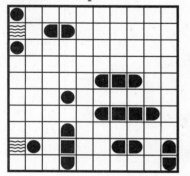

WORD WIT
GOPHER, ROACH

PAGE 166

Find the Ships

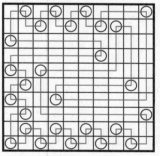

EQUATION CONSTRUCTION
8−3−3−1=1

PAGE 167

Kakuro

		7	1			1	4	
	3	4	2	1		1	3	2	4
	9	8	6	5	4	7		1	5
		9	7		1	2	4	3
			3	1		9	7	
		1	4	2	3		9	4
	1	5		8	9	1	5	2	6
	6	3	5	9		6	8	7	9
	2	1			6	3

IN OTHER WORDS
MISSTEP

PAGE 169

Whoa

D	A	B	S		C	A	R	T	E		A	G	E	R
D	I	R	T		I	V	I	E	D		M	A	M	E
T	R	O	Y		N	I	C	A	D		A	L	A	I
	H	O	L	D	E	V	E	R	Y	T	H	I	N	G
P	O	D	I	U	M				A	L	L	A	N	
A	L	E		P	A	S	T	I	N	G		E	T	E
S	E	D	E	R		H	O	S	T		S	E	E	D
			B	E	L	A	Y	T	H	A	T			
C	R	I	B		O	R	E	O		M	A	R	K	S
L	E	N		N	A	I	R	O	B	I		E	R	A
A	C	H	O	O				U	S	E	F	U	L	
S	T	O	P	R	I	G	H	T	T	H	E	R	E	
P	O	U	T		T	R	A	I	T		R	A	G	E
E	R	S	E		C	A	R	N	E		I	M	E	T
D	Y	E	D		H	Y	P	E	R		E	E	R	O

PAGE 170

Circular Reasoning

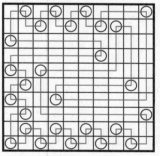

AND SO ON
CHAPTER and VERSE

PAGE 171

Islands

EQUATION CONSTRUCTION

$13 \times 11 = 143$

PAGE 172

Sweet Cinema

A	G	L	O	W		A	B	U	T		J	A	D	A
G	U	A	V	A		D	A	R	E		E	T	A	L
E	L	M	E	R	F	U	D	G	E		S	E	M	I
S	P	A	N	I	E	L		E	M	O	T	I	O	N
		N	E	T	S				P	E	N	N	E	
D	O	R	A	G	S		C	A	T	E	R			
O	V	A	L			S	O	L	A	R		P	A	R
P	E	R	I	L	S	O	F	P	R	A	L	I	N	E
E	R	E		L	O	A	F	S		Y	E	T	I	
	C	O	O	K	E		S	W	E	D	E	N		
D	E	L	A	Y		D	O	U	R					
A	M	A	N	D	A	S		P	R	E	S	O	R	T
N	A	P	A		F	O	R	R	E	S	T	G	U	M
T	I	E	D		E	D	N	A		T	E	R	S	E
E	L	L	A		W	A	S	H		S	T	E	E	N

PAGE 173

Pentagram

WORD WIT

SYDNEY and WENDY'S

PAGE 174

Hyper-Sudoku

6	4	1	9	8	2	7	3	5
2	3	8	4	5	7	1	9	6
9	5	7	1	3	6	4	2	8
7	9	2	6	4	8	3	5	1
1	8	3	2	9	5	6	4	7
5	6	4	3	7	1	2	8	9
8	2	5	7	1	3	9	6	4
3	1	9	8	6	4	5	7	2
4	7	6	5	2	9	8	1	3

TELEPHONE TRIOS

BEGONIA, JASMINE, PETUNIA

PAGE 175

Three or More

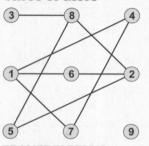

TRANSDELETION

CROISSANT

PAGE 176

Political Give-Ups

A	P	S	E	S		A	S	H		S	I	R	S	
C	R	E	E	P		P	E	A	R	T	R	E	E	
C	O	N	C	E	D	E	T	H	E	R	A	C	E	
E	M	O		C	O	X		A	B	E	T			
S	P	R	I	T	Z	E	R		W	E	E	D	S	
S	T	A	R	R		S	I	T	I	N		L	E	O
		K	A	N		G	I	N		T	M	A	N	
	Y	I	E	L	D	T	H	E	F	L	O	O	R	
T	O	D	D		A	R	T		O	E	R			
W	W	I		S	K	I	E	S		T	A	R	T	S
A	L	G	A	E		D	E	A	D	H	E	A	T	
	L	A	B	S		I	D	O		V	I	I		
S	U	B	M	I	T	A	N	E	W	B	I	L	L	
A	R	E	A	C	O	D	E		N	A	V	E	L	
G	L	E	N		P	O	S		S	H	E	D	S	

PAGE 177

Triad Split Decisions

EQUATION CONSTRUCTION

$(13 + 3) \div 8 = 2$

PAGE 178

One-Way Streets

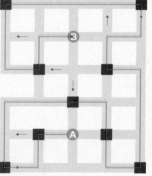

WORD WIT

PETER O'TOOLE

PAGE 179

Catch-All

M	O	D	E	S		U	T	A	H		G	E	T	S
E	V	E	R	T		N	O	N	E		O	L	E	O
S	E	C	R	E	T	C	O	D	E		U	S	E	R
A	R	C		R	O	L	L		D	I	R	E	S	T
S	T	A	B	I	L	E		S	L	A	M			
		A	L	L		W	H	E	N	E	V	E	R	
S	H	A	L	E		W	H	O	S		T	A	R	A
T	A	I	L		S	E	A	R	S		C	L	I	P
E	L	L	E		H	A	L	E		S	H	E	E	T
P	O	S	T	P	O	N	E		F	E	E			
		C	U	R	S		W	O	L	F	C	U	B	
S	C	U	L	P	T		A	I	R	E		A	P	E
T	I	N	A		C	A	D	E	T	C	O	R	P	S
O	A	T	S		U	T	I	L		T	O	L	E	T
W	O	O	S		T	E	N	D		S	P	A	R	S

PAGE 180

Train Maze

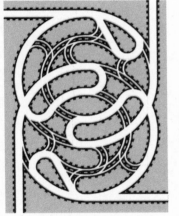

TRANSDELETION
MOUNT SINAI

PAGE 181

Star Search

		1	1			
	1	4	★	3		
2		★	★	★	4	★
★	★		★	★		1
4		3	4	★		2		1
★	★	★		★	★		★
2		3		3		2	2	
	1	★			★	
	1	1	1	1		

MIXAGRAMS
OBESE SURF
CIDER HOBO
FLUTE ORAL
LLAMA USED

PAGE 182

Sudoku

1	2	9	7	4	5	6	3	8
6	4	7	2	8	3	5	1	9
8	3	5	9	6	1	4	7	2
7	5	3	6	1	8	9	2	4
9	1	6	4	5	2	3	8	7
2	8	4	3	7	9	1	6	5
5	6	2	1	9	7	8	4	3
4	7	8	5	3	6	2	9	1
3	9	1	8	2	4	7	5	6

THREE OF A KIND
THE ENEMY OF AIRLINES THESE
DAYS IS THE FUEL MALADY.

PAGE 183

The Ex-Files

P	A	L	M		S	U	E	M	E		A	T	A	D
E	L	I	E		A	T	R	I	A		T	I	L	E
L	I	N	T		T	A	I	L	S		I	D	L	E
F	E	D	E	X	T	H	E	K	I	T	T	Y		
	N	A	O	M	I			E	L	S		I	R	A
		R	A	G	G	E	D	Y	A	N	N	E	X	
O	H	M		S	H	E	B			R	E	G	A	L
M	E	A	N		T	E	S	T	S		Y	U	L	E
E	L	S	I	E		E	R	I	C		P	M	S	
G	O	S	H	D	A	R	N	E	X	I	T			
A	T	M		I	F	I			T	A	R	O	T	
		E	X	T	R	A	C	T	H	O	U	S	E	S
M	A	D	E		A	T	E	A	M		S	A	N	A
E	R	I	N		M	A	L	T	A		T	K	O	S
N	C	A	A		E	S	S	E	N		S	A	N	E

PAGE 184

ABC

B			C	A
C			A	B
	A	B		C
	C	A	B	
A	B	C		

EQUATION CONSTRUCTION
$33 - 18 = 15$

PAGE 185

Find the Ships

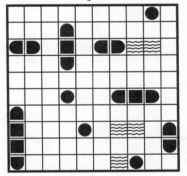

WORD WIT
STATE (ÉTATS)

PAGE 186

Shirt Stuff

P	O	S	H		D	A	N	T	E		M	B	A	S
O	M	N	I		O	L	E	A	N		A	L	G	A
G	A	I	T		B	O	A	R	D		J	U	A	N
O	N	T	H	E	B	U	T	T	O	N		E	N	D
		O	V	I	D			R	A	S	C	A	L	
Y	E	S	M	E	N		W	I	S	E	T	O		
A	L	I	E	N		K	I	T	E		E	L	M	S
L	I	D		T	O	N	E	A	R	M		L	E	E
U	S	E	R		F	E	L	L		I	S	A	A	C
		P	U	F	F	E	D		S	T	U	R	D	Y
B	I	O	T	I	C			A	M	E	N			
A	N	C		R	O	T	A	T	O	R	C	U	F	F
S	A	K	E		L	A	B	E	L		I	S	L	E
E	W	E	R		O	R	B	I	T		T	I	A	S
L	E	T	S		R	O	A	N	S		Y	A	M	S

PAGE 187

Four Kings

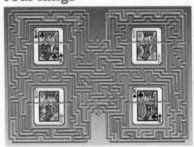

TELEPHONE TRIOS
CHUTNEY, KETCHUP, MUSTARD

PAGE 188

Kakuro

		1	3		6	9	8	
	2	9	7		2	1	7	5
2	3	8	6	4	1		6	4
1	5		4	3		8	9	
		2	5	1	3	4		
	3	8		2	1		7	1
6	2		1	7	4	3	5	2
7	5	2	4		2	1	8	
	1	3	2			2	9	

COMMON SENSE
LIGHT

PAGE 189
Circular Reasoning

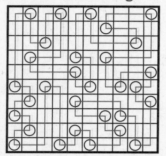

EQUATION CONSTRUCTION
$91 \div 7 = 13$

PAGE 190
Thievery

S	T	U	D		R	E	R	U	N		S	A	F	E
A	R	N	E		E	X	I	L	E		I	L	I	E
D	O	I	N	A	P	I	N	C	H		D	O	J	O
A	T	F	I	R	S	T		E	I	D	E	T	I	C
T	H	Y	M	E		V	E	R	S	U	S			
			S	O	I	L	S		S	W	E	A	R	
E	R	I	C		A	S	U		A	K	I	M	B	O
L	O	C	H		R	A	D	I	I		P	I	E	D
A	T	E	A	M	S		E	N	D		E	R	L	E
M	E	D	I	A		S	R	T	A	S				
			R	E	L	I	S	H		O	L	L	A	S
R	A	I	L	S	A	T		E	E	R	I	E	S	T
A	L	I	I		D	O	U	B	L	E	T	A	K	E
N	A	I	F		D	U	M	A	S		E	V	E	N
G	R	I	T		S	T	A	G	E		R	E	D	O

PAGE 191
Hyper-Sudoku

2	7	9	1	5	3	4	6	8
8	1	4	2	7	6	9	5	3
5	6	3	8	9	4	7	1	2
6	9	5	7	4	2	3	8	1
3	4	8	6	1	5	2	7	9
7	2	1	3	8	9	6	4	5
9	5	7	4	3	1	8	2	6
1	8	6	9	2	7	5	3	4
4	3	2	5	6	8	1	9	7

WORD WIT
GERMANIUM (GERANIUM)

PAGE 192
Split Decisions

EQUATION CONSTRUCTION
$(4+5) \div 9 = 1$

PAGE 193
Just Desserts

F	I	D	E		C	A	P	E	D		A	C	R	E
E	R	O	S		A	G	I	L	E		S	L	I	M
T	O	U	T		V	E	X	E	S		P	A	L	M
E	N	G		P	I	E	I	N	T	H	E	S	K	Y
	S	H	E	L	L		E	A	R	A	C	H	E	S
N	I	N	N	Y				O	T	T				
E	D	U	C		A	Y	E	A	Y	E		J	O	E
V	E	T		C	R	U	L	L	E	R		E	P	A
E	S	S		R	E	L	I	E	D		A	L	P	S
			B	A	A				A	L	L	O	Y	
A	D	V	A	N	C	E	S		S	W	A	Y	S	
P	I	E	C	E	O	F	C	A	K	E		R	E	F
H	A	R	K		D	R	O	N	E		T	O	D	O
I	N	G	E		E	E	R	I	E		A	L	T	O
D	E	E	D		S	M	E	L	T		B	L	O	T

PAGE 194
Labyrinth Cube

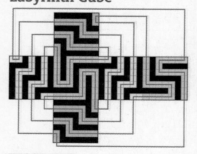

WORD WIT
PIANO PLAYER and PLAYER PIANO

PAGE 195
Three or More

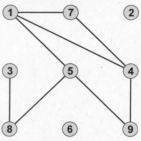

MIXAGRAMS
BEECH DRAW
AFTER OWLS
BERET LOCO
YANKS LIEU

PAGE 196
One-Way Streets

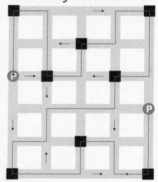

AND SO ON
MEAT and POTATOES

PAGE 197
Play-On Words

S	T	U	B		T	A	P	E		O	A	S	T	S
T	O	R	O		I	T	I	N		E	P	C	O	T
O	R	A	N		E	M	T	S		U	S	A	G	E
I	S	L	E		R	E	C	U	R	V	E	B	O	W
C	O	S	T	A	R		H	E	A	R				
			O	M	A	N	I		B	E	D	E	C	K
A	D	E	P	T		A	N	T	I		E	L	O	I
T	R	U	I	S	M	S		O	N	R	A	M	P	S
M	A	R	C		E	T	A	L		A	L	O	E	S
S	M	O	K	E	D		C	L	O	U	T			
			S	E	A	T		C	L	A	M	U	P	
S	K	I	P	S	A	B	E	A	T		B	O	Z	O
C	A	L	L	A		I	D	L	E		L	O	B	S
A	L	L	O	Y		D	O	I	T		O	L	E	S
N	E	S	T	S		E	N	D	S		W	A	K	E

PAGE 198

Sudoku

2	3	5	8	9	4	1	6	7
4	9	1	6	7	3	8	2	5
8	7	6	2	5	1	9	3	4
5	4	3	1	6	7	2	8	9
7	6	9	3	8	2	5	4	1
1	8	2	9	4	5	6	7	3
3	5	8	4	2	9	7	1	6
9	2	4	7	1	6	3	5	8
6	1	7	5	3	8	4	9	2

TRANSDELETION

MEMOIRS

PAGE 199

Star Search

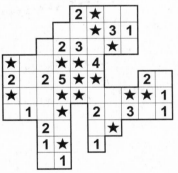

EQUATION CONSTRUCTION

$94 - 5 = 89$

PAGE 200

0 K's

J	A	D	E		S	C	H	E	D		E	V	A	N
A	G	E	S		P	A	I	G	E		L	A	R	A
M	E	N	T	A	L	B	L	O	C		A	C	A	T
E	N	S		B	E	E	T		I	V	T	U	B	E
S	T	E	E	L	E	R		A	D	I	E	U		
			Y	E	N		P	R	E	S	S	M	A	N
P	A	G	E	R		T	E	T	R	A		P	R	E
O	N	U	S		T	H	A	I	S		F	A	I	L
U	N	I		F	R	E	T	S		L	O	C	A	L
R	A	T	T	L	E	R	S		B	E	A			
		A	R	O	S	E		S	L	A	M	M	E	D
S	T	R	E	E	T		D	E	A	N		E	R	E
P	A	P	A		L	O	A	D	I	N	G	D	O	C
A	T	I	T		E	A	T	E	N		A	I	D	A
R	A	C	Y		S	T	A	R	E		G	A	E	L

PAGE 201

Poker Chips

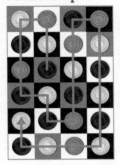

WORD WIT

CURRIER and IVES

PAGE 202

Line Drawings

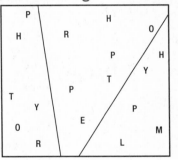

MIXAGRAMS

C R U S T   O G L E
A B O U T   L A R K
R O U G H   A M E N
D A I L Y   M E S H

PAGE 203

ABCD

A		D	B	C
A	B		C	D
C	D	A		B
	C	B		A	D
B		D	A	C
D		C	B		A

CLUELESS CROSSWORD

L	I	N	E	A	G	E
O		I		R		N
C	A	T	E	R	E	D
K		P		A		U
J	U	I	C	I	E	R
A		C		G		E
W	A	K	E	N	E	D

PAGE 204

Themeless Toughie

W	H	I	F	F	S		N	E	W	S	C	A	S	T
H	A	R	L	O	W		I	M	I	T	A	T	O	R
E	N	R	A	G	E		M	I	N	I	S	T	R	Y
E	D	I	T		D	E	B	T		R	A	I	D	S
D	I	G	S		E	L	L			L	I	T		
L	E	A		E	E	O		G	O	A	D	S		
E	S	T	A		M	A	R	C	H	E	S			
S	T	E	P	H	E	N		T	E	L	L	I	N	G
		S	O	L	O	M	O	N		O	M	A	R	
U	P	S	E	T		R	I	B			P	R	O	
N	O	T				S	E	A		F	O	R	A	
S	P	A	T	E		S	E	R	F		A	L	A	N
U	L	T	E	R	I	O	R		I	N	V	I	T	E
N	A	U	T	I	C	A	L		R	O	O	T	E	R
G	R	E	E	N	E	R	Y		E	G	R	E	S	S

PAGE 206

Find the Ships

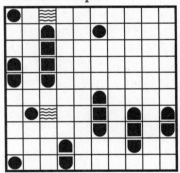

WORD WIT

COVERT (OVERT)

PAGE 207

Hyper-Sudoku

6	4	2	3	5	1	7	8	9
3	1	9	6	8	7	2	4	5
7	5	8	4	2	9	6	3	1
9	2	3	7	6	8	1	5	4
8	7	5	1	4	3	9	6	2
4	6	1	5	9	2	3	7	8
5	3	7	2	1	4	8	9	6
2	9	4	8	3	6	5	1	7
1	8	6	9	7	5	4	2	3

CITY SEARCH

ALIKE

PAGE 208
Themeless Toughie

E	G	O	T	I	S	T		A	T	T	I	R	E	D
N	A	N	E	T	T	E		B	A	R	N	O	N	E
S	W	E	N	S	O	N		D	R	I	S	T	A	N
I	K	I	D	Y	O	U	N	O	T		P	A	M	S
G	I	D	E		D	R	A	M	A		A	T	O	I
N	E	A	R		P	E	T	E	R	E	D	O	U	T
S	R	S		B	A	D	E	N		M	E	R	R	Y
			C	O	T				H	I	S			
S	T	A	R	Z		D	E	P	O	T		E	S	C
A	R	T	O	O	D	E	T	O	O		A	C	E	R
P	E	A	S		A	V	A	S	T		S	U	R	E
P	A	N	S		M	O	L	T	E	N	L	A	V	A
I	C	E	B	O	A	T		I	D	O	O	D	I	T
E	L	N	O	R	T	E		T	A	D	P	O	L	E
R	E	D	W	O	O	D		S	T	E	E	R	E	D

PAGE 211
Themeless Toughie

A	L	F	R	E	S	C	O		D	A	L	L	A	S
S	A	L	E	S	M	A	N		O	R	I	E	N	T
T	R	E	A	S	U	R	E		M	R	M	O	T	O
E	V	E	R		G	A	T	S		A	B	N	E	R
R	A	C	E	D		T	I	P	P	Y		A	R	M
S	E	E	D	E	D		M	I	I		T	R	O	I
			C	A	T	E	R	S		I	D	O	L	
M	A	R	C	O	N	I		E	C	O	N	O	M	Y
O	V	E	N		C	E	A	S	E	D				
N	E	O	N		E	S	T		S	E	A	L	E	D
A	R	C		A	D	I	T	S		S	P	A	R	E
L	A	C	E	S		N	A	T	L		P	S	A	T
I	G	U	A	N	A		C	R	E	V	A	S	S	E
S	E	R	V	E	R		K	I	N	D	L	I	E	R
A	S	S	E	R	T		S	P	O	T	L	E	S	S

PAGE 214
Themeless Toughie

I	M	P	O	S	E	R	S		B	E	M	I	R	E
M	A	L	A	P	R	O	P		R	A	I	N	E	D
P	R	E	T	E	N	T	I	O	U	S	N	E	S	S
A	S	N	E	W		A	N	N	I	E		V	U	E
C	H	I	S		F	R	O	S	T		M	I	L	L
T	A	P		B	U	Y	U	P		P	U	T	T	S
S	L	O	P	E	S		T	E	R	E	S	A	S	
			T	U	N	E	D		C	A	R	I	B	
G	E	N	T	E	E	L		R	E	C	I	F	E	
D	O	N	T	S		N	U	N	E	Z		L	O	X
E	F	T	S		C	A	N	O	E		W	I	L	T
P	O	I		S	A	L	U	D		S	A	T	I	E
T	R	A	N	Q	U	I	L	I	Z	A	T	I	O	N
H	I	R	A	M	S		A	C	I	D	T	E	S	T
S	T	Y	M	I	E		R	E	P	A	S	S	E	S

PAGE 209
Egyptian Maze

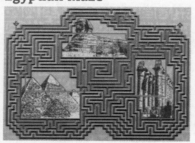

EQUATION CONSTRUCTION
$840 \div 14 = 12 \times 5$

PAGE 210
Circular Reasoning

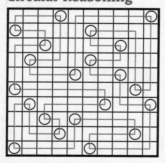

TELEPHONE TRIOS
FRIGATE, GONDOLA, TUGBOAT

PAGE 212
Kakuro

WORD WIT
JACK LEMMON or JACK KLUGMAN

PAGE 213
Islands

IN OTHER WORDS
RADIOED

PAGE 215
Three or More

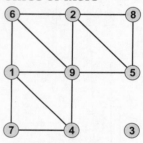

COMMON SENSE
SLOW

PAGE 216
Monkeys and Bananas

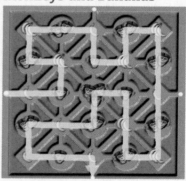

WORD SQUARE JIGSAW

P	E	A	L
A	X	L	E
P	A	T	E
A	M	O	K

PAGE 217

Themeless Toughie

K	E	T	C	H	U	P			M	A	I	L	E	D
I	S	R	A	E	L	I		W	E	L	C	O	M	E
S	C	A	L	I	N	G		I	L	L	E	G	A	L
S	A	C		R	A	M	B	L	E		S	I	N	E
E	P	I	C	S		E	I	D	E	R		C	A	T
R	E	N	E		I	N	K		S	E	D	A	T	E
S	E	G	M	E	N	T	E	D		P	I	L	E	D
			E	A	S	E		O	B	O	L			
M	E	A	N	T		D	E	M	I	T	A	S	S	E
U	L	S	T	E	R		V	I	N		T	U	N	A
S	E	T		R	I	P	E	N		S	E	N	O	R
T	A	R	A		V	A	L	I	S	E		R	O	N
A	N	I	S	E	E	D		C	A	P	S	I	Z	E
R	O	D	E	N	T	S		A	L	I	A	S	E	S
D	R	E	A	D	S			N	E	A	T	E	S	T

PAGE 218

Split Decisions

WORD WIT
SHREW and PIGEON

PAGE 219

Sudoku

3	5	7	4	1	9	6	8	2
9	8	4	2	7	6	5	3	1
1	2	6	5	8	3	4	9	7
4	9	2	7	6	1	8	5	3
5	7	8	9	3	2	1	4	6
6	1	3	8	4	5	2	7	9
7	6	9	1	5	4	3	2	8
8	3	5	6	2	7	9	1	4
2	4	1	3	9	8	7	6	5

AND SO ON
LADIES and GENTLEMEN

PAGE 220

Themeless Toughie

C	O	S	T	U	M	E	S		C	S	H	A	R	P
A	L	L	I	N	O	N	E		H	O	O	P	E	R
R	E	A	S	S	O	R	T		A	N	T	O	N	E
L	A	N	C	E	L	O	T		N	A	P	L	E	S
E	N	T	H	R	A	L	L	S		T	A	O		
				E	A	T	I	N	G	I	N			
A	S	H		S	H	O	R	T	O	N	T	I	M	E
B	U	Y	S	O	U	T		E	R	A	S	E	R	S
C	E	D	A	R	C	H	E	S	T	S		S	E	T
S	T	R	I	C	K	E	N							
		O	L	E		R	E	S	I	S	T	O	R	S
P	R	F	I	R	M		M	A	N	T	O	M	A	N
L	O	O	N	I	E		I	N	T	O	N	A	T	E
U	N	I	T	E	S		E	Y	E	L	I	N	E	R
G	A	L	O	S	H		S	O	L	E	C	I	S	T

PAGE 221

One-Way Streets

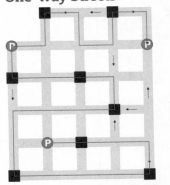

EQUATION CONSTRUCTION
$5(9+4)=65$

PAGE 222

Line Drawings

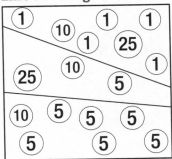

TRANSDELETION
TABERNACLE

PAGE 223

Themeless Toughie

R	U	T	T	E	D		A	P	P	E	A	S	E	S
E	N	E	R	G	Y		F	I	E	R	C	E	S	T
A	D	M	I	R	E		F	A	L	S	E	T	T	O
P	E	P	P	E	R	M	I	N	T		S	T	A	R
P	R	E	S	S		A	R	O	S	E		E	T	E
E	A	R		S	H	I	M	S		C	R	E	E	D
A	G	A	R		I	N	S		F	R	I			
R	E	S	E	R	V	E		T	A	U	N	T	E	D
			P	O	E		H	O	T		D	E	M	O
S	H	O	O	T		C	A	N	E	S		L	U	G
T	E	D		S	N	A	R	K		C	A	L	L	S
A	R	E	S		O	R	N	A	M	E	N	T	A	L
N	O	S	E	D	I	V	E		I	N	N	A	T	E
D	I	S	P	O	S	E	S		R	E	E	L	E	D
S	C	A	T	T	E	R	S		A	S	S	E	S	S

PAGE 224

Block Maze

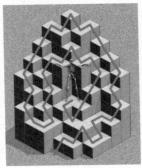

THREE OF A KIND
WHO TOLD THE CHAIRMAN THAT HIS UNRULY OUTBURST SURPRISES NO ONE?

PAGE 225

Star Search

(star placement grid)

MIXAGRAMS
DOWEL BIAS
ALONE SHAH
IRONY FLUE
HIDES WORD

PAGE 226

Themeless Toughie

G	O	D	S	E	N	D		P	L	A	S	T	I	C
E	C	U	A	D	O	R		R	O	B	E	R	T	O
M	A	S	T	E	R	Y		E	N	C	L	A	S	P
I	N	T	E	R		H	O	T		S	E	G	A	L
N	A	B	S		N	O	D	E	S		S	E	L	A
I	D	I		S	I	L	E	N	T	S		D	I	N
S	A	N	T	A	F	E		D	E	L	A	Y	E	D
		O	U	T				P	A	R				
F	R	A	N	C	I	S		C	O	N	C	E	P	T
R	E	D		Y	E	L	L	I	N	G		M	R	I
A	L	V	A		S	I	E	V	E		M	I	E	N
P	I	A	N	O		M	T	V		M	A	T	C	H
P	A	N	G	R	A	M		I	N	E	R	T	I	A
E	N	C	L	A	V	E		E	A	S	I	E	S	T
S	T	E	E	L	E	R		S	P	H	E	R	E	S

PAGE 229

Themeless Toughie

C	H	A	R	I	S	M	A		E	R	R	A	T	A
R	E	L	A	T	I	O	N		R	E	U	B	E	N
E	L	E	C	T	R	O	N		A	U	B	U	R	N
W	E	R	E		S	L	O	G		P	E	D	R	O
E	N	T	R	Y		A	Y	A	H	S		H	A	T
L	A	S	S	O	S		E	V	E		N	A	P	A
			L	E	A	D	E	R		O	B	I	T	
S	K	U	L	K	E	D		I	M	A	G	I	N	E
M	A	N	E		K	I	D	N	E	Y				
O	L	I	O		E	E	O		S	E	R	I	A	L
O	A	F		G	R	U	N	T		S	U	M	M	A
T	H	O	S	E		S	A	R	A		S	P	U	R
H	A	R	K	E	D		T	E	L	L	T	A	L	E
E	R	M	I	N	E		E	N	T	A	I	L	E	D
D	I	S	M	A	L		S	T	A	C	C	A	T	O

PAGE 232

Themeless Toughie

C	L	A	S	S	A	C	T		V	I	S	A	G	E
O	U	T	T	O	S	E	A		A	R	A	B	I	A
G	A	M	E	R	O	O	M		L	E	V	E	L	S
S	U	S	P	E	N	S	E		K	N	O	T	T	Y
			A	L	E		S	P	I	E	R			
L	A	S	S	O		C	T	R	L			C	D	C
A	R	T	I	S	T	E		E	M	A	N	U	E	L
T	R	A	D	E	O	N		P	E	T	E	R	I	I
T	O	R	E	R	O	S		P	R	O	V	I	S	O
E	W	E			T	O	R	Y		M	E	E	T	S
			M	A	H	R	E		F	I	R			
T	A	R	O	T	S		P	E	A	C	E	F	U	L
A	P	O	L	L	O		E	X	C	A	V	A	T	E
N	O	M	A	A	M		L	I	E	G	E	M	E	N
S	P	A	R	S	E		S	T	T	E	R	E	S	A

PAGE 227

Islands

INITIAL REACTION
9 = SYMPHONIES WRITTEN BY
LUDWIG VAN BEETHOVEN

PAGE 228

Anagram Crossword

CLUE ANSWER	ANAGRAM OF ANSWER
ROLES	LOSER
LARGE	LAGER
ANGEL	GLEAN
GRINS	RINGS
STERN	RENTS
TINES	STEIN

L	A	G	E	R
O		L		E
S	T	E	I	N
E		A		T
R	I	N	G	S

PAGE 230

Triad Split Decisions

EQUATION CONSTRUCTION
$45 \div 9 = 5$

PAGE 231

Twilight Maze

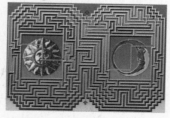

CLUELESS CROSSWORD

T	R	A	I	P	S	E
Y		D		L		T
P	H	A	R	A	O	H
I		M		T		I
C	H	A	O	T	I	C
A		N		E		A
L	I	T	E	R	A	L